AF291234

# IN SEARCH OF
# BAWA
## Master Architect of Sri Lanka

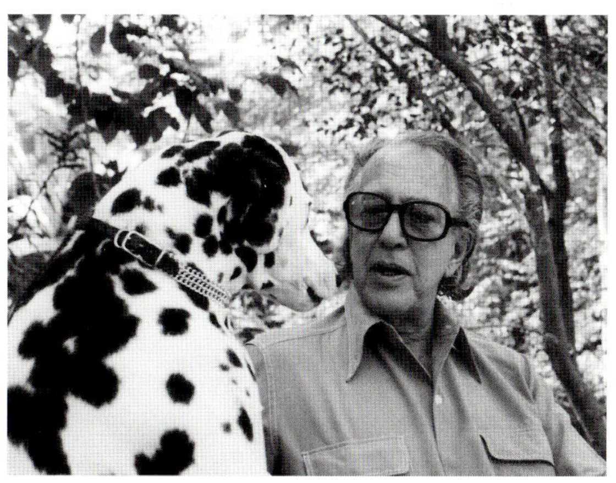

David Robson

Photography
Sebastian Posingis

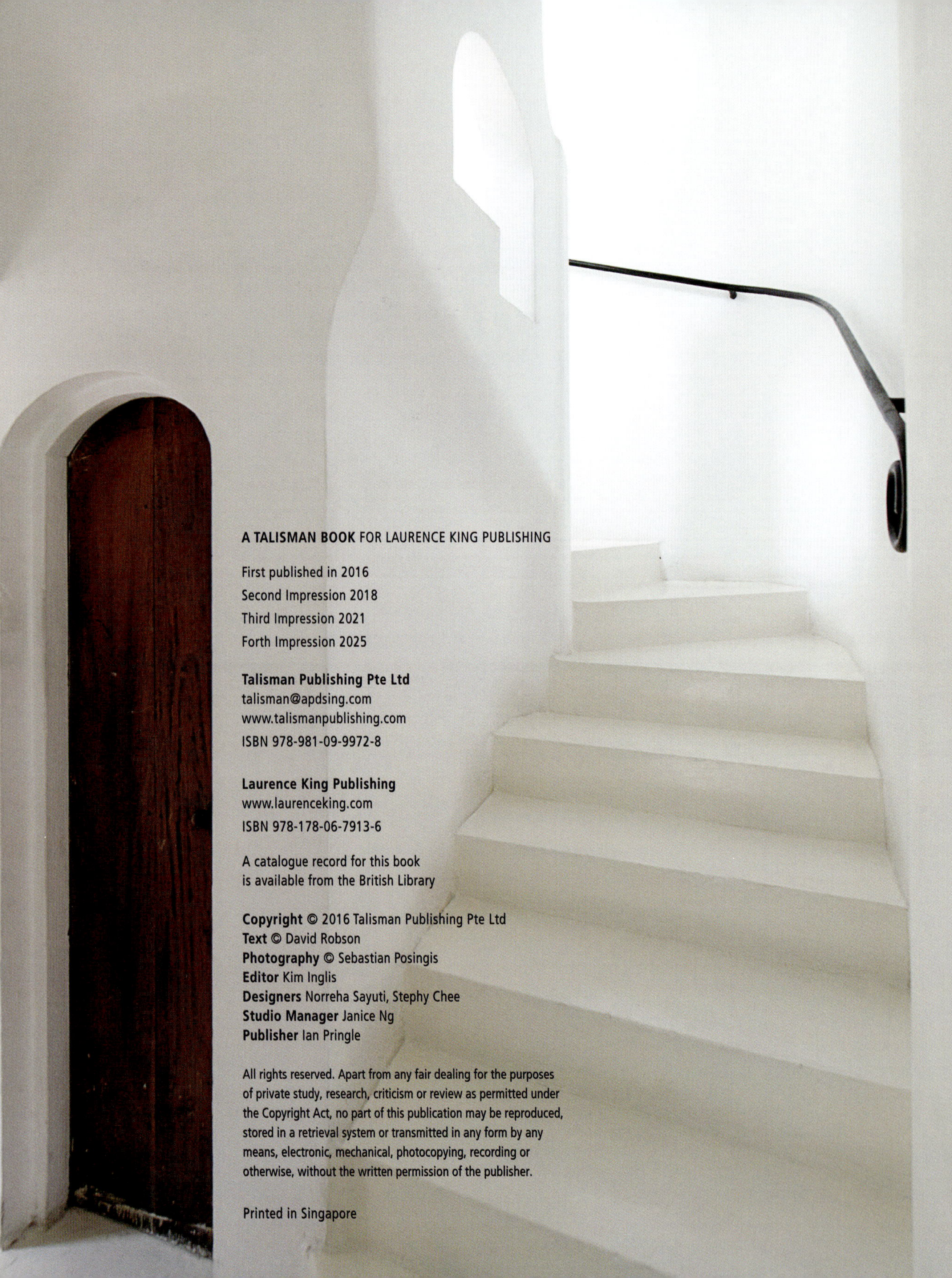

**A TALISMAN BOOK** FOR LAURENCE KING PUBLISHING

First published in 2016
Second Impression 2018
Third Impression 2021
Forth Impression 2025

**Talisman Publishing Pte Ltd**
talisman@apdsing.com
www.talismanpublishing.com
ISBN 978-981-09-9972-8

**Laurence King Publishing**
www.laurenceking.com
ISBN 978-178-06-7913-6

A catalogue record for this book
is available from the British Library

**Copyright** © 2016 Talisman Publishing Pte Ltd
**Text** © David Robson
**Photography** © Sebastian Posingis
**Editor** Kim Inglis
**Designers** Norreha Sayuti, Stephy Chee
**Studio Manager** Janice Ng
**Publisher** Ian Pringle



Printed in Singapore

# CONTENTS

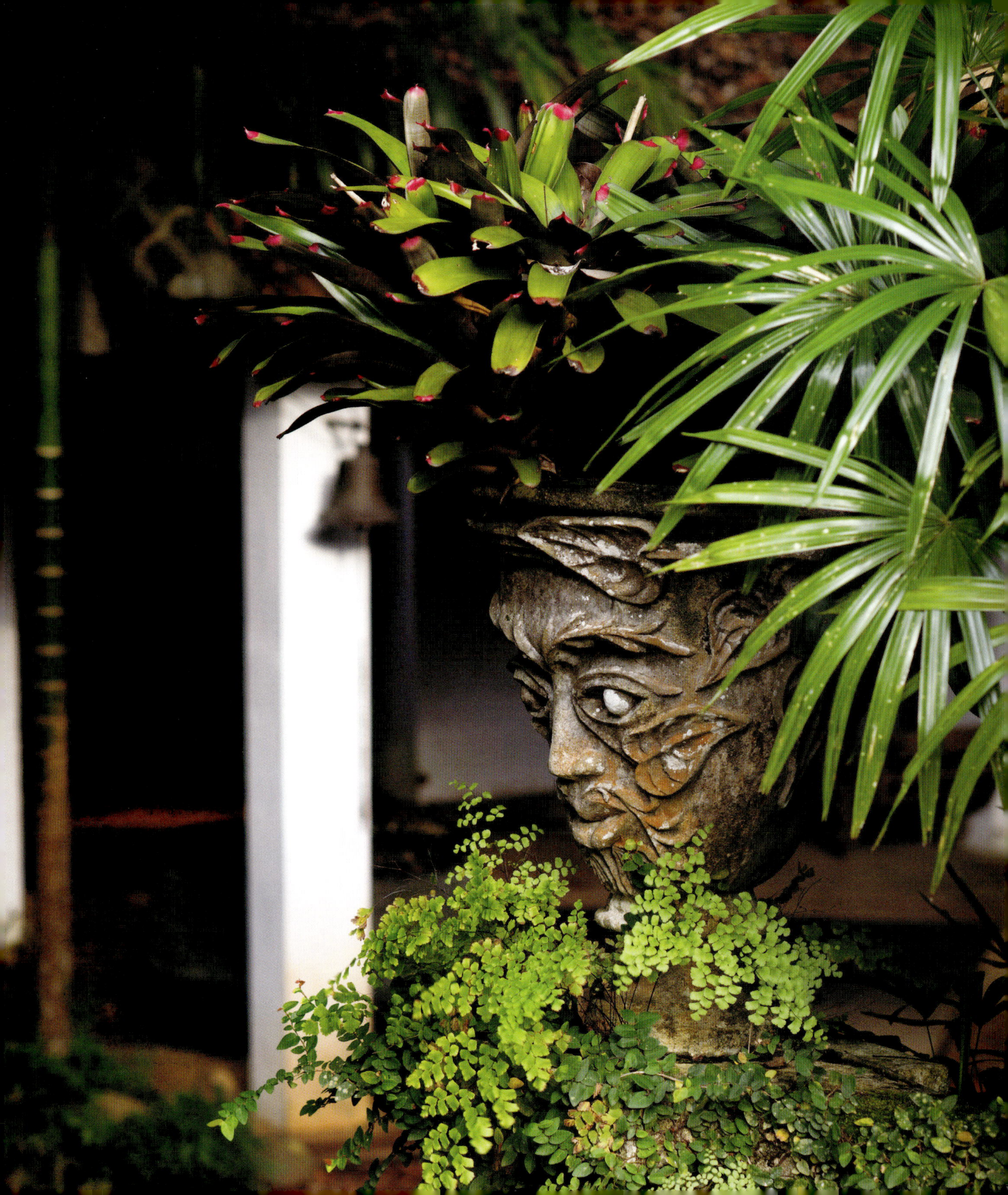

# Preface

Some 20 years ago Geoffrey Bawa, then approaching the end of his career, asked me to help him write a monograph on his work. We started on this in 1997, but our collaboration was nipped in the bud in early 1998 when he was felled by a stroke that left him almost totally incapacitated. However, the Bawa Trust encouraged me to continue with the project and the book finally appeared in 2002 under the title *Bawa the Complete Works* (Thames & Hudson). Geoffrey survived to see the book finished and attended its launch, though we don't know what he thought of it. Although I tried to present his point of view, it's certain that, had he been able to take part in its production, it would have become a different book.

Bawa died in 2003 and his practice ceased to exist. Since then many of his buildings have been altered by their owners, some beyond all recognition, while a number have been demolished or have fallen prey to termites and the relentless cycle of tropical sun and monsoon rain.

This book came about at the suggestion of photographer Sebastian Posingis and is intended to complement the much larger book of 2002. It focuses primarily on Geoffrey Bawa's built works in Sri Lanka and offers a catalogue of those that have survived the depredations of two decades while issuing warnings about those that no longer fairly represent his original design intentions. They are arranged, not chronologically, but geographically, as a series of circuits: one within Colombo, one around its outskirts and one around the island.

The book also seeks to address some recurring questions: who was Geoffrey Bawa? What inspired his shift in mid life from mediocre lawyer to master architect? What were the qualities that distinguished his work? It doesn't attempt to describe his unbuilt designs — many of these were featured in *Bawa, the Complete Works* — nor does it speculate about his influence on other architects — this was discussed in the book *Beyond Bawa* (Thames & Hudson, 2007).

There can be little doubt that Geoffrey Bawa was a towering figure in post-independence Sri Lanka and, indeed in the wider context of South and South East Asia. It's also clear that he exercised a huge influence on succeeding generations of architects. For this reason it is indeed regrettable that so many of his buildings have been altered or lost during past decades. This book will hopefully help to draw attention to their plight and will result in at least a few of them being conserved to delight future generations.

Bawa believed that architecture could never be fully understood through written descriptions or pictures and should be experienced face-to-face. We hope that this book will encourage you to visit his buildings and explore them for yourselves.

**Page 1** Geoffrey Bawa with his dog Leopold, 1985.
**Previous page** The staircase in Geoffrey Bawa's town house.
**Left** Donald Friend urn in the Lunuganga garden.
**Overleaf** The veranda of the Claughton Bungalow.

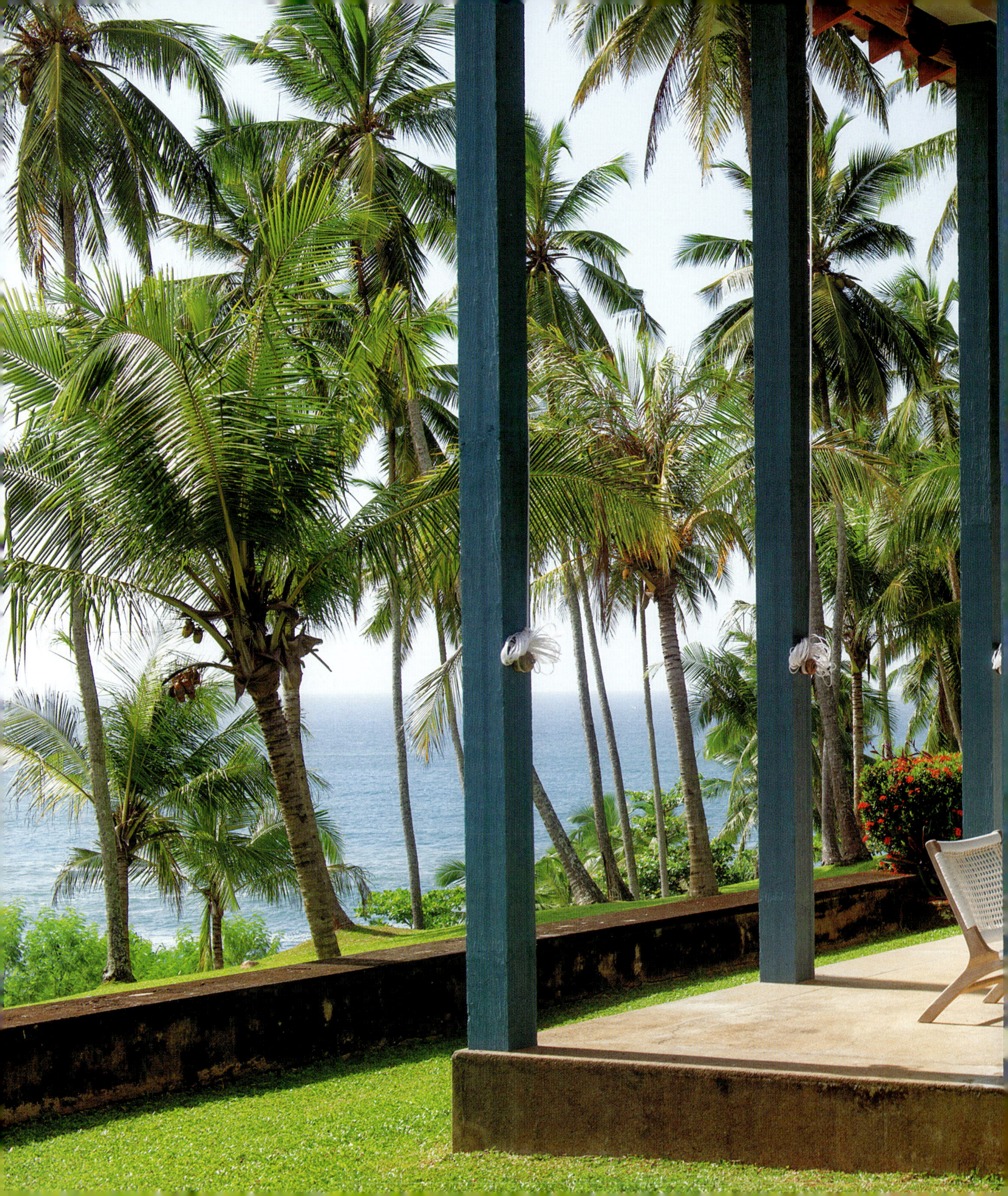

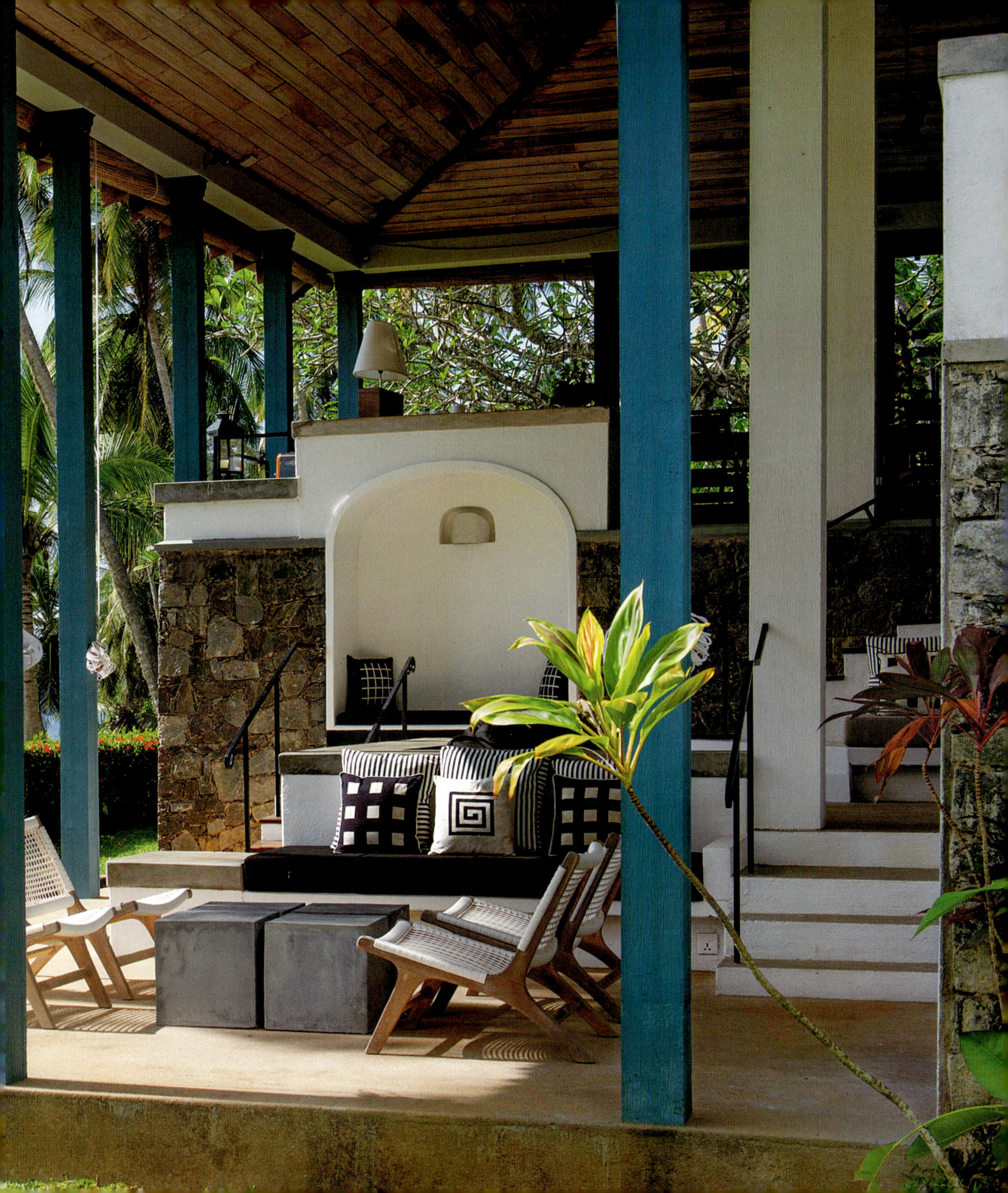

# Introduction

Geoffrey Bawa believed that architecture could never properly be described in words and that it was ill-served by theoretical discourse; for him buildings had to be experienced. We hope that this book will inspire the reader to visit and experience at least a few of his buildings.

This is not a book aimed at specialists: it avoids jargon and arcane theorising. Nor is it a travel guide or gazetteer, though it can be used as a travellers' handbook. The 40 or so buildings that are featured have been organised along imagined routes: a clockwise circuit around Colombo starting from Bawa's former office, now the Gallery Café, and a clockwise circuit around the island, taking in Anuradhapura and the Hill Country and following the sweep of the south coast to end at a seminary in Piliyandala.

Geoffrey's career ran from the end of the 1950s until he was felled by a stroke in 1998. The book focuses on those of his built designs in Sri Lanka that still survive in something approximating to their original state. Many of the public buildings that are featured can be visited, though sometimes only by appointment. Private houses can't be visited without special permission.

Today, 17 years after his career ended and a dozen years after his death, a number of his buildings have disappeared altogether and many have been altered, some beyond recognition. Buildings that have been altered are described here in such a way as to clarify the extent to which they still represent Bawa's original design intentions and to dispel any false claims to a lost authenticity. His buildings were 'total works of art' and their final state reflected the way in which he controlled their construction to the very end, adding that special quality that is all too susceptible to insensitive change.

In a recent article the travel writer Royston Ellis[1] questioned why Geoffrey's Bentota Beach Hotel could not be admired in its present, much altered, state. The hotel, dating from 1969 and one of Sri Lanka's first purpose-built resorts, was a work of pure genius, but it was massively remodelled by its present owners in the mid 1990s and now bears only a vestigial resemblance to the original. Its tiled roofs were replaced by green plastic sheeting, its entrance staircase and lobby were remodelled, its central

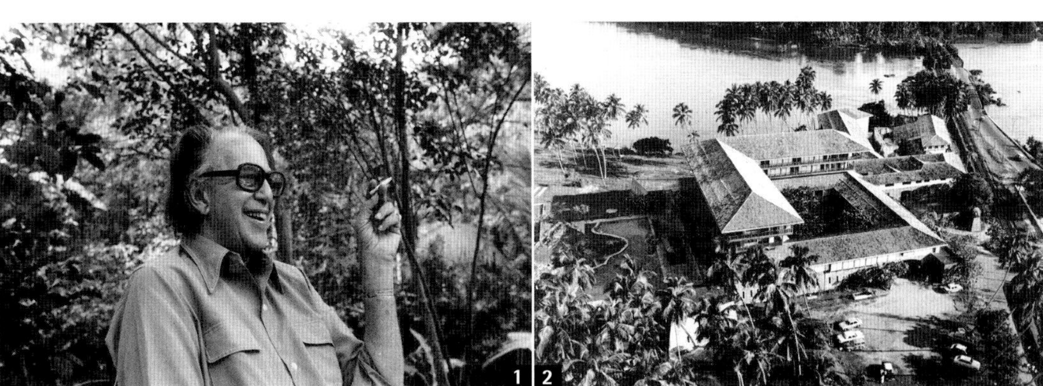

1 Geoffrey Bawa at Lunuganga in 1986.
2 Bentota Beach Hotel, 1972. Bawa Archive.

courtyard was stripped of its landscape, its reception rooms were chintzified and its bedrooms restyled. Like a scarred and moustachioed Mona Lisa, the Bentota Beach Hotel has lost its essential qualities and no longer adequately represents Bawa's original design intentions.

## Who Was Bawa?

Geoffrey Bawa was something of an enigma, even to those who claimed to know him. One question remains almost impossible to answer: what was the source of his undoubted genius?

Although he enjoyed good company and moved freely around Colombo society he remained a very private person and had few close friends. Indeed, towards the end of his life he was often lonely and related to other people mainly through his work, the contemplation of which filled almost every waking moment of his life.

From his parents he inherited a liking for meandering anecdotes, and was a master of the witty off-the-cuff aphorism. He enjoyed participating in barbed and often spiteful gossip, as for instance, when driving into Colombo and encountering a heavy stream of traffic coming in the other direction, he quipped that this was a sure sign that the architect Minnette de Silva was in town.

Nonetheless, Geoffrey had a generous spirit and was always happy to encourage younger architects. But he could also be quite mean with money and failed to pay his staff adequately. He would often try to persuade friends to buy a property or a piece of furniture or a painting, so that he could enjoy vicariously both the excitement of the transaction and the pleasure of ownership. But he was always ready to help friends and colleagues in moments of need. He lived quite simply and his main indulgences were foreign travel, his motorcars and his garden at Lunuganga, in which he invested most of his spare money and time over a period of almost 50 years.

He was gay and, from his time in Cambridge, quite openly so. Denys Johnson-Davies, a contemporary at St Catherine's College, recalled[2]: "He was from Ceylon and flaunted the fact that he was gay. He dressed in flamboyant style and spent as little time as possible in the college."

Bawa avoided lasting relationships and never entered into a long-term partnership. Indeed when friends got too close, as was the case with Ulrik Plesner and Christoph Bon, he would push them away, as if he viewed companionship as an invasion, or perhaps a distraction from architecture.

He was very tall, though less so than his elder brother, Bevis, and was quite ungainly, as if his frame had outgrown his muscles. Strikingly handsome with fair hair and blue eyes, he paid close attention to his personal appearance, in later life often wearing strong-coloured loose-fitting shirts over well-ironed slacks.

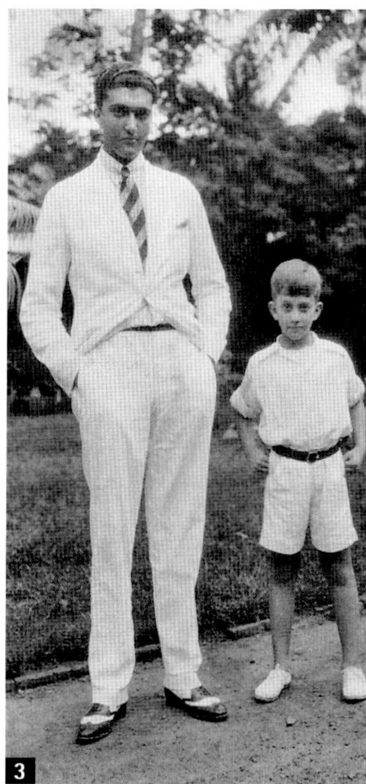

**3** Geoffrey with his elder brother Bevis, *circa* 1927. Bawa Archive.

[1] Royston Ellis, Domus 5 (Sri Lanka) 2015

[2] Denys Johnson-Davies, 'Memories in Translation'. Cairo 2006, quoted in Robert Aldrich's *Cultural Encounters and Homoeroticism in Sri Lanka*, Routledge 2014

Both he and his brother had distinctive voices and affected the somewhat languid English of the late-colonial British, referring to Kurunegala as 'Kurnigalle' and Bentota as 'Bentot' and employing such superlatives as 'splendid' and 'superb'. Both spoke 'kitchen Sinhala' with decidedly English accents.

Ignoring the example of his father, who was a keen sportsman, he eschewed all forms of physical exercise. Although he designed some of the 20th-century's most inventive swimming pools, he was unable to swim and never ventured near water. For much of his life he was an addicted smoker, often lighting the next of his preferred Peacock cigarettes from the last.

## Towards Architecture

The young Geoffrey Bawa was a literary rather than a visual person. During his teens he composed short stories and entertained ambitions to be a writer, though his mother was determined that he should follow his father and become a lawyer. Unlike his brother he showed no talent for drawing and little interest in the visual arts. He enjoyed listening to music of all sorts but was not himself musical. He played with a Meccano construction set and, having inherited a passion for motor cars from his parents, became a reasonably competent mechanic.

An avid traveller, he seems to have retained vivid mental images of the places that he visited, though he never kept a sketch book. During his early years he used a camera and installed a darkroom in his Colombo home, but he seems to have given up photography during the mid-1960s and none of his photographs survive from after that date.

How was it that a man who had shown almost no interest in architecture during the first three decades of his life should suddenly transform himself in his mid–thirties from failed lawyer and feckless dilettante to committed architect? We shall probably never know the answer to this conundrum.

There was no Damascene moment but rather a long period of hesitation which ran from his return to Ceylon as a qualified lawyer in 1946 to his departure in 1954 to study architecture at the Architectural Association (AA) in London. This was marked by two events: his purchase of Lunuganga, an abandoned rubber estate near Bentota, in 1948, and his encounter with his first client, Mrs Prini Deraniyagala in 1951. He bought the rubber estate in order to create an Italian garden but soon discovered that he lacked the technical knowledge to put his ideas into practice and, after struggling to provide Mrs Deraniyagala with the design she craved, he finally declared himself unequal to the task.

Geoffrey came to architecture through his interest in gardens. He was first attracted to English landscaped gardens during his time at Cambridge when he was often invited to stay in country houses. Later, during a visit to Italy immediately after World War II, he was introduced to Italian Renaissance gardens. Later still he discovered for himself the wonderful landscape traditions of Sri Lanka — from the great water gardens of the classical period to the estate gardens of the colonial period.

For him a building had to be conceived as part of the surrounding landscape; it should reach outwards to create outdoor rooms and should draw outside space in towards itself. Today this might seem unremarkable, but 60 years ago it was not so. In Sri Lanka the British had built introspective bungalows that were sealed off from what was perceived as an alien environment. In the West the main exponents of International Modernism preferred to indulge in abstract form-making, ignoring the specifics of site and context and developing general solutions to universal problems rather than specific designs for particular places.

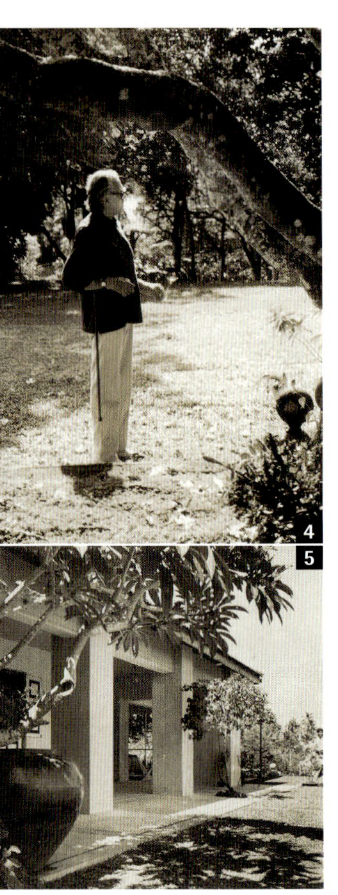

4 Geoffrey Bawa at Lunuganga in a favourite shirt with a Peacock cigarette, *circa* 1989.
5 An early view of the bungalow at Lunuganga, 1958. Bawa Archive.

Geoffrey's approach to architecture was also influenced by his legal training which instilled in him a healthy disregard for cant. A design should proceed from a clear statement of needs — the 'brief' — and should develop 'logically'. His literary interests, meanwhile, inspired him to adopt a narrative or scenographic approach to the design process: he would imagine the life to be led and would conceive of a building as a sequence of spatial *tableaux*, enlivened by views and animated by light and shadow.

In the final analysis he was a pragmatist, believing that a building must first fulfil the needs of those who would use it, and that use and beauty were inextricably linked.

## Childhood

Geoffrey Manning Bawa was born in 1919, the second son of a wealthy and successful lawyer, in what was then the British Crown Colony of Ceylon, and died 84 years later in the Democratic Socialist Republic of Sri Lanka. Having grown up in a small corner of a large, tottering empire he pursued his architectural career in a newly independent country. His life straddled the divide between the late-colonial and post-colonial periods.

His father, Benjamin Bawa, was half Ceylon Moor (a mixed descendent of Arab seafarers) and half British while his mother, Bertha Marion Campbell Schrader, was what was known as a Dutch Burgher — the mixed-race descendent of a European employee of the Dutch East Indies Company.

Geoffrey's immediate ancestors included adherents of at least three religions and between them represented many of Ceylon's ethnic strands. He was baptised as an Anglican Christian and at a school roll-call once identified himself as a "sort of Christian Moslem Burgher", for which flippancy he was severely caned. His family was English-speaking and European in outlook, but he was brought up by a Sinhala-speaking *aya*. In the final analysis he was probably half Asian and half European: one of the 'people in between', patronised by the colonial British and mistrusted by the Sinhalese.

Benjamin Bawa died when Geoffrey was only three leaving him and his brother Bevis to be brought up by their mother and two maiden aunts. They all lived in Chapman House, a large villa on Darley Road, then a fashionable tree-lined avenue that linked the suburb of Cinnamon Gardens to the Hultsdorf legal district.

**6** Benjamin and Bertha Bawa in front of Chapman House, *circa* 1908. Bawa Archive.
**7** The wedding of William Manning, 1920. Benjamin Bawa is standing at the left, Manning is centre right. Bawa Archive.
**8** The front veranda at Kimbulupitiya, 2000.

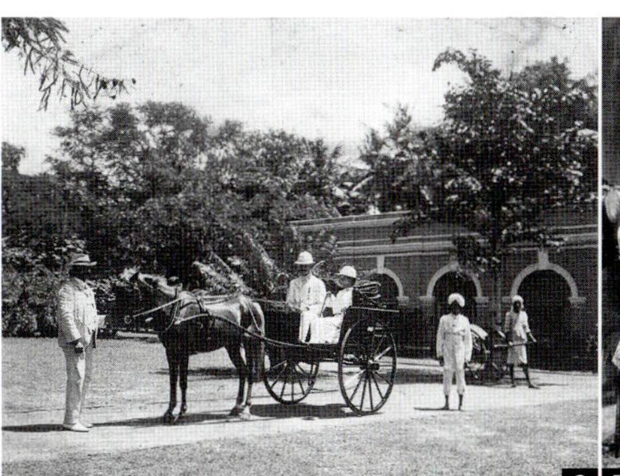

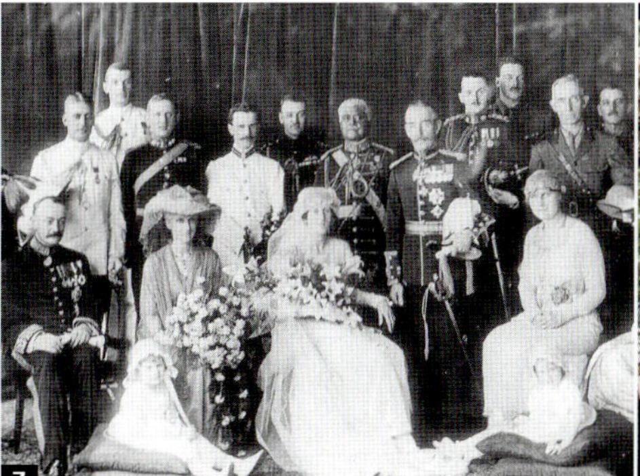

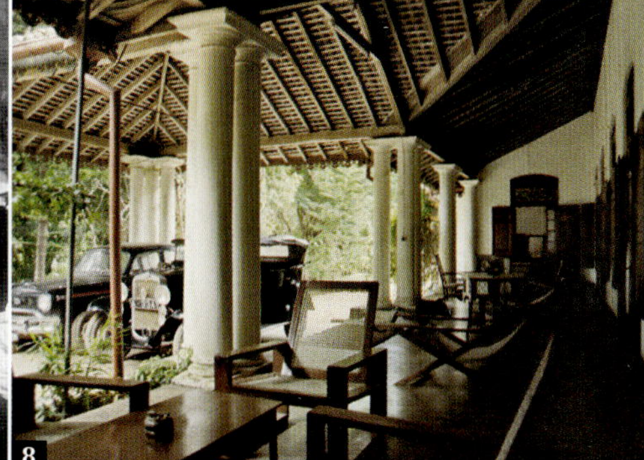

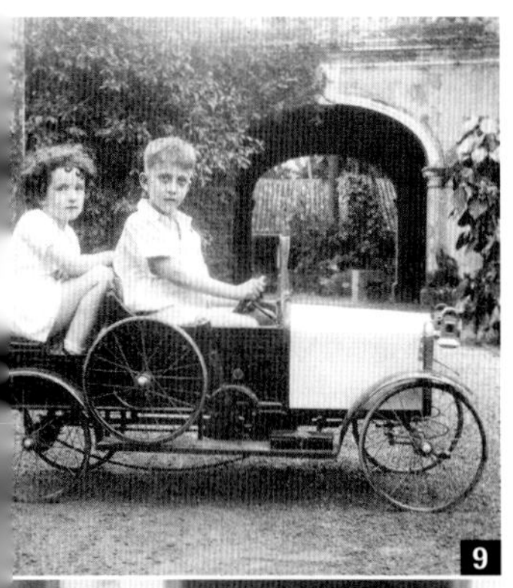

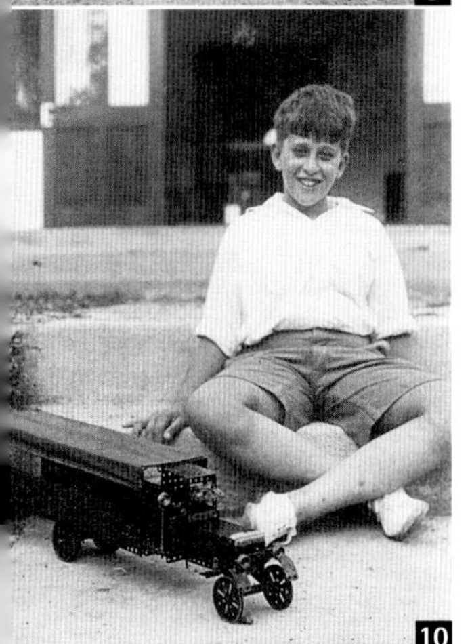

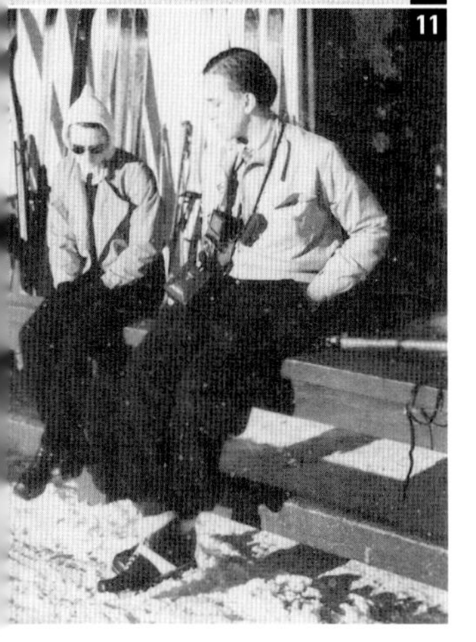

Geoffrey took his middle name from his godfather Sir William Manning, who was the British Governor and a close friend of the Bawas. It was rumoured that Manning was his real father and a portrait that hangs in the National Archive does reveal a certain resemblance. That Geoffrey was of fair complexion while his brother was dark simply fuelled speculation. During his time in Cambridge, it is said that Geoffrey often boasted that he was the illegitimate son of an 'English gentleman', and once suggested to the writer Olivia Manning that they must be related. The Schrader family, according to a niece of Mrs Bawa, believed the rumours, but we shall never know the truth.

Geoffrey's early life was divided between Chapman House with its spacious and airy first-floor rooms and generous gardens, and the deep verandas of the Schrader family's estate bungalows at Kimbulupitiya and Wester Seaton near Negombo. He attended Royal College, a monumental building of red brick with stone dressings, and his daily journey to school took him past Colombo's newly completed white neo-classical Town Hall, a design of Edwards, Reid & Booth. Some of his earliest architectural memories were gleaned from a trip to China with his mother and brother when he was 15 years old. He later recalled "walking through dusty Chinese squares, yellow walls, big doors".[3]

Geoffrey's brother Bevis was 10 years his senior and their early lives barely touched: no academic, Bevis quit school at the age of 17 when Geoffrey was only seven. Despairing of her elder son's lack of ambition, their mother bought him a rubber estate near Aluthgama, which she renamed 'Brief', and set him up as a planter. Following in his father's footsteps, Bevis became a part-time officer in the Ceylon Light Infantry and, thanks more to his height and bearing than to any military prowess, was made aide-de-camp to a succession of four British governors, spending more time playing at toy soldiers than tending to his rubber trees.

Geoffrey was more studious and in 1937 enrolled at University College Colombo to study English. In that year Mrs Bawa decided to invest in property for her two sons. Having given Bevis a house in Colombo's Deal Place, she bought a piece of land in Buller's Lane for Geoffrey and commissioned architect Oliver Weerasinghe to design a house for him. Bevis was friendly with Arthur van Langenberg, an up-and-coming theatre designer, and the two persuaded Geoffrey to take an active interest in the project, much to the frustration of the architect. Weerasinghe's design was in conventional Art Deco style, but Geoffrey and his co-conspirators inserted a modern staircase with open concrete treads and a flowing tubular steel handrail. Geoffrey never lived in the house and sold it in 1946. It now houses the Dutch Consulate, though the staircase was recently removed.

Geoffrey's mother was determined that he should become a lawyer like his father, and in 1938 sent him away to study in England. Having won a place for the following year to read English at St Catherine's College Cambridge, he went to stay in Paris with a distant cousin of his father called Georgette Camille. Georgette had made a name as a translator of English novels and moved in avant-garde circles. She took him to parties where he met such luminaries as Braque and Léger and caught glimpses of what he would later describe as "alternative possibilities". From Paris, seemingly oblivious to the threat of war, he moved on to spend the summer of 1939 in Italy. There he seems to have devoted himself to writing short stories, a folio of which, called *Florence August 1939* and dedicated to his brother Bevis, recently came to light by chance at a London jumble sale.

<hr>

[3] In conversation with Channa Daswatte, 1997

## Cambridge and London

Geoffrey's time at Cambridge coincided with the first three years of World War II and many of his contemporaries gave up their studies to enlist. He avoided those he called the 'ruggerites' and the debaters and joined the aesthetes, decorating his rooms on King's Parade in faux Georgian style with gilt mirrors and chandeliers. His friends were members of the minor aristocracy and he enjoyed weekending in their country houses and exploring their landscaped parks.

After completing his degree in 1942, he moved to London to study for the Bar at the Middle Temple and shared a flat in Belgravia with his Cambridge friend the Honourable Guy Strutt. He passed his final law exams in 1944, but put off returning to Sri Lanka.

At the end of the War in 1945, Geoffrey accompanied Guy Strutt on a visit to Guy's aunt, the Duchesse della Grazia, who lived in a villa overlooking Lake Garda. An architect friend of the Duchesse took Geoffrey on excursions around the Veneto visiting renaissance gardens and some of the villas of Andrea Palladio.

Geoffrey's life in London was putting a big strain on the family finances and he came under increasing pressure from his brother to return to Ceylon. Bevis, as equerry to the British Governor, managed to get Geoffrey a seat on an RAF transport plane that flew into Ratmalana Airport at the end of January 1946.

Reunited with his family after an exile of eight years, Geoffrey moved back into Chapman House, took a job with the law firm of Noel Gratiaen, and bought his first Rolls Royce, a 1925 Phantom I. However, his mother, who had been ill for some time, died three months later. Disposing of much of his property, including his share in Chapman House and his newly acquired Rolls, Geoffrey quit Ceylon at the end of 1946 and set off on a year-long world tour that would take him to Europe via the Far East and across the United States.

In Britain he paused to buy his second Rolls Royce — a 1925 Silver Ghost — and arranged for it to be shipped back to Ceylon. He then headed back to Italy and the shores of Lake Garda where his hopes of buying a villa and creating his own Italian garden were eventually dashed by machinating lawyers. Forced to accept that his money was running out, he returned disconsolately to Ceylon in 1948, just as it was throwing off the shackles of empire.

**9** Geoffrey Bawa in his toy car at Chapman House, *circa* 1929. Bawa Archive.
**10** Geoffrey Bawa with his Meccano, *circa* 1933. Bawa Archive.
**11** Geoffrey Bawa with Georgette Camille, 1939. Bawa Archive.
**12** Geoffrey Bawa in his rooms in Cambridge, *circa* 1940. Bawa Archive.
**13** Geoffrey Bawa in Italy, 1945. Bawa Archive.
**14** Geoffrey Bawa's first Rolls Royce,$ 1946. Bawa Archive.

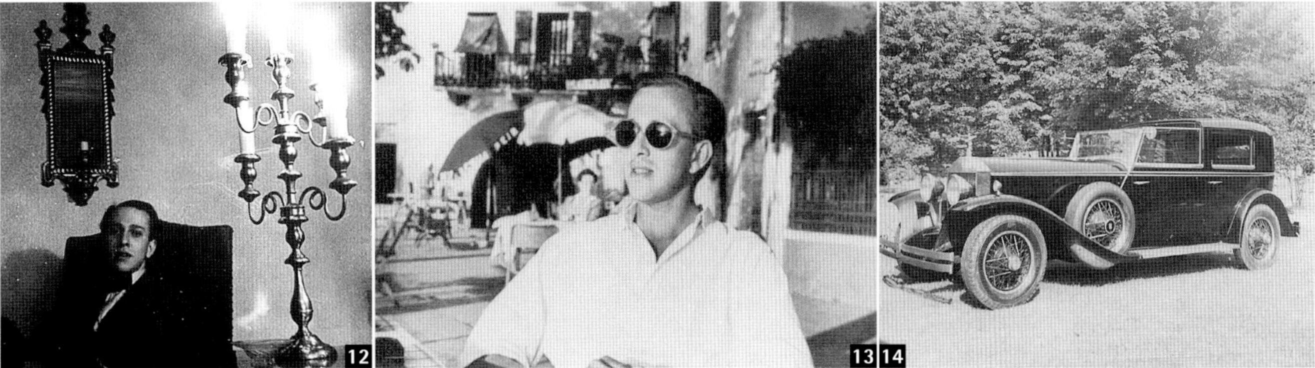

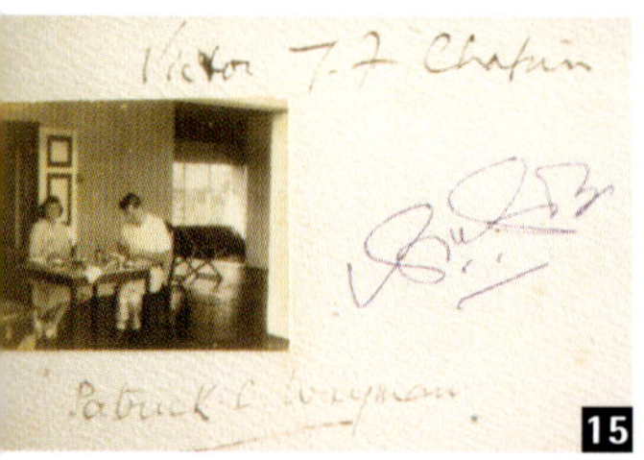


**15**

## Lunuganga

Bevis had sold off much of his rubber estate at Brief during the War, and had used the money to develop a landscaped garden on the land around its bungalow. As the garden matured it attracted visitors from far and wide, encouraging Bevis to start a plant nursery and, with his friend Arthur van Langenberg, to set up a garden design consultancy. When Geoffrey returned in 1948, he no longer had a home of his own and went to stay at Brief.

Bevis wrote in his memoirs: "We were more or less strangers at the time of (Geoffrey's) return: I Eastern in outlook and Geoffrey British. Geoffrey was happier with Europeans, hardly remembering his few school friends in Ceylon. His whole life was tied up with the arts, beauty and culture: good taste in everything from vintage cars to snuff boxes."

Geoffrey was impressed by his brother's garden which seemed to match his dreams for the villa on Lake Garda. But Bevis's achievement stirred up old rivalries and he resolved to create a garden that would be bigger and better than that of his brother. Searching for a suitable piece of land he stumbled across an abandoned rubber estate that straddled two hills across a promontory in the Dedduwa Lagoon, a couple of kilometres inland from Bentota. Having negotiated its purchase from a complex clan of shareholders, Geoffrey became the proud owner of his own country estate and renamed it 'Lunuganga' or 'Salt River'.

The development of the garden would occupy him for the best part of half a century and hardly a year passed without him undertaking some new improvement. However, although brimming over with ideas, he found that he lacked the necessary technical knowledge. His cousin Georgette from Paris was one of his first visitors in 1949 and it was she who advised him to study to become an architect "so that you can use other people's money to do what you like doing best".

## The Deraniyagalas

Geoffrey went back to work in Noel Gratiaen's law firm and rented a flat overlooking the Galle Face Green in a building that had been designed in 1931 by architects Edwards, Reid & Booth. During 1951, however, he also worked intermittently as an unpaid intern with HH Reid, the firm's sole surviving partner. The practice had been founded in 1924 by SJ Edwards, a partner in the Penang practice of

**15** The first visitors at Lunuganga: Georgette Camille and Victor Chapin. Lunuganga Visitors' Book, 1949. Bawa Archive.
**16** Aerial view of Lunuganga, *circa* 1955. Bawa Archive.
**17** The ha-ha at Lunuganga, *circa* 1960. Bawa Archive.

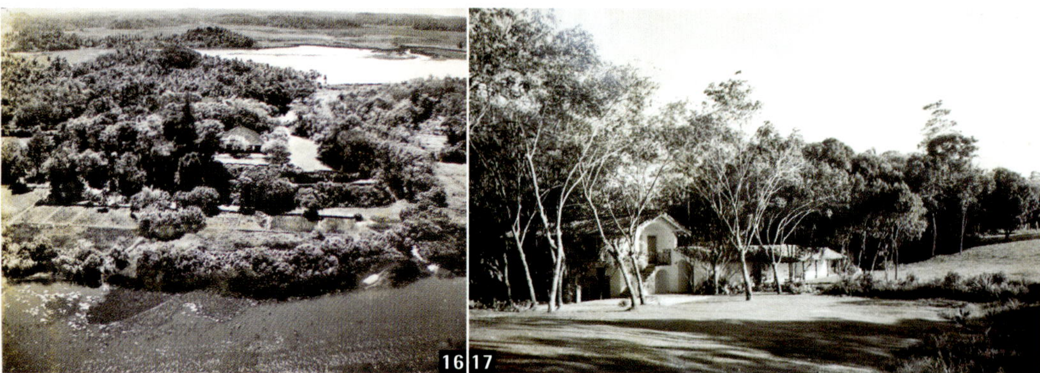

**16 17**

Booty & Edwards, after winning the competition to build the new Colombo Town Hall. With a portfolio that included the Hong Kong and Shanghai Bank, the rebuilding of the Kelaniya Temple, the Colombo Art Gallery and the Nuwara Eliya Hill Club, it became the most prolific in colonial Ceylon. Edwards, Booth and his successor Begg had all quit the firm before the outbreak of World War II, but Reid stayed on and took in a Colombo Parsee called Jimmy Nilgiria as his 'local partner'. The firm occupied offices in the Prince Building in the heart of the Colombo Fort.

Little is known about Geoffrey's brief sojourn with Reid but it coincided with him meeting the Deraniyagalas. Paul Deraniyagala was a zoologist and the Director of the Colombo Museum, whilst his wife Prini came from the Mollamure family and was heir to the famous Ecknelligoda manor house at Kuruwita. His brother Justin Deraniyagala, one of Sri Lanka's leading painters, lived in another famous manor house at Nugedola, near Pasyala.

Paul's maternal grandmother, Lady Hilda Obeyasekere, owned a large tract of land between Reid Avenue and Guilford Crescent. She decided to divide up and share this amongst her grandchildren, giving each of them the princely sum of 100,000 rupees with which to build a house. Architects were in short supply and the Deraniyagalas failed to find one who could satisfy their ambitions. Lady Obeyasekere was impatient for them to get started and told them of a young lawyer called Bawa who was now apprenticed to a firm of architects. Geoffrey was summoned to a meeting in the Deraniyagala's home in Castle Street and their son Arjun has a clear memory of returning home from school to find a Rolls Royce parked in the drive and a tall man in lawyer's rig seated with his mother. Mrs Deraniyagala wanted a contemporary house that would also capture the spirit of the family's ancient manor houses and she sent Geoffrey off with her younger son Siran on a visit to Ecknelligoda.

Geoffrey agreed to design the Deraniyagala's house, but was again plagued by his lack of technical skills. When he suggested to Mrs Deraniyagala that she should find another architect, she encouraged him to go and study, assuring him that she would postpone the project until he was qualified.

## The Architectural Association (AA)

This encounter with Prini Deraniyagala pushed Geoffrey towards a career as an architect. Leaving Lunuganga in the safe hands of his friend Neville Wynne-Jones, he returned to Britain at the end of 1952, accompanied by his third Rolls Royce, a 1934 Drophead Coupé. Having no clear plan, he rented rooms in Cambridge, where he engaged a private tutor to teach him construction and structural design. After spending the winter of 1953 in Ceylon, he applied to the AA School in London and managed to persuade the Principal, Michael Patrick, to take into account his age and allow him to join the third year of the five-year course in 1954.

His time at the AA coincided with a seismic shift towards Modernism, and Geoffrey rubbed shoulders with students and lecturers who would become the leading British architects of the day. However, he remained detached from the polemics of the various modernist factions in the school, using his lawyers' skills to demolish their arguments. He claimed to be interested in the "whole history of architecture" arguing, unfashionably, that Vignola was every bit as important as le Corbusier.

His second year was spent in John Killick's Studio and he took part in a study of housing in Islington that was later published in the journal 'Architectural Design'. He also took a close interest in a new

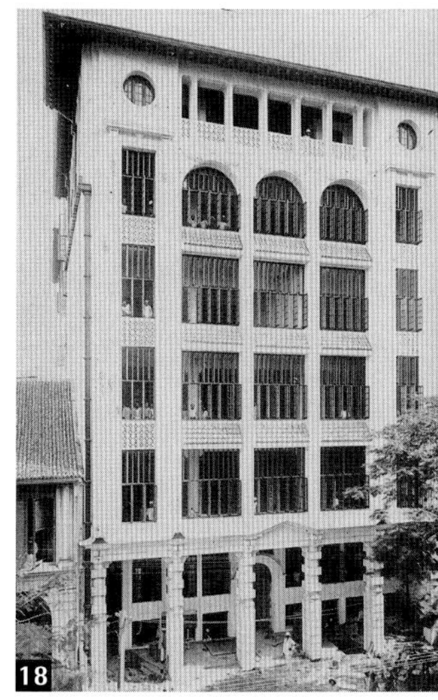

**18** The Prince Building, Colombo, *circa* 1920. Bawa Archive.

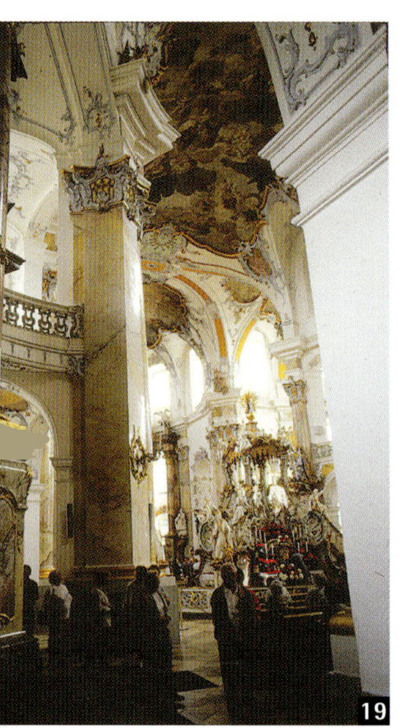

**19** Vierzehnheiligen Church,
Balthasar Neumann.
**20** From left to right: Booth,
Edwards and Reid, *circa* 1932.

tropical architecture course that was being offered by Maxwell Fry and, though he didn't join the course, became a friend of Fry and his wife Jane Drew.

Of his teachers, one of the most influential was John Summerson, the author of *The Classical Language of Architecture* (first published 1965) who convinced him that buildings are not themselves possessed of intrinsic meanings, but that meanings are attributed to them through use.

Tiring of student life, Geoffrey spent much of his final year in Italy and wrote his dissertation on the German Baroque architect Balthazar Neumann[4]. Neumann started out as a canon founder and became a military engineer before turning to architecture at about the age of 30. Geoffrey could not resist observing: "In these days of academic professionalism, it is a little difficult to see how it would profit a man like Neumann to come so late to architecture. The answer is that by that time he had had a thorough grounding in all sorts of crafts and trades, both practical and theoretical, without which he would not have been able to deploy the abilities of his various associates to such good effect."

He reflected at length on the apparent contradiction between the need for each generation to build on the achievements of the past and the imperative to challenge the past and initiate change: "In art a decade or two are the limits of a generation. Each new generation finds its instincts are for change and self assertion; each newcomer looking at the achievements of his predecessor feels varying degrees of dissatisfaction...".

He admired Neumann's innovative structural designs, and his resolution of the conflict between the need for centrality and axiality in church planning. But most of all he admired his use of light to articulate space: "The light in a Neumann church is astonishingly even in its distribution. This is true of Vierzehnheiligen: the windows are deep set and glazed in plain glass and the deep embrasures modify the midday sun. Light is handled like an omnipresent but subtle fluid."

Geoffrey also lauded Neumann's staircases: "Neumann's palace designs, in their junctions and reflections of plan-spaces and in the handling of staircases, owe a debt to the early joint work of Bernini and Borromini in the Barberini Palace in Rome."

His dissertation was accepted and in June 1957 he passed the final examinations of the AA and was elected a member of the Royal Institute of British Architects.

## Edwards, Reid & Begg

Back in Ceylon, Geoffrey re-joined the now much reduced firm of Edwards, Reid & Begg which was still based in the Prince Building. HH Reid had died suddenly in 1952, leaving Jimmy Nilgiria as the principal partner.

His return coincided with that of Valentine Gunasekara, an architect 10 years his junior who had been his contemporary at the AA where they had carefully avoided each other. Nilgiria was keen to recruit London-qualified architects and offered them both 'ten-per-cent' partnerships. From the outset they worked on different jobs and recruited their own assistants.

Geoffrey had had no practical experience of working in an architect's office, apart from his brief internship with Reid. His team included Turner Wickremasinghe and Nihal Amerasinghe, who would later complete their studies in England, and Stanley Perera, a seasoned technician who was a cousin of the important Socialist politician NM Perera.

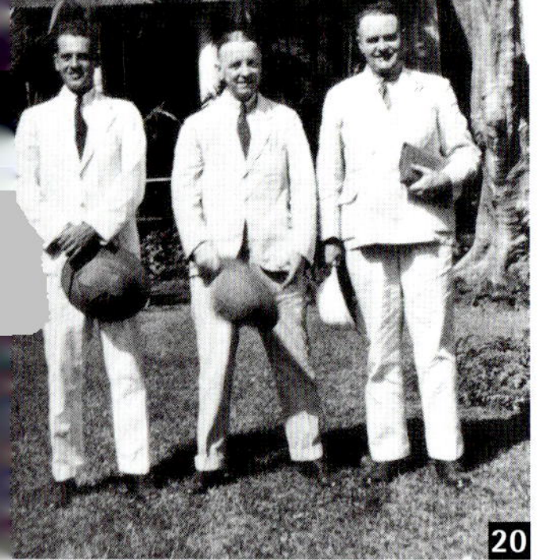

[4] 'Balthazar Neumann and His Architecture', History Thesis submitted by Geoffrey Bawa to Architectural Association, June 1957

He was allocated a number of commercial projects — an office building and workshops for Baur Ltd and a factory for Lipton, both in Grand Pass, and an industrial estate at Ekala, near the airport. But he also renewed contact with the Deraniyagalas and quickly finalised the design for their house in Guilford Crescent.

## Ulrik Plesner

At the end of 1958 Geoffrey was invited to a grand party given for the composer Benjamin Britten and his partner Peter Pears on a tea estate in the hills above Kandy. Stopping off for a drink at the Queens Hotel in Kandy he met a young Danish architect called Ulrik Plesner and invited him to tag along. Plesner had been working during the previous year in the Kandy office of the architect Minnette de Silva. Minnette was renowned as the first Asian woman to have become an associate of the Royal Institute of British Architects, and had been practising in Kandy for almost a decade, producing a number of innovative buildings. She was one of the first architects to attempt a fusion of modernist and traditional tropes and formulated her own theory of 'a Modern Regional Architecture for the Tropics'. Ulrik admired her progressive ideas, but she didn't pay his salary and he was bored by provincial life. When Geoffrey offered him a job in Colombo, he jumped at the opportunity.

Ulrik worked initially as a freelance consultant on the various factory projects that had been assigned to Geoffrey and quickly became his close associate and friend. Although only 28 years old, he had already worked with architects in Copenhagen and London, gaining the professional experience that Geoffrey lacked. As collaborators they complemented each other: Ulrik was an inventive designer with practical skills, while Geoffrey had a profound knowledge of the culture of architecture gleaned from his years of travel.

The two were soon almost inseparable. During the week they worked together long into the night, dined together, talked architecture together. At weekends they travelled around the island looking for old buildings or they retired to Lunuganga to work on the garden.

The common approach which they first developed was influenced both by Ulrik's grounding in Danish modernism and by Geoffrey's interest in the Tropical Modernism that had been promulgated by Fry and Drew. It was characterised by their designs for classroom blocks for St Thomas' Prep School and Bishop's College in Colombo, both of which employed simple white cubic forms, exposed concrete structures, and geometrically patterned sun-screens.

Ulrik undertook a handful of projects off his own bat, including a house for the lawyer Maurice Perera and an annexe for the textile designer Barbara Sansoni. These employed gently sloping clay-tiled roofs with double-height volumes and made subtle references both to Ceylonese vernacular traditions and to the simple abstract functionalism of Scandinavia. Barbara Sansoni became a friend and together they started to record old buildings, recruiting the artist/architects Laki Senanayake and Ismeth Raheem to help produce the beautiful measured drawings that they would later publish.

However, Geoffrey and Ulrik soon became disenchanted with their early designs, having discovered that the Tropical Modern approach created as many problems as it solved. Pure white forms deteriorated quickly in the humid climate and sun-screens produced stuffy and claustrophobic interiors. They concluded that the roof was the most important element of a building in the tropics and that interiors should be protected by deep overhanging eaves and cooled by cross-ventilation. Inspired by Minnette de Silva, they also turned to traditional buildings for inspiration.

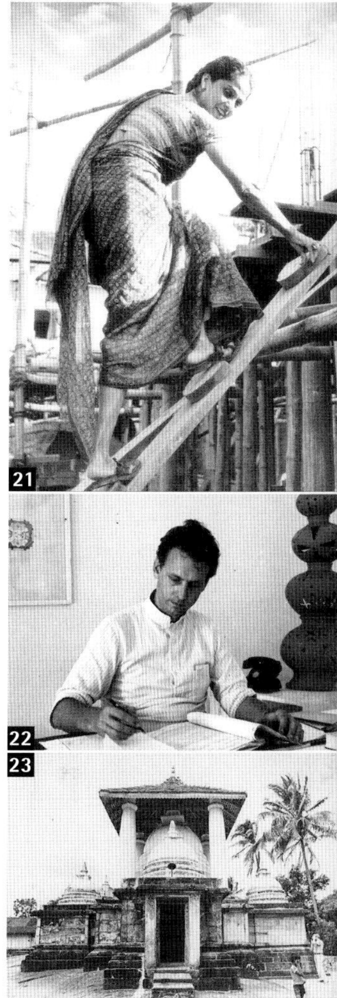

**21** Minnette de Silva, 1958.
**22** Ulrik Plesner, 1962.
**23** Geoffrey Bawa's photograph of the Gadaladeniya Temple with Plesner on the right, *circa* 1962.

The imperative to develop a new approach was also encouraged by economic necessity. Imported building materials, like metal or glass, were expensive and in short supply, and cement and reinforcing bars, though manufactured locally, were also costly. Air-conditioning was in its infancy, was expensive to run and was compromised by intermittent power supplies. It made absolute good sense to use locally produced materials like stone, brick, clay-tile, timber and lime plaster and to develop alternative ways to cool buildings.

Their first 'roof' house was built for a Dr ASH de Silva in Galle. This consisted of a cluster of linked pavilions on a hillside that defined a series of partially enclosed garden courts and was unified by a single over-sailing roof plane. Their second was the remarkable Polontalawa Estate Bungalow in which the main part of the house was reduced to a simple roof without walls that spanned between a pair of massive boulders.

Their first 'contemporary vernacular' house was the courtyard house they designed for the batik designer Ena de Silva that was a reworking of a traditional manor house. The second was a house for a Dr Bartholomeusz in Colombo that, having been abandoned by the client before it was finished, was quickly transformed into a new office for the practice.

During the mid 1960s Geoffrey was joined by talented young assistants including Anura Ratnavibushana, Ismeth Raheem, Vasantha Chandraratne and Pheroze Choksy; they were all graduates of the new school of architecture at Katubedde.

Geoffrey now found himself at the centre of a circle of enthusiastic people, including batik artist Ena de Silva, textile designer Barbara Sansoni and artist Laki Senanayake. They had skills that he lacked, but he acted as their lynch pin, as the conductor of their small orchestra. He offered a panoramic view of architectural history, a deep-rooted awareness of the culture of architecture, and a clear appreciation of what constituted good design.

The group came together to produce *Gesamtkunstwerke* or 'total works of art'. The Bandarawela Chapel was designed by Geoffrey and Ulrik using materials gathered from the surrounding area. The Stations of the Cross and the panels depicting the 23rd Psalm were made by Barbara Sansoni, the furniture was designed by Ulrik and the priest's vestments were designed by Laki Senanayake. The Bentota Beach Hotel, Sri Lanka's first purpose-built resort, used only one strategically placed lift and was originally cooled by natural ventilation. Ismeth Raheem and Pheroze Choksy designed the furniture, Ena de Silva made the batik ceiling panels, Barbara Sansoni supplied the bed and table linen, and Laki Senanayake and Ismeth Raheem created the artworks.

Senanayake and Raheem were skilled draftsmen and together developed the graphic drawing style that became the hallmark of the office. Both were influenced by the topographical paintings of Bevis Bawa's long-term house guest, the Australian artist Donald Friend. A section through the Ena de Silva House drawn by Senanayake in 1960 was typical of the new approach. At the time architects were wont to draw in a manner that emphasised the abstract qualities of their designs, and landscape was represented by stylised symbols — trees were drawn as circles in plan and lollypops in elevation, for example. Senanayake's drawing offers a phenomenological image of the house as it might be experienced by its occupants: the trees are drawn accurately to represent the actual species and a tiny tortoise can be seen crossing the veranda. This method formed the basis of what later became the Bawa office drawings style.

Senanayake later drifted away from architecture to concentrate on art and design, contributing paintings and sculptures to many of Bawa's buildings. With Ulrik's assistance Ratnavibushana, Raheem,

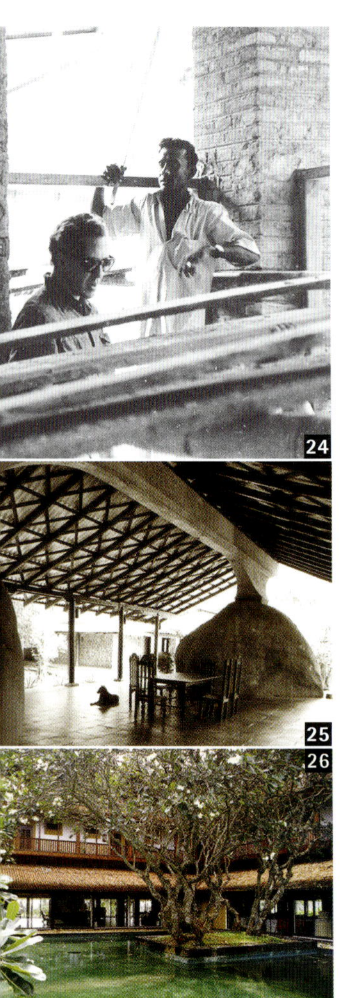

**24** Geoffrey Bawa on site with Dr AHS de Silva, 1959.
**25** The main pavilion at Polontalawa, *circa* 1985.
**26** The courtyard of the Bentota Beach Hotel, 1990.

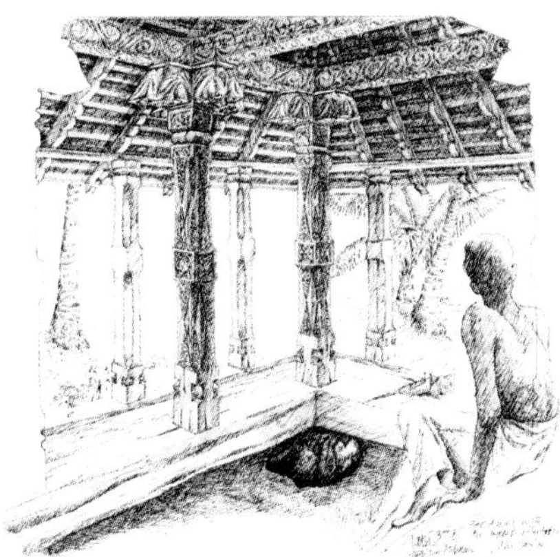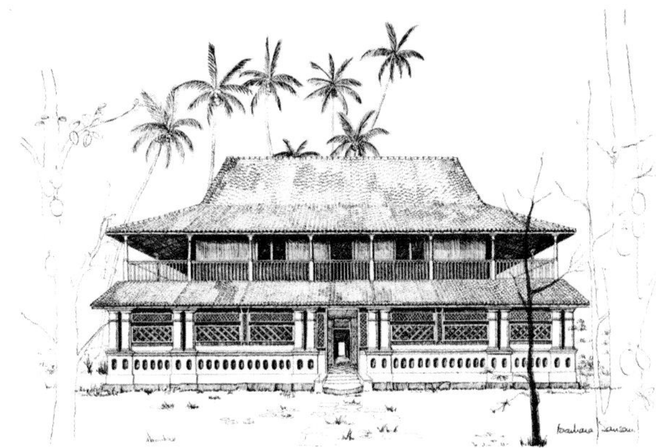



Chandraratne and Choksy were able to complete their training in Denmark, rejoining the office at the end of the 1960s.

The first articles to feature Geoffrey's work on an international stage appeared in two successive issues of the Danish Journal 'Arkitekten' in 1965 and were written in Danish by Ulrik Plesner. These were followed a year later by a major article in English that appeared in the 'Architectural Review' in 1966 under the title 'Ceylon Seven New Buildings – Geoffrey Bawa and Ulrik Plesner'. The article featured seven projects, each of them illustrated with haunting black and white photographs and expressive drawings executed in what was fast becoming the office's trademark drawing style.

There can be no doubt that Geoffrey relied heavily on Ulrik's skills during their eight years together and that Ulrik contributed both to the projects that they conceived together and to Geoffrey's development as an architect. However, their relationship soured during 1966, in part because Geoffrey felt that Ulrik was getting 'too big for his boots' and in part because Ulrik resented Geoffrey's reluctance to acknowledge the full extent of their joint working. Things were not helped by the arrival in Colombo of Tamar Liebes, Ulrik's girlfriend and future wife.

During 1966 Ulrik was sidelined into working on abortive projects and, in 1967, following the cancellation of the Colombo Hilton, he returned to Europe. After an acrimonious separation the two agreed to attribute certain projects, such as Polontalawa, to Ulrik, and others, such as the Ena de Silva House, to Geoffrey. The truth, however, was certainly much more complicated and each of them contributed to varying degrees in different ways to all of the projects that passed through the office during the period of their collaboration.

Ulrik's departure coincided with the emergence of Dr K Poologasundram or 'Poologs' as a major player in the office. Poologasundram was a brilliant structural engineer who had been moonlighting for several years as Geoffrey's consultant. When Geoffrey invited him to become a partner in the practice, Poologs stipulated that Nilgiria be bought out, that Gunasekara be persuaded to 'go it alone' and that Ulrik be encouraged to leave. Geoffrey agreed and gave Poologs a free hand in exorcising the partnership's ghosts. Soon, Poologs was established as Geoffrey's equal partner with responsibility for engineering and office management.

A version of the 'Architectural Review' article was later published in 'The Times of Ceylon Annual' of 1968, though Plesner's name was expunged. It was accompanied by a reflective text written by Geoffrey entitled 'A Way of Building'. This was the closest that he ever came to setting out his personal philosophy and formed the basis of an essay which appeared in the later monograph of 1986. In it he proposed a simple reiteration of the Vitruvian virtues of 'Commodity, Firmness and Delight' in the form of three simple rules: that a building 'should satisfy the needs that give it birth'; that there must be a 'knowledgeable and true use of the materials with which you build'; that 'a building in Ceylon must be in accord with the country's ambience'.

Ulrik Plesner spent some time in London before moving with his Israeli wife to Jerusalem. Over the years he published several articles about his work in which he claimed a number of the Edwards, Reid & Begg projects as his own. In 2012 he published his own delusional account of their joint working some 50 years after the events it portrays[5]. In it he describes his life in Ceylon, boasting of his sexual exploits — amongst them his alleged seduction by the architect Minnette de Silva and his purchase of a concubine from a village headman — and of his Bond-like dealings with Israeli arms-dealers. A reviewer in the 'Architectural Review' aptly labelled him 'the Playboy of the Eastern World'.

Plesner paints a scathing picture of Bawa's lack of technical knowledge and claims hubristically, that 'the only architecture school Geoffrey ever had was the one I put him through'. He describes a total of 16 projects, implying that he was their main, if not sole, designer. In fact, while he was undoubtedly the lead designer on a few projects, the majority were designed collaboratively, and several are solely attributable to Geoffrey.

Plesner's collaboration coincided with only eight of Bawa's 40 years as an architect. When he quit in 1967 there were many who expected Bawa to founder. In fact Bawa went from strength to strength, developing highly innovative designs for the Bentota Beach Hotel and the Hanwella Farm Convent before the end of the decade.

## The Middle Years

The office had moved out of the Prince Building in 1963 and occupied the unfinished Bartholomeusz House in Alfred House Road. At more or less the same time Geoffrey gave up his flat in Galle Face Court and moved into the third of a row of four tiny cottages in an alley off 33rd Lane. By the end of the decade he had managed to buy all four and had converted them into the labyrinth of small courtyards topped by a Corbusian tower that would be his home for the next 30 years.

[5] Plesner, Ulrik. 'In Situ'. Denmark: Aristo, 2012

**27** The sanitorium of the Yahapath Endera Farm Orphanage, 1978.
**28** The aluminium Rolls Royce in front of Keith Lodge, Geoffrey Bawa's home in Madras, *circa* 1975.
**29** The pool court of the Madurai Club, 1975.

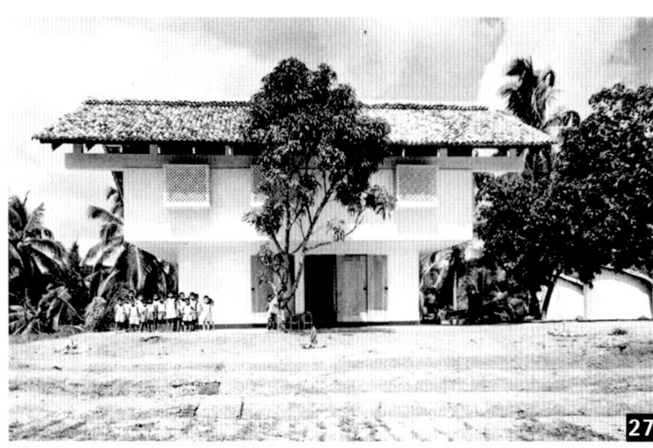

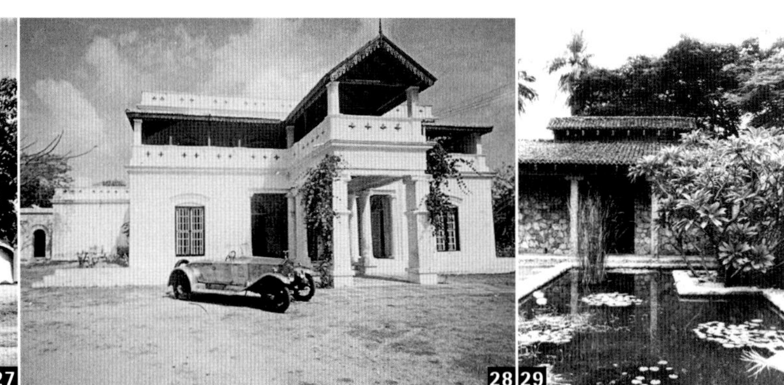

During the late 1960s Geoffrey and his team of young assistants produced a series of innovative projects in 'contemporary vernacular' mode, and the practice became the most prolific and the most versatile in the land.

Any complacency was shattered, however, by the election of Mrs Bandaranaike's Nationalist Socialist government in 1970 and the violent armed insurrection that followed a year later. These events threatened the minority communities and the newly established middle classes and many educated people chose to emigrate.

Fearing that his practice may fail to find work, Geoffrey established a bolthole in Madras, renting a substantial house and buying an aluminium-clad Rolls Royce while he touted for work. During the early 1970s his Indian office was moderately successful, producing designs for a substantial extension to the Connemara Hotel in Madras and a beautiful staff club in Madurai.

At the same time Geoffrey picked up commissions in Bali and Mauritius. His client in Bali was the Australian artist Donald Friend who had been his brother's tenant at Brief for some five years at the end of the 1950s. Friend, now a Bali resident, was seeking to develop an estate of beachside properties at Batujimbar and invited Bawa to be his architect. Bawa threw himself into the project with gusto and, although only three of the projected villas were built, the project established his reputation in South East Asia. In Mauritius his client was an ex-Colombo tea-broker called Peter White for whom he converted an abandoned sugar factory into a magical holiday home.

Much to his surprise, Geoffrey became a favourite architect of the Bandaranaike Government. In the space of five years, he designed an industrial estate near Kandy, the science faculty of the new Vidyodaya University in Nugegoda, the Agrarian Research and Training Institute near Independence Square and the astonishing Mahaweli tower opposite his parents' former home in Darley Road.

In 1976, whilst on a site visit to the Connemara Hotel, Geoffrey was introduced to an unlikely architectural trio from Britain: Joe Chamberlin, his wife Jean and their companion Christoph Bon. These three had formed the rump of the firm Chamberlin, Powell & Bon and had recently completed the huge Barbican development in London. Geoffrey invited them to join him on a trip in his silver Rolls Royce to visit the recently completed Madurai Club. His guests were impressed by what they were shown and resolved to visit Sri Lanka in the following year to see more of his work. This they did and, as a result, they persuaded their friend Michael Brawne to write a critical appraisal of Bawa's designs in the 'Architectural Review'.

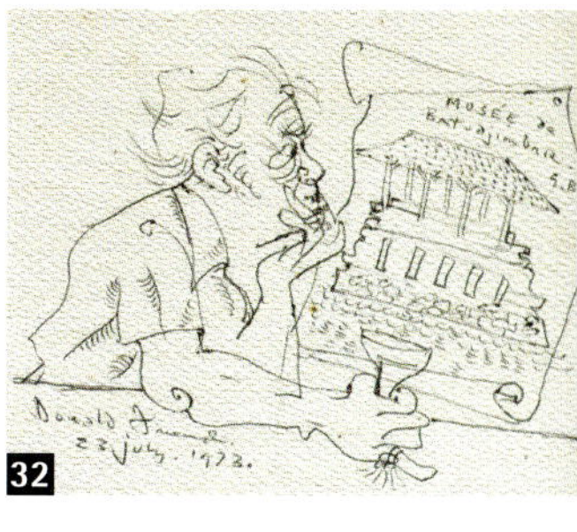

**30** House No 11, Batujimbar, Bali, 2006.
**31** Geoffrey Bawa with Jean Chamberlin and Christoph Bon, *circa* 1990.
**32** 'Dreaming of Batujimbar', Donald Friend's self-portrait in the Lunuganga Visitors' Book, 1973. Bawa Archive.

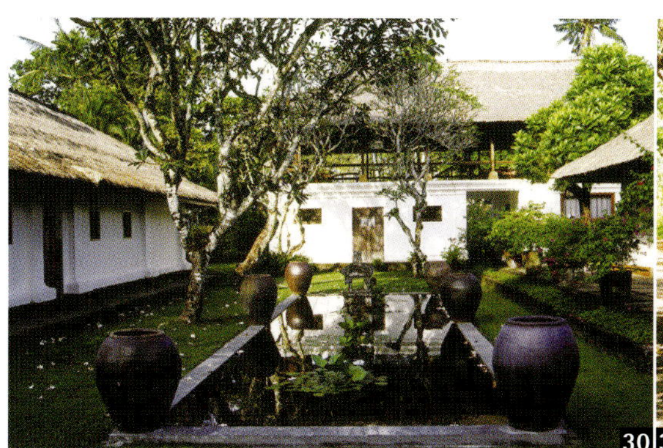
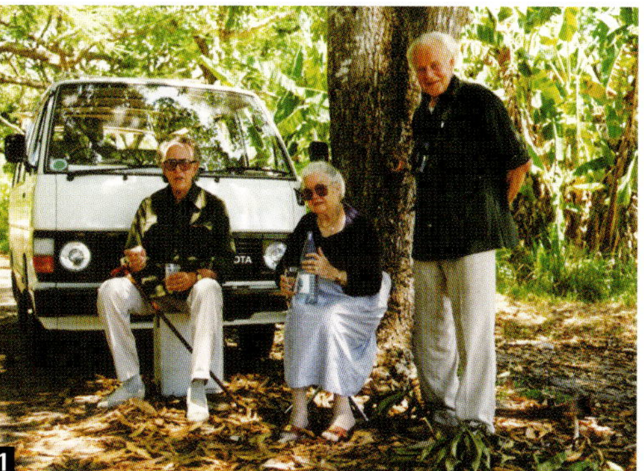

When Joe Chamberlin died suddenly in 1978, Geoffrey was invited to take his place in the trio and the three became close friends, sharing their various homes and embarking on ambitious architectural tours together. Their friendship lasted for almost two decades, spawning several books and articles, until Geoffrey dissolved it in an inexplicable fit of pique.

## The Big Projects

In 1977 the Bandaranaike government was swept aside by JR Jayawardene's United National party, heralding a period of economic liberalisation and rapid development. Like the Vicar of Bray, Geoffrey soon ingratiated himself with the new government. In quick succession he received commissions to build a new Parliament at Kotte, a prestigious hotel at Ahungalla and a massive new university campus near Matara.

By now most of his early assistants had left to pursue independent careers: Turner Wickremasinghe had become Chief Architect to the State Engineering Corporation; Ismeth Raheem and Pheroze Choksy had started their own practice; Anura Ratnavibushana had joined the firm of Mihindu Keerthiratne; and Laki Senanayake continued to paint while running his own landscaping consultancy.

Only Vasantha Jacobsen-Chandraratne remained from the group that had joined Geoffrey in the early 1960s and it was she who took on the onerous task of managing the Parliament project alongside Dr Poologasundram. Working with Mitsui, the Japanese contracting company, they managed to complete the project on time and to budget. Soon after, however, Vasantha and her Danish husband disposed of all their worldly goods and entered separate Buddhist monasteries, where they remain to this day.

On a visit to Australia, Geoffrey was introduced to a young Sri Lankan architect called Nihal Bodhinayake and invited him to join him on the Ruhunu University project. Bodhinayake then spent the next six years as the sole project architect on a development that comprised over 50 separate buildings with a combined area of around 40,000 square metres.

## Broadcasting Bawa

In 1986 a monograph on Bawa was published in Singapore by Concept Media, the publishing arm of the Aga Khan Trust for Culture[6]. The book had been the dream of Joe Chamberlin before his death in 1978 and was given its initial impetus by Christoph Bon and Joe's widow Jean. They had planned to publish it in London with the Architectural Press and persuaded 'Architectural Review' editor Jim Richards to write the Foreword. Geoffrey didn't approve of Richards' text, however, and the project stalled. Then Hassan Udin Khan, the joint editor of the Aga Khan journal 'Mimar', appeared in Colombo and proposed taking on the project with his colleague Brian Brace Taylor as the lead writer. The architect Anjalendran, who acted as Geoffrey's unpaid assistant and amanuensis throughout the 1980s, took on the role as go-between and was largely responsible for the book's content.

Geoffrey had always practiced under the aegis of Edwards, Reid & Begg, but the book was given the title *Geoffrey Bawa*, implying that he was the sole author of all that it contained. That it omitted any reference to Ulrik Plesner came as no surprise, but the fact that it failed to acknowledge the contribution of Dr Poologasundram, Geoffrey's partner of 20 years' standing, caused consternation.

[6] Brace Taylor, Brian et al. *Geoffrey Bawa*. Singapore: Concept Media, 1986

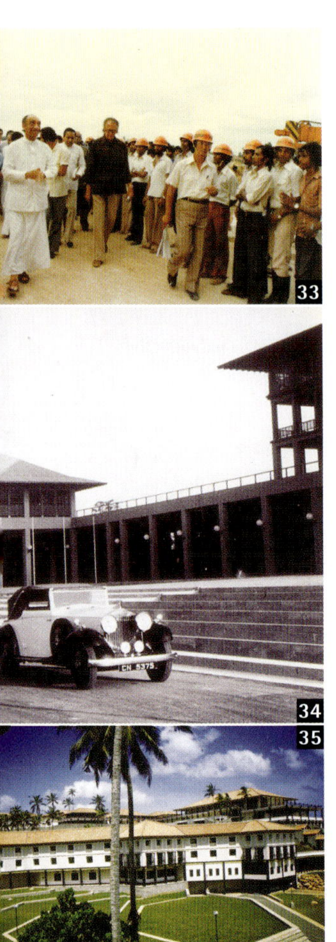

**33** An official site visit to the Parliament with Sri Lankan President JR Jayawardene (on left), 1981.
**34** Geoffrey Bawa's Rolls Royce parked in front of the newly-built Parliament, 1983.
**35** Ruhunu University Campus, 1985.

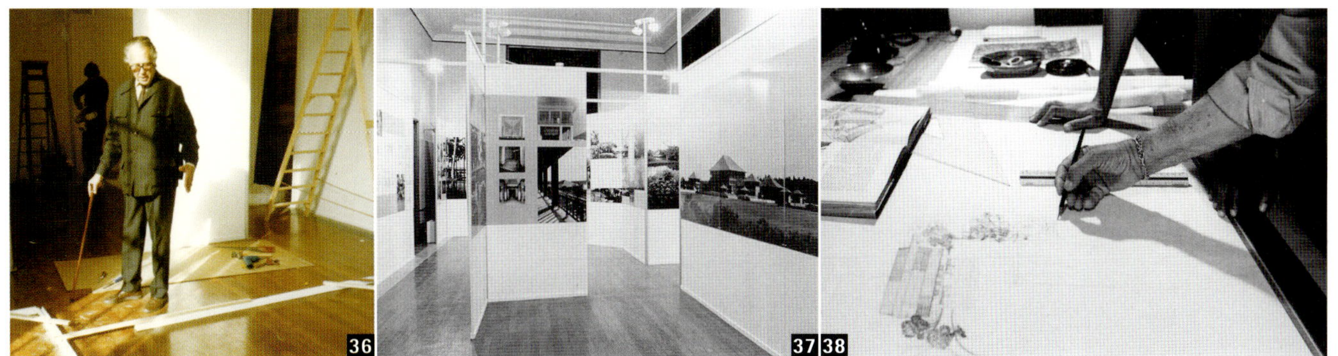

The book, which came to be known as the *White Book*, was the first of its kind to feature the work of a contemporary Asian architect and contained a unique combination of photographs, pithy texts and explicit drawings. It was an immediate success in Singapore where Bawa's blend of modernism and tradition struck a chord. Soon copies were to be seen in every architect's office and the revolutionary way of drawing was widely copied, becoming the *lingua franca* of what came to be known as 'Tropical Regionalism'.

The publication of the book coincided with an exhibition of Bawa's work at the RIBA in London that had been the brainchild of a young British architect called Christopher Beaver. However, neither exhibition nor book attracted much attention in Britain and the exhibition panels were stored away in 33rd Lane and forgotten.

## The End of the Beginning

Geoffrey was now approaching the age of 70 and the large projects had left him exhausted. Early buildings like the Bentota Beach Hotel had been built with just a few drawings and many key decisions were taken on site with the craftsmen. In contrast, the Parliament project had necessitated hiring in a team of assistants from India who, alongside the technicians from Mitsui, produced around 5,000 drawings. Geoffrey longed to return to the simpler world that his success had banished.

This period was marked by an escalation of the Civil War in the North and by a resurgence of home-grown terrorism in the South. Geoffrey was himself threatened by a terrorist group at Lunuganga. He considered moving to Australia and went so far as to visit his friend Chris Raffel in Sydney. When asked upon his return if he was planning to settle there, he replied: "Good Lord no! It's a terrible place. D'you know poor Chris even has to iron his own shirts!"

As the decade drew on, he simply stopped making the short journey from his house at 33rd Lane to Alfred House Road and one day finally terminated his partnership agreement with Dr Poologasundram. Friends assumed that he had retired and that he would eke out the rest of his days in his beloved garden at Lunuganga. Nothing could have been further from the truth.

## The $10,000 Projects

In 1988 Geoffrey established a small design studio in the front section of his Colombo town house and enlisted Sumangala Jayatilleke and Dilshan Ferdinando to work with him. At around the same time he was invited by the Singapore Tourist Promotion Board to design a 'Cloud Centre' in the Singapore

**36** Geoffrey Bawa helping to set out the RIBA exhibition in London, 1986.
**37** The RIBA exhibition in London, 1986.
**38** Geoffrey Bawa posing with the bird's eye view of No 87, 1985.

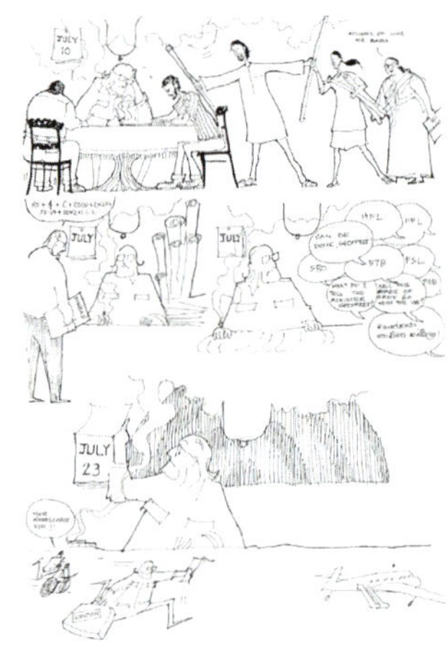

Botanical Gardens to house a simulated montane forest environment. For this he proposed creating a large glass pyramid surrounded by a cluster of smaller pyramids, set within a wooded hillside. The design was eventually turned down because it did not conform to the clients' preconceptions of what a Bawa building should be and was considered too modern. Christoph Bon later maintained that, had it been built, it would have been one of his greatest achievements.

The Singapore Cloud Centre was the first of a series of unbuilt commissions that came to be known as the $10,000 Projects. They included proposals in 1989 for an extension to the Bali Hyatt Hotel that developed ideas from the earlier Batujimbar project and took the form of a village of clustered court-yard houses linked to the beach by a 200-metre-long swimming pool. This was followed in 1991 by a commission from the Banyan Tree Group to prepare a master plan for a group of three hotels on the island of Bintan. The project was temporarily shelved, but Bawa's design later formed the basis of the main Banyan Tree Hotel. Other unbuilt projects followed in India: a house on the outskirts of Ahmedabad for the mill-owning Sarabhai family, a huge party house in Delhi for Lalith and Minar Modhi, and the conversion of a fort near Bangalore for the Poddar family.

This moment of hiatus was also marked by the publication of a beautiful book of black and white photographs and drawings of the garden at Lunuganga, funded by Jean Chamberlin. Simply entitled *Lunuganga* (first published 1990), it was photographed by Christoph Bon and Dominic Sansoni and the drawings, in the main, were done by Sumangala Jayatilleke. It became one of the most evocative garden books of all time.

## The Last Years

Geoffrey had now passed the age of 70 and his health was failing. A series of minor strokes had limited his mobility and he took to using a wheelchair. He was joined by a group of young assistants, all of them more than 40 years his junior, including Channa Daswatte, Amila de Mel and Murad Ismail. Together they embarked on a series of projects of breathtaking originality.

The first of these, commissioned in 1992, was for a new hotel near Dambulla, sited high on an isolated ridge overlooking the Kandalama Reservoir with distant views of Sigiriya. This was followed in quick succession by hotels at Galle, Kalutara and Wadduwa. These were interspersed with designs for

**Above** Geoffrey Bawa dreaming of his next trip abroad. Office cartoon by Sumangala Jayatilleke, *circa* 1989.
**39** Plan of the unbuilt Bali Hyatt extension, 1989. Bawa Archive.
**40** Visualisation of the unbuilt Singapore Cloud Centre, 2007. Tan Beng Kiang, NUS.
**41** Geoffrey Bawa and Christoph Bon during work on the Lunuganga book, 1989.

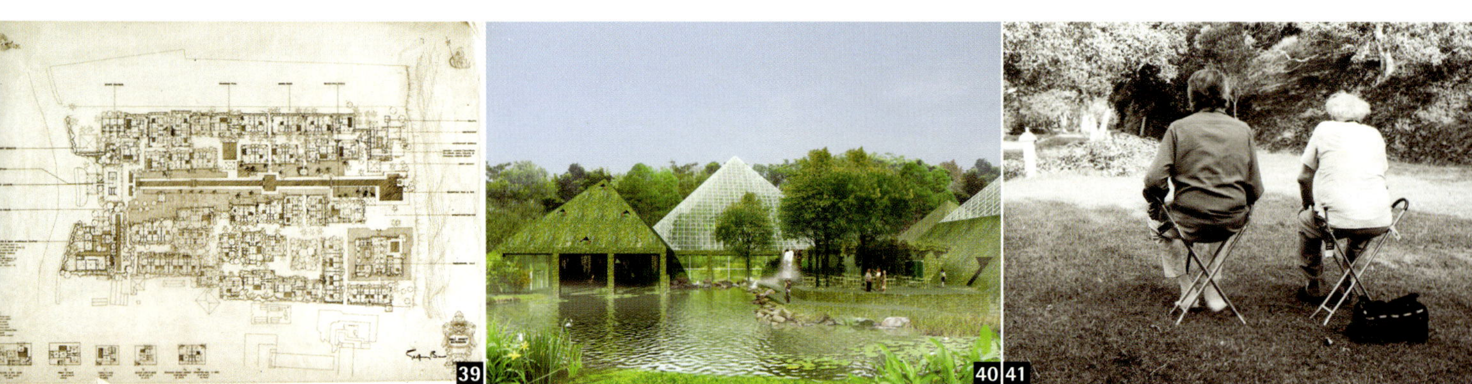

private houses: the Jayakody House and the David Spenser House in Colombo and the Jayawardene House on the Red Cliffs at Mirissa. Finally, in 1997, he was commissioned by President Kumaratunga to design a new Presidential Secretariat and Residence on the southern edge of the lake that he had created in 1980 to surround the new Parliament. With the exception of the Presidential Secretariat, all of these were carried forward to completion with Geoffrey still at the helm.

In 1995, when a request for an exhibition came out of the blue from Sao Paulo, the old RIBA exhibition from 1986 was taken out of its wrappers, brushed down and dispatched. Geoffrey travelled to Brazil for the opening to discover that what had been ignored in London was now creating a storm of admiration. He was treated like a celebrity and later told friends: "I felt like one of the Beatles". The tired old exhibition was now sent to Brisbane in Australia and to Singapore and in both places received rapturous welcomes.

1998 marked the 50th anniversary of Sri Lanka's independence from Britain and Queen Elizabeth sent her son Charles Windsor to represent her at the celebrations. A keen student of architecture, he had heard of Geoffrey Bawa and asked at the last minute if he might see the garden at Lunuganga. This unscheduled visit caused a flurry of frenetic preparation: a security cordon had to be thrown around the estate, the narrow road across the paddy fields had to be cleared, cucumber sandwiches had to be brought in from the Serendib Hotel at Bentota, and Geoffrey had to be rushed down from Colombo. The visit was a great success, but the excitement was too much for its host. Two weeks later he succumbed to a massive stroke that left him paralysed and unable to speak.

A new edition of the *White Book* had appeared in London in 1995. While it carried some revisions, it failed to cover the full range of Geoffrey's work. With Christoph Bon's encouragement, Geoffrey asked British architect David Robson to help him put together a new monograph. Work on this began in 1997 but was nipped in the bud by Geoffrey's stroke in 1998. Robson was persuaded by Bawa's trustees to continue without him, and took the opportunity to fashion a text that re-established the roles of Bawa's collaborators. However, as the work neared completion, it proved to be difficult to find a publisher.

In 2001, the jurors of the triennial Aga Khan Award for Architecture selected Kerry Hill's design for the Datai Hotel on the island of Lankawi in Malaysia for one of the seven awards. Raj Rewal, one of the jurors, pointed out that the Datai was very much a homage to Geoffrey Bawa, none of whose buildings had previously been selected. Glenn Murcott, another juror, then proposed that the Aga Khan should

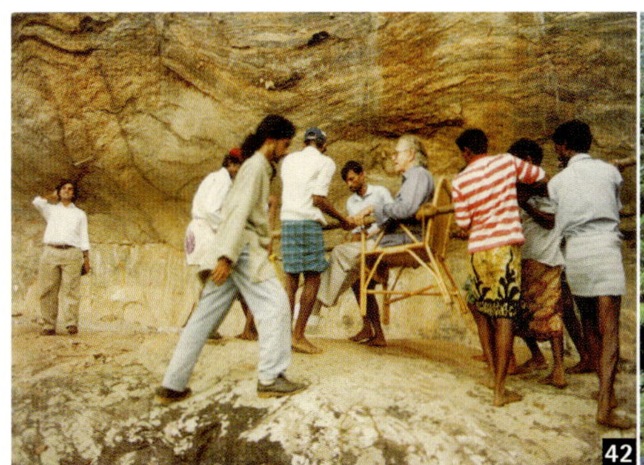
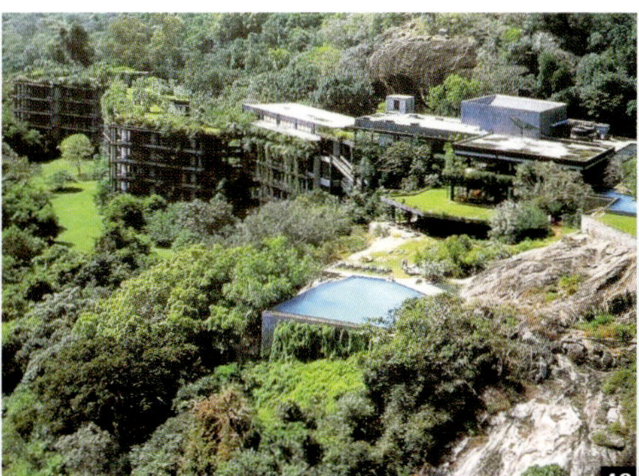
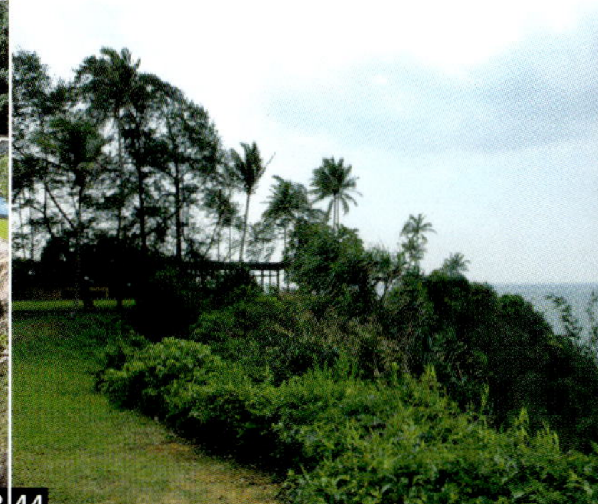

**42** An early site visit to the Kandalama Hotel, 1990.
**43** An aerial view of the Kandalama Hotel, 1995. Bawa Archive.
**44** The Jayawardene House on the Red Cliffs overlooking Weligama Bay, 2000.

confer a Lifetime's Achievement Award on Geoffrey. And so it came to pass. Geoffrey was too ill to travel to Aleppo to receive the Award, but architects C Anjalendran and Channa Daswatte accepted it on his behalf.

The Award put Geoffrey's work on the map and persuaded Thames & Hudson to publish Robson's monograph under the title *Bawa, The Complete Works* in 2002. Geoffrey lived to see the book completed and attended its launch in Colombo, but he died in 2003 after suffering five years of paralysis.

The book inspired Ingeborg Flagge, the Director of the Deutsches Architektur Museum in Frankfurt, to commission a retrospective exhibition of his work. The exhibition filled the whole of the Museum for three months of 2004, attracting record numbers of visitors.

Since then Geoffrey's work has featured in several books as well as myriad journal articles in many different languages, and he has come to be recognised as one of the most significant Asian architects of his generation.

## Bawa in Practice

When British architects Joe Chamberlin and Christoph Bon visited Bawa in Sri Lanka in 1977, they had recently retired from practice, having battled for 20 years with the massive Barbican development in London, running a huge team of architects and consultants and navigating around strikes, lock-outs, programme changes and budget revisions. They were astonished to discover that Geoffrey employed only a small team of designers and technicians and produced relatively small numbers of drawings, specifications and contract documents. This direct approach may have been in part the result of Bawa's ignorance of more conventional procedures, but it had a significant effect on his buildings and added immeasurably to their quality. Aided by Dr Poologasundram's managerial skills, projects moved quickly from inception through design to construction.

Geoffrey placed a high value on his relations with craftsmen and many key decisions were taken on site as building progressed. In those halcyon days there were few planning constraints or building regulations and Geoffrey's clients, both private and public, having set out their basic requirements, gave him a relatively free hand.

The Bentota Beach Hotel, Ceylon's first purpose-built resort hotel, was built with about 30 drawings and the interior fittings and furnishings were designed on site as the building neared completion. Later President Jayawardene entrusted the design of the Sri Lanka Parliament to Bawa and allowed him to determine both the site strategy and the configuration of the main chamber, while Aitken Spence were happy to shift the Kandalama Hotel some 10 kilometres away from Sigiriya at his behest.

Throughout his career Geoffrey was assisted by a succession of highly talented architects, though none of these remained with him for more than a decade. They all contributed in their different ways to the body of work that we associate with the name Geoffrey Bawa, though it is almost impossible to indentify or quantify the contribution made by each individual. The only constant presence during the 40 years from 1957 to 1998 was Geoffrey himself, who acted throughout as figurehead, impresario, instigator, innovator, inspiration and final arbiter.

## Art and Artefact

Although not himself a great draftsman, Geoffrey was an art-lover and a great supporter of artists. He went out of his way to incorporate good design in his buildings and to persuade his clients to buy works of art. In one of his very first projects, the classroom blocks for St Thomas' Prep School, he commissioned

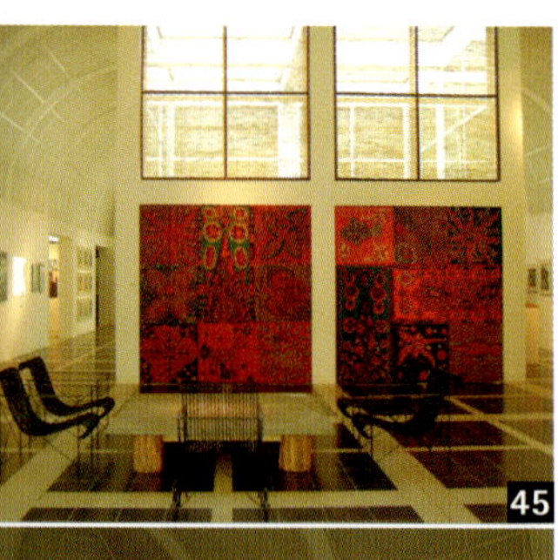

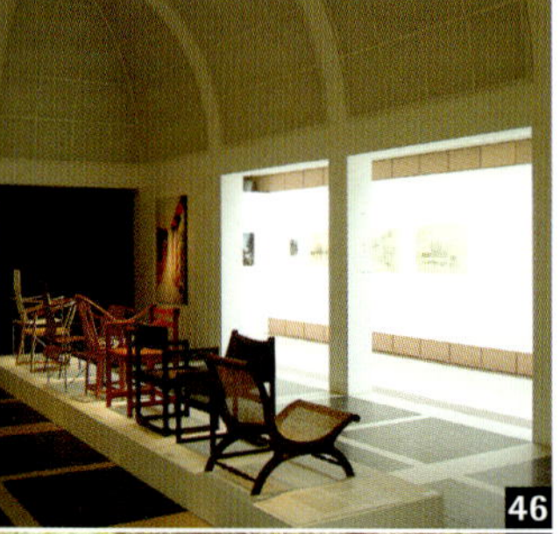

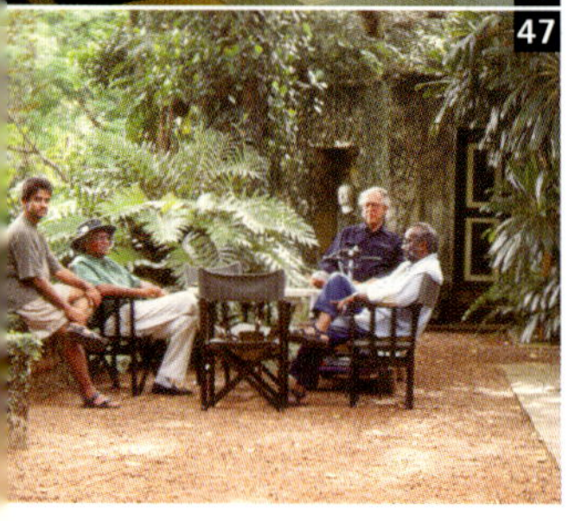

**45** Geoffrey Bawa exhibition in the German Architecture Museum in Frankfurt: panels of Ena de Silva ceiling batiks. 2004.

**46** Same exhibition: a display of Bawa chairs. 2004.

**47** Geoffrey Bawa at Lunuganga in 1997 with three generations of his collaborators: From left to right, Channa Daswatte, Ismeth Raheem, C Anjalendran.

Anil Jayasuriya, son of his friend Ena de Silva, to create a massive concrete relief that ran in a band around the first floor. The result was impressive and much loved by the pupils, though it was later attacked by the corrosive sea air. Geoffrey intended to use the same technique on his proposed tower for the Hilton Hotel, but this was never built. Later, he employed artist Laki Senanayake to design and construct the massive chandelier that hangs over the debating chamber of the Parliament and to create the writhing warrior staircase of the Lighthouse Hotel in Galle.

Geoffrey also appreciated good furniture, both ancient and modern. Early on in his career he realised that it was impossible to import well-designed furniture from Europe, but he soon learned that he could work with local craftsmen to produce reasonable copies. These copies took into account the limitations of local material and craftsmanship and developed a character of their own. The process inspired Geoffrey and his colleagues to make original furniture and light fittings inspired in part by Scandinavian design, and he went on to produce a whole range of locally produced furniture for his various hotels.

## After Bawa

Today, Geoffrey's estate is managed by the Geoffrey Bawa Trust. This originally comprised Sunethra Bandaranaike, Michael Mack, Chris Raffel, Ward Beling and Channa Daswatte, though Eugenie Mack and Suhanya Raffel have now replaced their respective fathers. The trustees are concerned primarily with the conservation of Geoffrey's town house in 33rd Lane and his garden at Lunuganga — and in this they have been spectacularly successful. The house now serves as a Bawa archive and museum and is open to the public. The garden is also open the public and functions as a boutique hotel.

The Trustees, urged on by architect C Anjalendran, have also respected Geoffrey's wish to support the cause of architecture in Sri Lanka. To this end they have invited a series of luminaries, including Senake Bandaranayake, Kerry Hill, Mok Wei Wei and Cecil Balmond, each to deliver an annual memorial lecture, and they have organised a triennial Award for Architecture. The Award has been a great success, attracting over 50 entrants in each of its three iterations and it has demonstrated the extent of Bawa's legacy.

Geoffrey belonged to the heroic First Generation of Sri Lankan architects that also included Minnette de Silva, Valentine Gunasekara and Justin Samarasekera. The Second Generation included former Edwards, Reid & Begg associates: Anura Ratnvibushana, Ismeth Raheem and C Anjalendran. Now a Third Generation has moved towards centre stage. This comprises architects born after 1960 who received their training wholly or partly in Sri Lanka and includes Channa Daswatte, Amila de Mel, and Vinod Jayasinghe, all of whom worked with Bawa, as well as Pradeep Kodikara, Thisera Thanapthy, Philip Weeraratne and Palinda Kanangara, who have been shortlisted for Bawa Awards. There can be no doubt that Sri Lanka, one fiftieth the size of neighbouring India in terms of area and population, punches well above its weight in the field of architecture, thanks in no small measure to the influence of Geoffrey Bawa.

When Geoffrey returned to Sri Lanka in 1957, there was no Institute of Architects or School of Architecture and all the qualified architects could be sat around a single table. Today there is an Institute with over 1,000 members and there are two schools of architecture. The Third Generation has been influenced by Geoffrey's example, though the better architects are those who have been inspired by his approach rather than those who have fallen into the trap of copying a style.

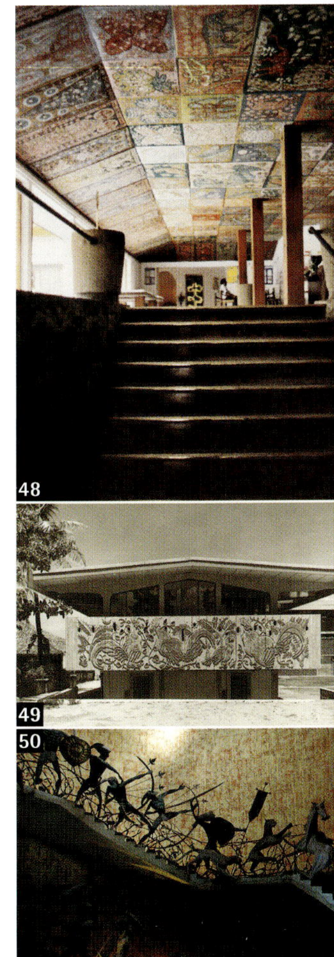

**48** The main entry staircase in the Bentota Beach Hotel, 1990.
**49** The east gable of St Thomas' Prep School showing relief panel by Anil Jayasuriya, *circa* 1962.
**50** Part of the staircase at the Lighthouse Hotel by Laki Senanayake, 2000.

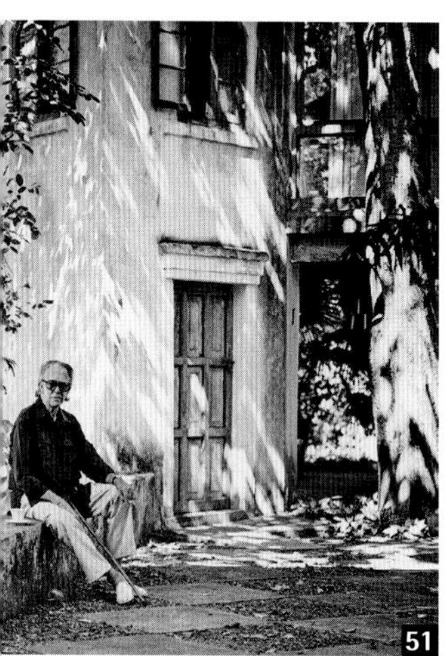

51 Geoffrey Bawa at Lunuganga, *circa* 1992.

Geoffrey was not a teacher, though he did support the new school of architecture at Kattubedde when it was founded by Justin Samarasekera in the early 1960s. He never regarded himself as a guru and his aim was not to set an example, but simply to make each building as good as it could be.

However, he succeeded in changing the perceptions of the people of Sri Lanka, revalidating their threatened traditions and demonstrating that contemporary buildings could reflect an existing culture while still exploiting new technical possibilities and meeting new needs. And he established a range of new prototypes for a variety of building typologies: schools, hotels, offices and houses. Today his influence can be seen, not only in architect-designed buildings, but in the ordinary buildings of the towns and villages, and even in the latest wave of public buildings to have been built by the Urban Development Authority, such as the new Kandy Law Courts. Indeed many of his innovations — courtyards, deep verandas, overhanging roofs of clay tile on cement sheeting — have become so commonplace that few people are aware that these have not always existed.

During the late 1980s and 1990s, Geoffrey also had a considerable influence on the emerging architectures of Asia. When it was published in Singapore in 1986, the *White Book* had a big impact on a new generation of architects who were concerned by the increasing globalisation of architecture. Bawa's ideas were taken up by the Singaporean guru William Lim and influenced such up-and-coming architects as Kerry Hill, Mok Wei Wei and Ernesto Bedmar. Bedmar took his whole office on a Bawa pilgrimage to Sri Lanka; Hill went so far as to buy his own estate bungalow a few kilometres from Lunuganga; and the WOHA office developed computer software to produce Bawa-type drawings. In his numerous books on the new houses of Asia, the writer Robert Powell demonstrated the full extent of Bawa's influence and even drew his illustrations in the Bawa style.

Sri Lankans have been more concerned with their problematic present and precarious future to worry about preserving the past. A number of Geoffrey's buildings have been demolished, others have been badly treated by their owners and only a few buildings survive in their original state. Hotels, of course, are regularly 'upgraded' to meet changing demands — in some cases this has been done with great sensitivity, in others disastrously. Houses have been demolished or turned by their owners into restaurants, banks or hairdressers; school and university buildings have succumbed to the ravages of time; religious buildings have been allowed to crumble. Hopefully, steps will soon be taken to protect and indeed maintain at least a few of the surviving gems — the Sri Lanka Parliament, the Chapel at Bandarawela, the Ruhunu University Campus, the Kandalama Hotel and the Agrarian Research and Training Institute.

## Bawa Is.... Not a Style

Bawa is not a style. During a career that spanned over 40 years he refused to be straight-jacketed, never confining himself to one architectural language and always refusing to become a prisoner of his own success. He had a consistent approach to design and a determination to treat each new project as a unique problem requiring a unique solution. Every design was for him an experiment and he never repeated himself.

It is possible to identify a whole series of what might be described as stylistic positions which he adopted at various times. First was his tentative espousal of Tropical Modernism as exemplified by the classroom block for St Thomas' Prep School; then came the Contemporary Vernacular of the Yahapath

Endera Farm Convent; the stripped Minimalism of the rugged Polontalawa Estate Bungalow and its elegant counterpart the Martenstyn House; the Brutalist Modernism of the Mahaweli Tower; the Modern Regionalism of the Kotte Parliament; the Late Modernism of the Kandalama Hotel; and, finally, the elegant simplicity of the Jayawardene House at Mirissa.

There are signature elements in every project that seem to transcend style and to capture the essential wit of a Bawa design: the geometric elegance of the facade of the Bishop's classroom block; the inexplicable offset entry axis of the Ena de Silva House; the water-tower *campanile* of the Blue Lagoon Hotel; the sensuous curves of the tiny staircase in his town house at 33rd Lane; the simple jettying of the small sanatorium at Yahapath Endera; the mock chapel that serves as the loggia of the Cinnamon Hill House.

## Bawa Is.... Not a Brand

Bawa is not a 'brand', though it is clear that, during the decade since his death, others have sought to make him one. Certainly he never gave his name to a pepper grinder like Zumthor or a lemon squeezer like Starck and somebody has yet to market I love Bawa tee-shirts. But the property magazines of Colombo regularly advertise houses 'in the Bawa style' and claim Bawa authorship for houses on which he never clapped eyes, while dubious hotels offer 'Bawa hospitality'. At the East Coast Park in Singapore there is even a Bawa MacDonalds with frangipani trees on square stone plinths in a reflecting pool and hipped roofs of round clay tiles.

## Place, Pleasure and Architecture

What were the essential ingredients of Geoffrey Bawa's architecture? A main preoccupation was the choreography of space — the space within a building, the space surrounding it and the connections between the two. But space does not exist in a vacuum: it is defined by surface, texture and materiality and is modulated by light and shadow and by rhythm and proportion, all qualities that Bawa discovered in his study of Balthazar Neumann. And space is not static: Geoffrey was a scenographer, conceiving a building as an enfilade of linked spaces to be moved through at will, playing with axes and cross-axes, denying and creating views. His aim was also to imbue each space with a sense of place, to give every

52 The bath house court at Yahapath Endera Farm Orphanage, 1977.
53 Bishop's College, Colombo, 1962.
54 The veranda of the Cinnamon Hill House with its echoes of the Bandarawela Chapel, 2015.

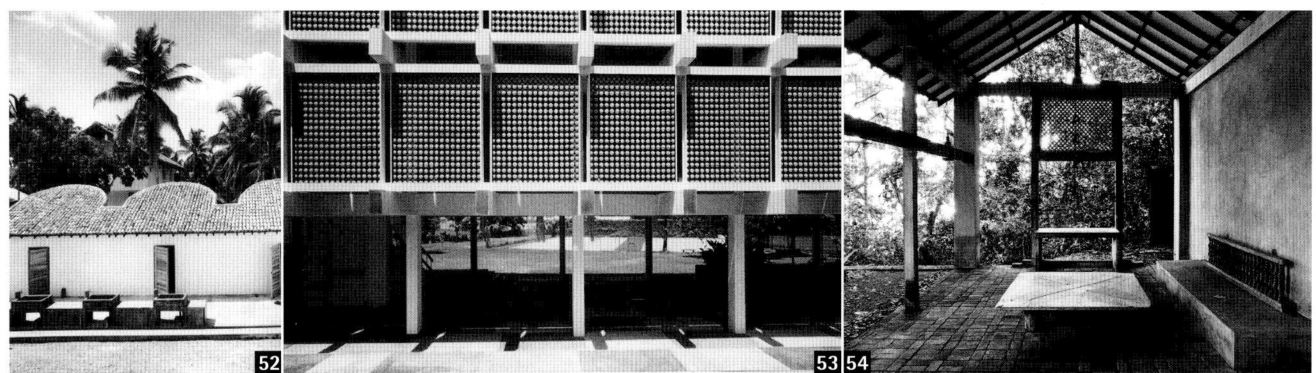

part its own unique identity. One thinks of Alexander Pope's advice to Lord Burlington: "Consult the Genius of the Place in all; / That tells the waters or to rise, or fall."

Thus the Ruhunu University campus straddles three hills and comprises over 50 substantial buildings, all built by necessity from a limited vocabulary of materials. And yet every part of the vast campus develops its own unique sense of place from the way that it is detailed and from its interactions with view, topography and vegetation.

The Ruhunu campus also serves as a reminder that almost all of Geoffrey's buildings were planned orthogonally: he rarely used curves and his occasional non-right angles were usually 45°. In this he was following not only the example of such neo-classical architects as Andrea Palladio, but also the architecture of Sri Lanka's great Anuradhapura Period. And, whilst he would begin from a symmetrical *parti*, he would delight in breaking symmetries and playing games with major and minor axes. Nowhere is this more apparent than in the organisation of the masses of the Sri Lankan Parliament.

Geoffrey was also concerned with responding to people's needs. For him a building was a human artefact, built to fulfil a purpose. Thus, when designing the Madurai Mills Staff Club he grilled his client Martin Henry for two complete days in order to understand the complex interactions of the building's users.

Amongst the needs that had to be met, one important one was the need for comfort. Geoffrey was all too aware of the discomforts of a tropical climate and was determined to build in such a way as to discourage solar gain and to encourage cross-ventilation. He was determined to break down the barriers between inside and outside, between building and landscape, and forswore the use of air-conditioning because it created a sealed interior, cut off from the sounds, smells and gentle breezes of the outside world.

He was an inveterate traveller and had visited buildings in all corners of the world. During his twenties he had accumulated a profound knowledge of European architecture and later, through his friendship with archaeologist Senake Bandaranaike, he developed a deep understanding of Sri Lankan and South Asian architecture. He believed implicitly that a contemporary architecture must be rooted in the past, insisting on the importance of learning from history and developing a sense of historic continuity, while steering well clear of pastiche: "In my personal search I have looked into the past for the help

**55** Model of the Ruhunu Campus at the Frankfurt exhibition, 2004.
**56** The train in the window: Mohoti Walauwe, 1985.
**57** The Debating Chamber, Sri Lanka Parliament, 2015.

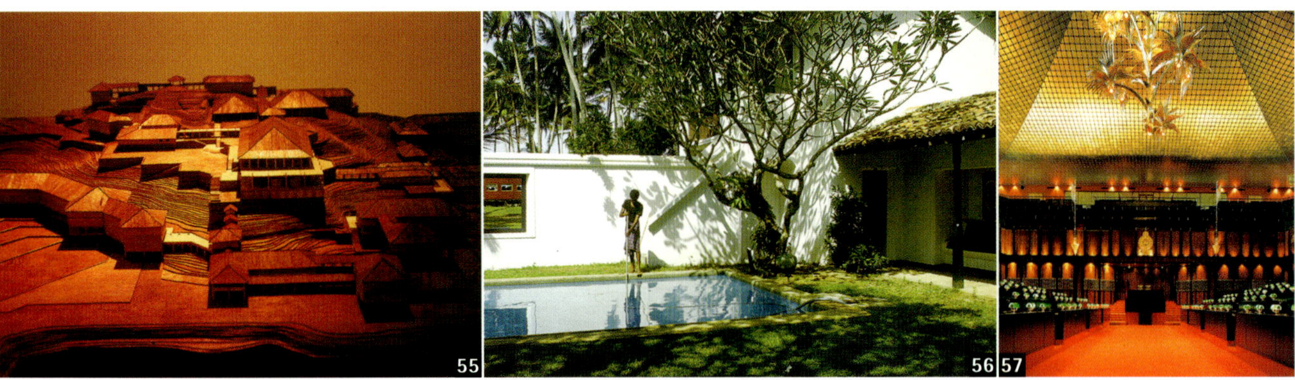

that previous answers can give and at the pointers of previous mistakes. By that I mean all the past from Anuradhapura to the latest building in Colombo – the whole range of effort, the peaks of beauty and simplicity and the deep valleys of pretension. And it seems to me that mistakes have been made when these rules are ignored."[7]

It has been said of Geoffrey Bawa that he only designed for the wealthy and that his buildings were overly expensive. Neither of these assertions is true. As well as building private houses he designed and built a number of public housing projects. But he also built schools and university campuses as well as social and public buildings. A number of his buildings, such as those for the Catholic Church were built to minimal budgets, and his hotels, though they exuded a sense of luxury, were built within strict cost limits. As his friend C Anjalendran would later demonstrate in his designs for the SOS Children's Villages, a building can be precious, but still cheap! Geoffrey's two largest projects – the Sri Lanka Parliament and the Ruhunu University – were delivered on time and within budget.

Wit is an essential ingredient of good design. Geoffrey's buildings are full of wit and imagination: a window in the courtyard wall of the Mohoti Walauwe Hotel gave glimpses of passing trains; the ceremonial staircase in the Parliament brought the President up, head first, between the rows of seated parliamentarians; the entrance sequence of the Bentota Beach Hotel led travel-weary visitors up from a dark stone cavern into a sparkling water-court and offered them views of the ocean through swaying coconut palms.

One need that he regarded as paramount was the need to experience beauty and feel pleasure. Bad buildings certainly inflict misery while beautiful buildings can support happiness. Many of Geoffrey's buildings have achieved lasting beauty and continue to please the eye: one thinks, for instance, of the interior of the chapel at Bandarawela, the entrance corridor at 33rd Lane, or the Sandela Pavilion at Lunuganga.

Geoffrey derived enormous pleasure from the act of creating a building and even more pleasure from the knowledge that it brought pleasure to the people who used it. By the same token we hope that you, the reader, will derive pleasure from this book and from the contemplation of the buildings it describes.

[7] Geoffrey Bawa. 'A Way of Building'. Times of Ceylon Annual, 1968

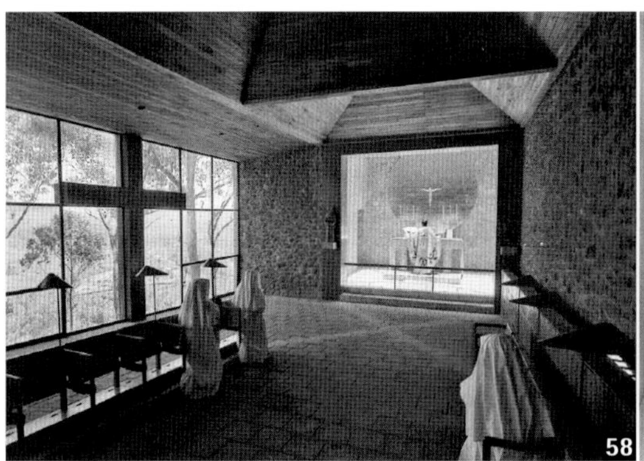

**58** The Nazareth Chapel, Bandarawela, 1963. Bawa Archive.

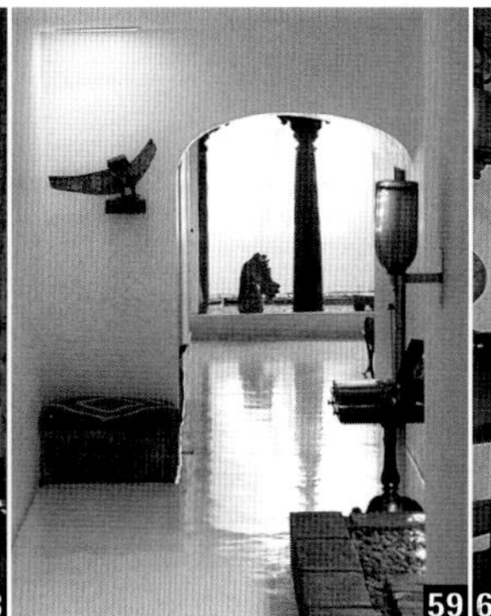

**59** The main corridor in Geoffrey Bawa's townhouse, 2015.

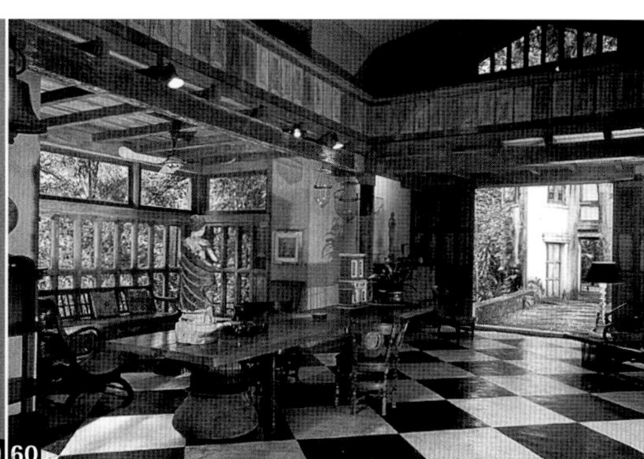

**60** The interior of the Sandela Pavilion, Lunuganga.

# The Gallery Café

### 4 Alfred House Gardens

First built in 1961/Transformed into a café in 1998

The Gallery Café was opened by Udayshanth (Shanth) Fernando in 1998. Functioning both as a private art gallery and a bistro, it has become one of the city's most popular meeting places.

The premises occupy a succession of separate pavilions that between them form three open-to-the-sky courtyards: an entrance court, the gallery court and the final garden court with the dining loggia. Uniquely, the various galleries and dining spaces are open-sided and naturally ventilated.

Today the Gallery Café has the well-worn look of somewhere that was tailor-made to accommodate its present functions but, as they tuck into his Chocolate Nemesis, few of Fernando's clients are aware of the building's checkered history.

In 1961 a Dr Bartholomeusz commissioned Geoffrey Bawa to design a house in Alfred House Gardens on land belonging to art-lover Harold Pieris. Bawa designed the house as a series of pavilions separated by courtyards, in a manner that owed much to traditional Sinhalese *walauwe* and to the town houses of the Dutch Period. Before it was completed, however, Bartholomeusz disappeared to Australia.

In a canny move that anticipated the south-ward shift of the business district out of the Fort, Bawa persuaded his partners to buy the incomplete shell to use as their offices. The house-

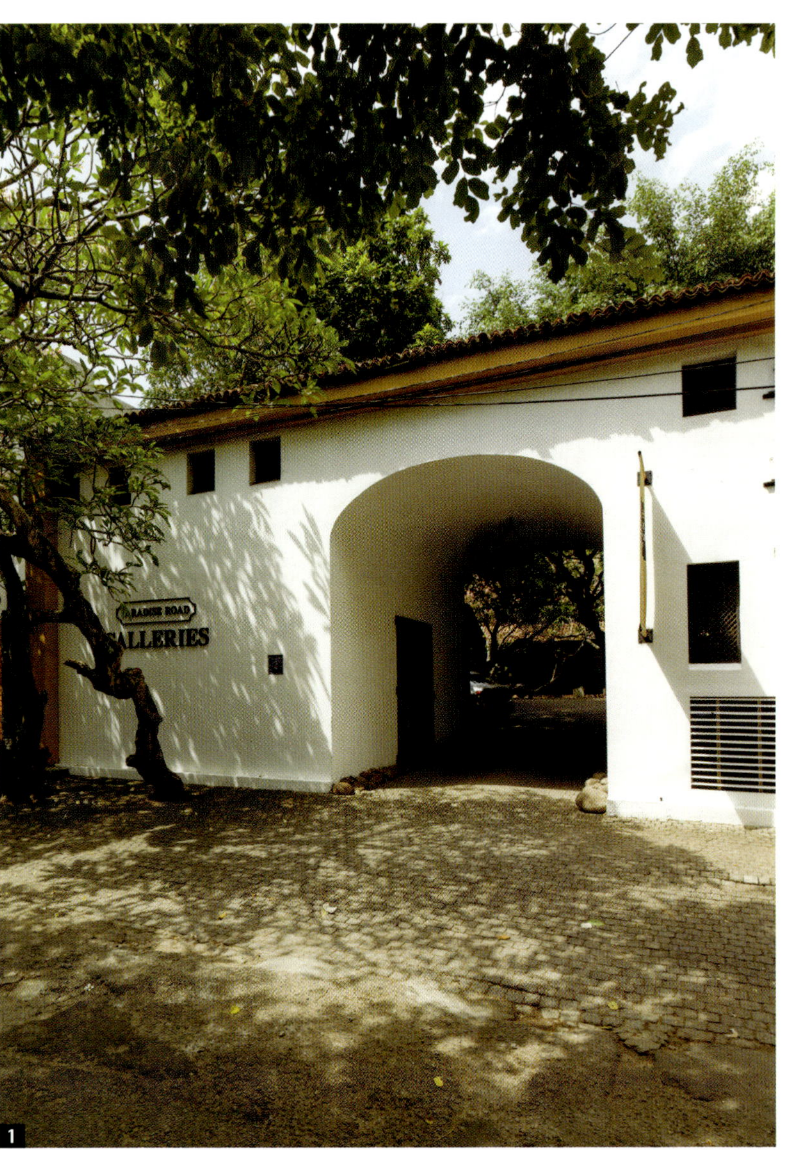


1 The entrance archway.

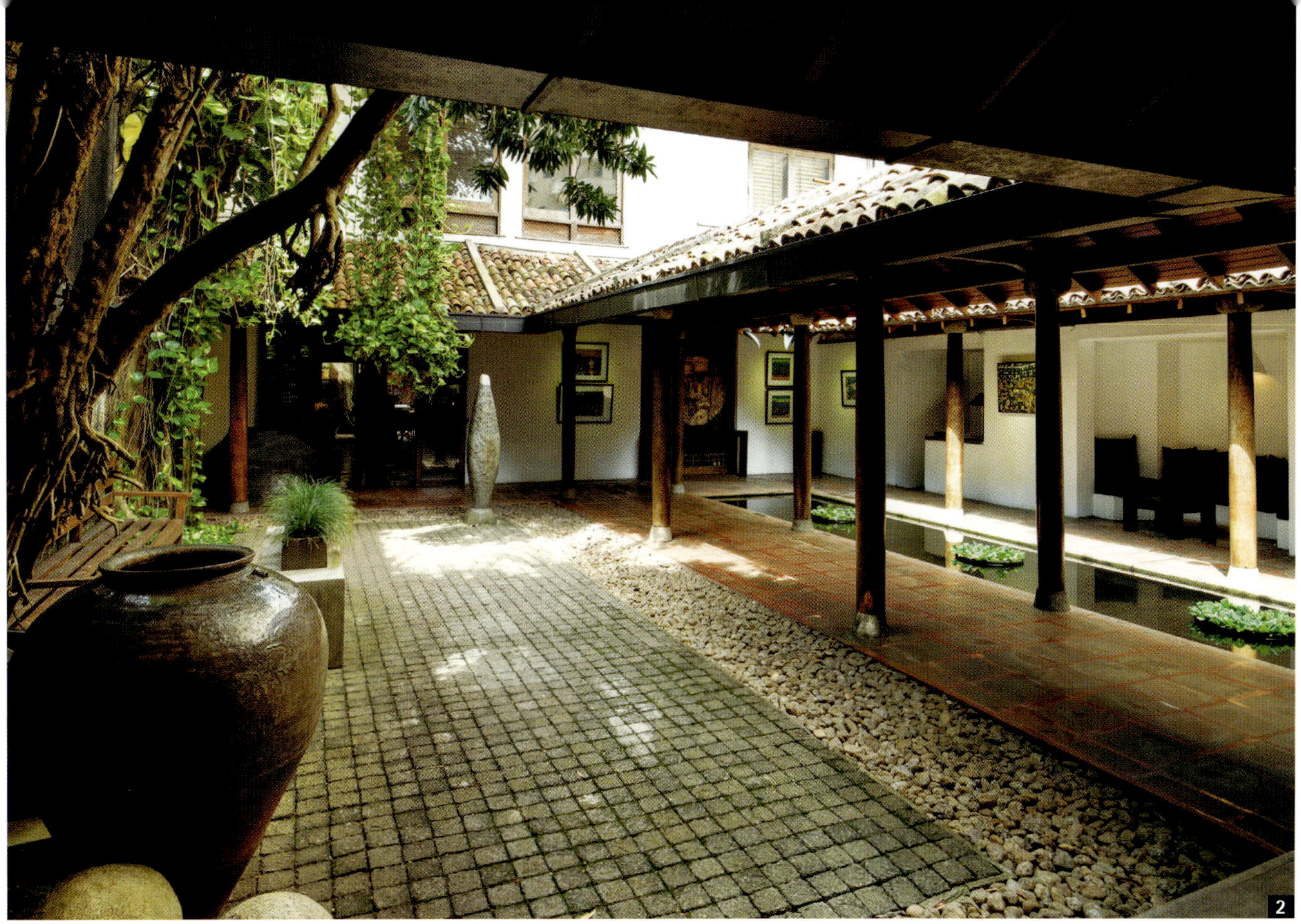

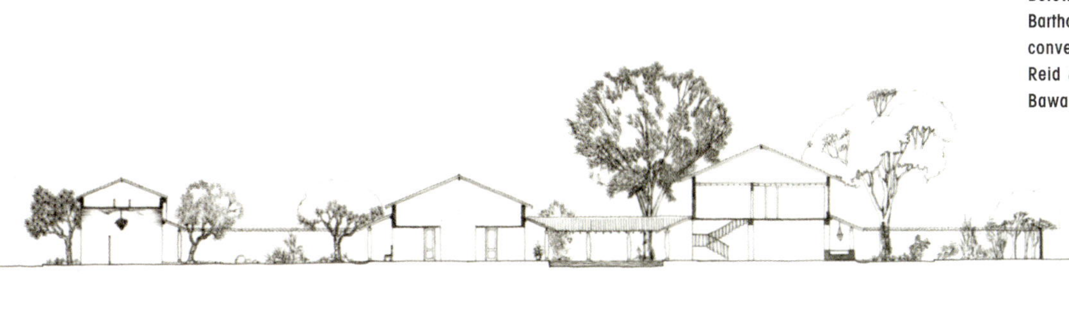

2 The central gallery court.
**Below** Plan and section of the Bartholmeusz House after its conversion to the Edwards, Reid & Begg office, 1964, Bawa Archive.

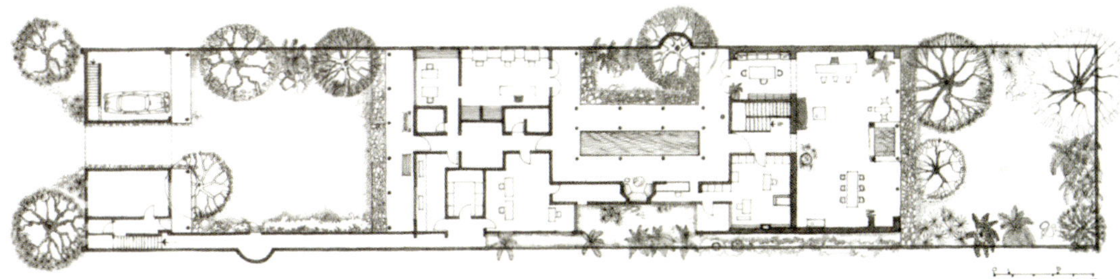

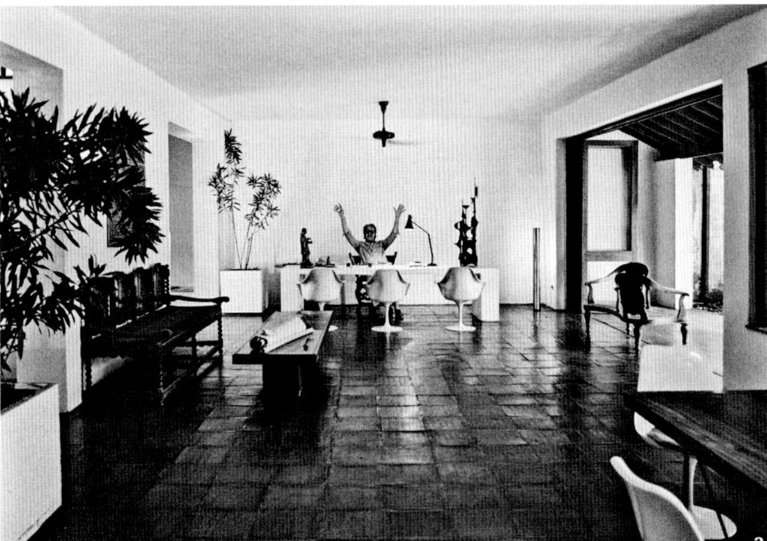

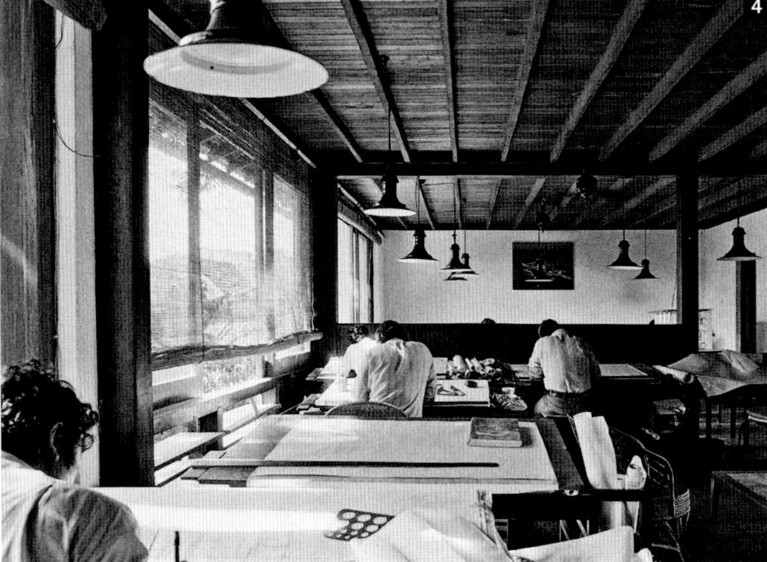

turned-office became a showcase for Bawa's architecture and the central courtyard with its reflecting pool functioned as a waiting room for clients. The design incorporated a number of Bawa's characteristic innovations: turned timber columns with granite bases and capitals; roofs formed from half-round clay tiles laid on corrugated cement sheets; projecting windows with lattice shutters.

Bawa installed himself with his associate Ulrik Plesner in what would have been the generous sitting room of the Bartholomeusz residence, relegating partners Valentine Gunasekara and Jimmy Nilgiria to small rooms in the outer pavilion. He placed himself strategically at a concrete desk against the south wall, from where he enjoyed a commanding view of the whole office; when unwelcome visitors appeared in the reception court, he would escape down the hidden service corridor that ran along the north wall to the entrance court. Both corridor and desk still survive, the desk serving ironically as a cake stand.

A doorway in the far corner of the dining court connected to a club called 'Next Door' that Bawa and his colleagues ran for a few short years in a bungalow on Galle Road during the early 1970s. This had a magical white interior of verandas and pool courts, quite unlike anything seen in Colombo, before or since.

In 1989 Bawa reached his 70th year and, disbanding the Edwards, Reid & Begg partnership, closed the Alfred Gardens office and set up a

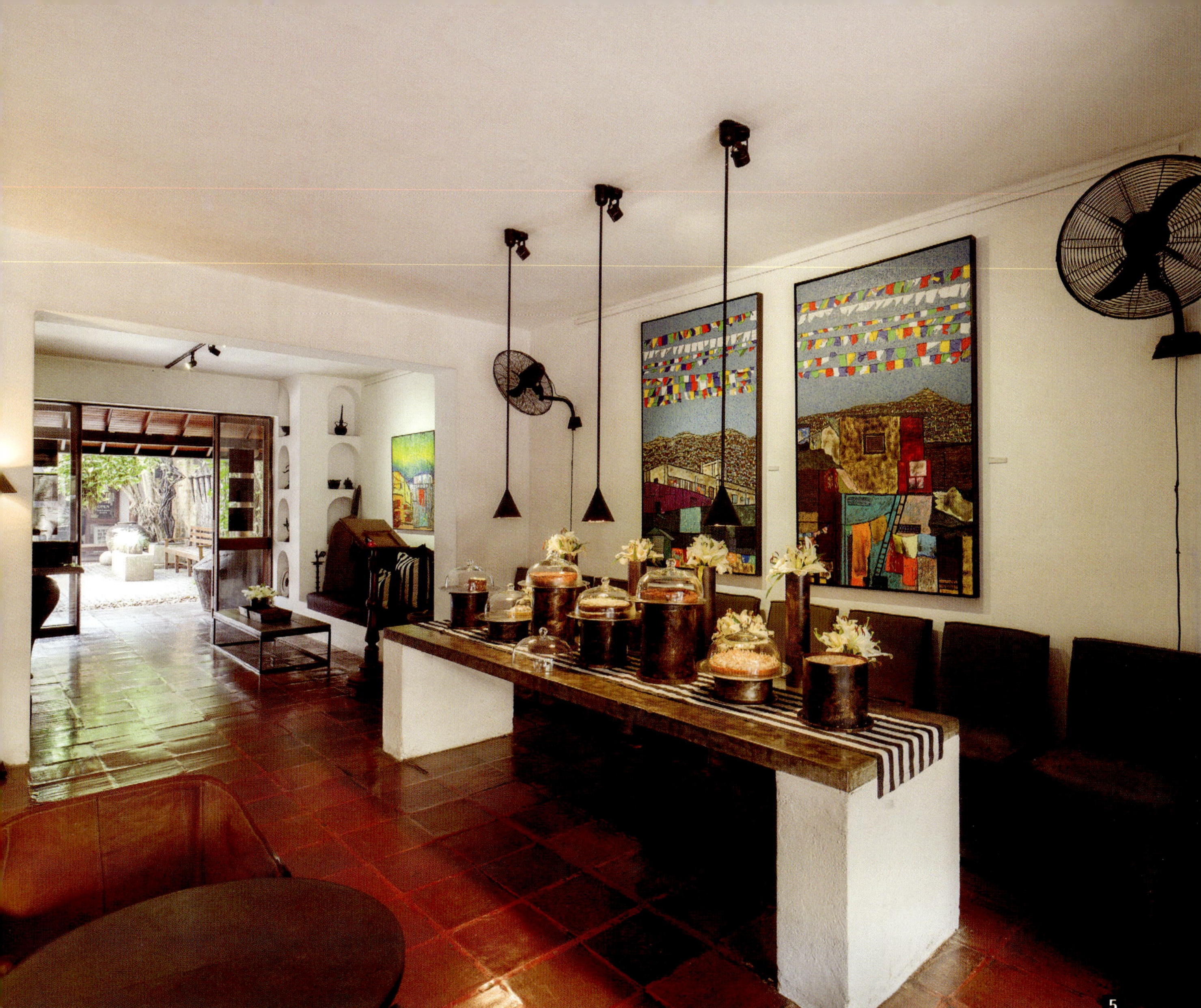

small studio in his 33rd Lane home. By 1997 it was apparent that his health was failing and he decided to clear out the office building in order to rent it out. Shanth Fernando, the proprietor of the Paradise Road boutiques, stepped in and persuaded Bawa to let him turn the office into a restaurant, promising that he would always run a part of it as an art gallery.

In March 1998 Bawa suffered the massive stroke that left him paralysed until he finally died in 2003. Soon after, Fernando opened his restaurant, making relatively few alterations to the building: a new dining pavilion, designed by Bawa associate Channa Daswatte, was added to the far court and Bawa's office became a bar.

**3** Geoffrey Bawa at his desk, 1985.
**4** The first-floor drawing office, 1985.
**5** Geoffrey Bawa's former desk, now a cake stand in the Gallery Café.

# Geoffrey Bawa's Town House



11, 33rd Lane, Bagatelle Road
1962–1968

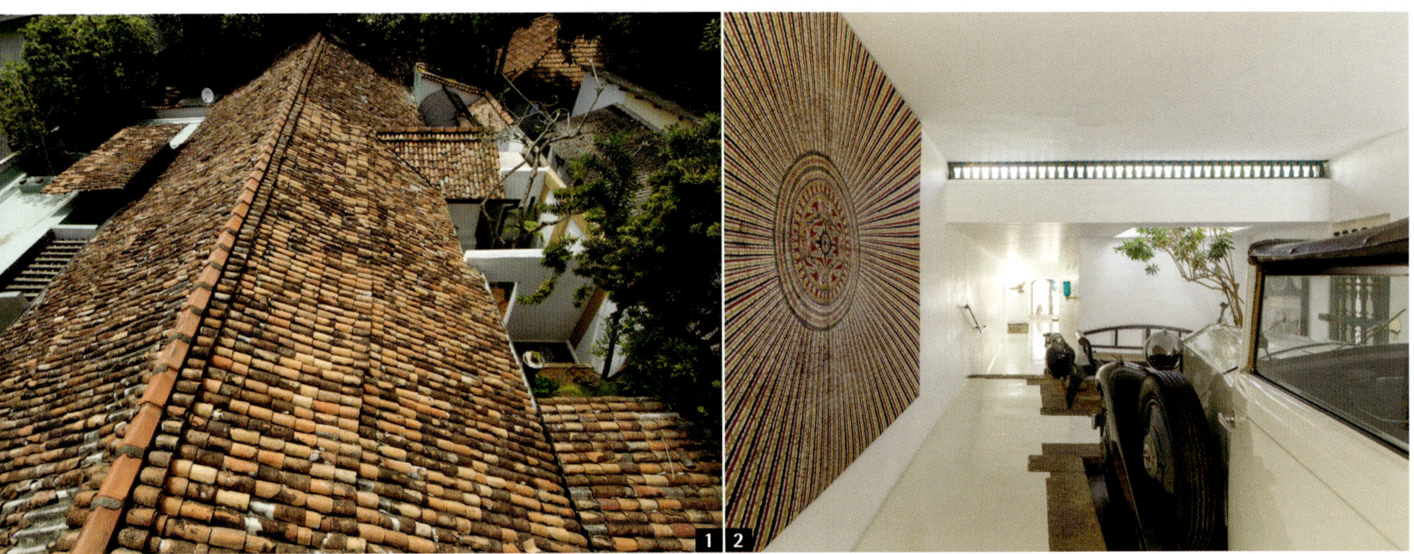

As the Edwards, Reid & Begg office was being transplanted from the Fort to Colpetty, Bawa gave up his Galle Face Court apartment and rented the third of a row of four tiny bungalows in a narrow alley at the end of 33rd Lane. His landlord was Harold Pieris, the owner of the Alfred House estate, and his neighbour in the fourth bungalow was Sooty Banda, a Marxist journalist and leading light in the Lanka Sama Samaja Party (LSSP).

Bawa created a *pied à terre* with a sitting room, a bedroom, a tiny kitchen and a miniscule bedroom for his manservant Miguel. Later, when Sooty Banda moved out, he expanded into the fourth bungalow, creating a formal drawing room and a dining room. Finally, in 1968, when the other tenants showed signs of moving, he persuaded Pieris to sell him the whole row. He then demolished the first bungalow and erected in its place a Corbusian tower, with a first-floor sitting room and guest suite and a second floor loggia and roof terrace. The alleyway, meanwhile, was reconfigured as a meandering corridor, lit by tiny lightwells, that led to the heart of the house. In its final form the house functioned as a space laboratory where Bawa could experiment with lighting effects, induced ventilation and tricks of scenography.

The result at ground-floor level was an introspective labyrinth of rooms and verandas, lit and ventilated from open-to-the-sky courtyards,

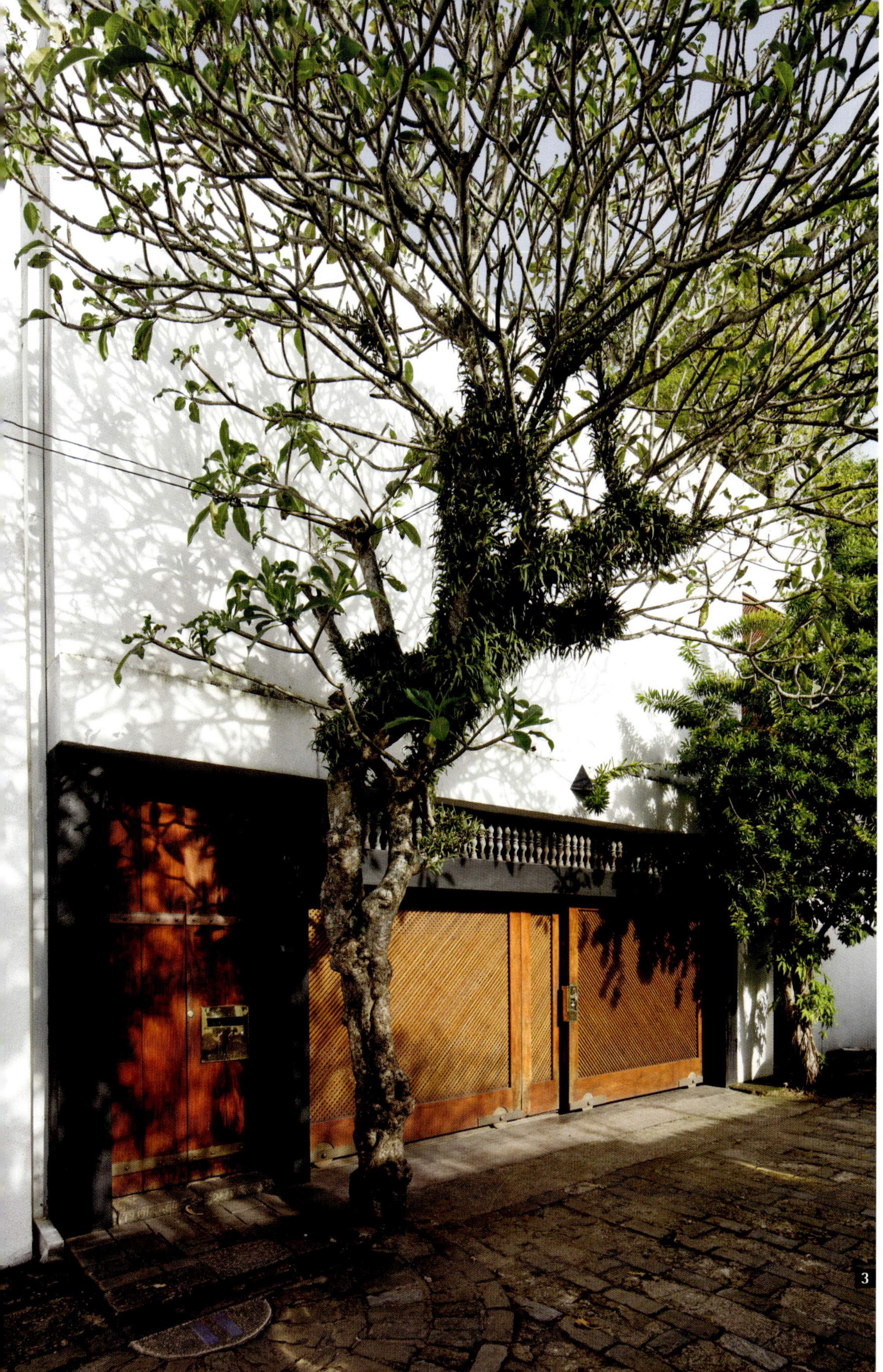

1 A view over the roofs from the tower.
2 The car port showing the Rolls Royce and an Ena de Silva 'Sunburst' batik, with the long corridor.
3 Street view.

whilst the new tower functioned as a periscope, its upper roof terrace giving views across the surrounding rooftops towards the sea.

Visitors entered via a glass door etched with a sunburst by Laki Senanayake into a car port occupied by Bawa's two prized cars: his 1934 Rolls-Royce Coupé and his 1953 Mercedes Cabriolet. From there a long corridor led to a distant pool court where a terracotta horse-head signalled a right turn towards the epicentre of the house. Here Geoffrey Bawa would offer a welcome from his Braganza chair, a Peacock cigarette in his extended hand, like the Minotaur at the centre of the maze.

For a number of years the second bungalow served as an autonomous apartment that was rented out to friends, but after closing the Alfred House Office in 1989 Bawa turned this into his home-office. Here, working with a team of young architects, he produced the amazing designs of his final decade.

As his health deteriorated, however, he was no longer able to climb the narrow winding stair to the roof terrace and a lift was inserted into one of the lightwells. After suffering a stroke in 1998, he was confined to his bed, and the subterranean rooms became a prison, from which he would escape occasionally for brief sojourns in his beloved garden at Lunuganga.

Today the house is maintained by the Geoffrey Bawa Trust as a museum and the drawing office functions as an archive.

**4** Painted doors by Donald Friend (the originals are now in the Art Gallery of New South Wales) and Chettinad columns.
**5** Veranda and pool court.
**6** The sitting room.
**7** Brass and aluminium door by Ismeth Raheem with the main staircase.
**8** The main corridor with an owl by Laki Senanayake.
**Opposite** Ground-, first- and second-floor plans with section, 1997. Bawa Archive.

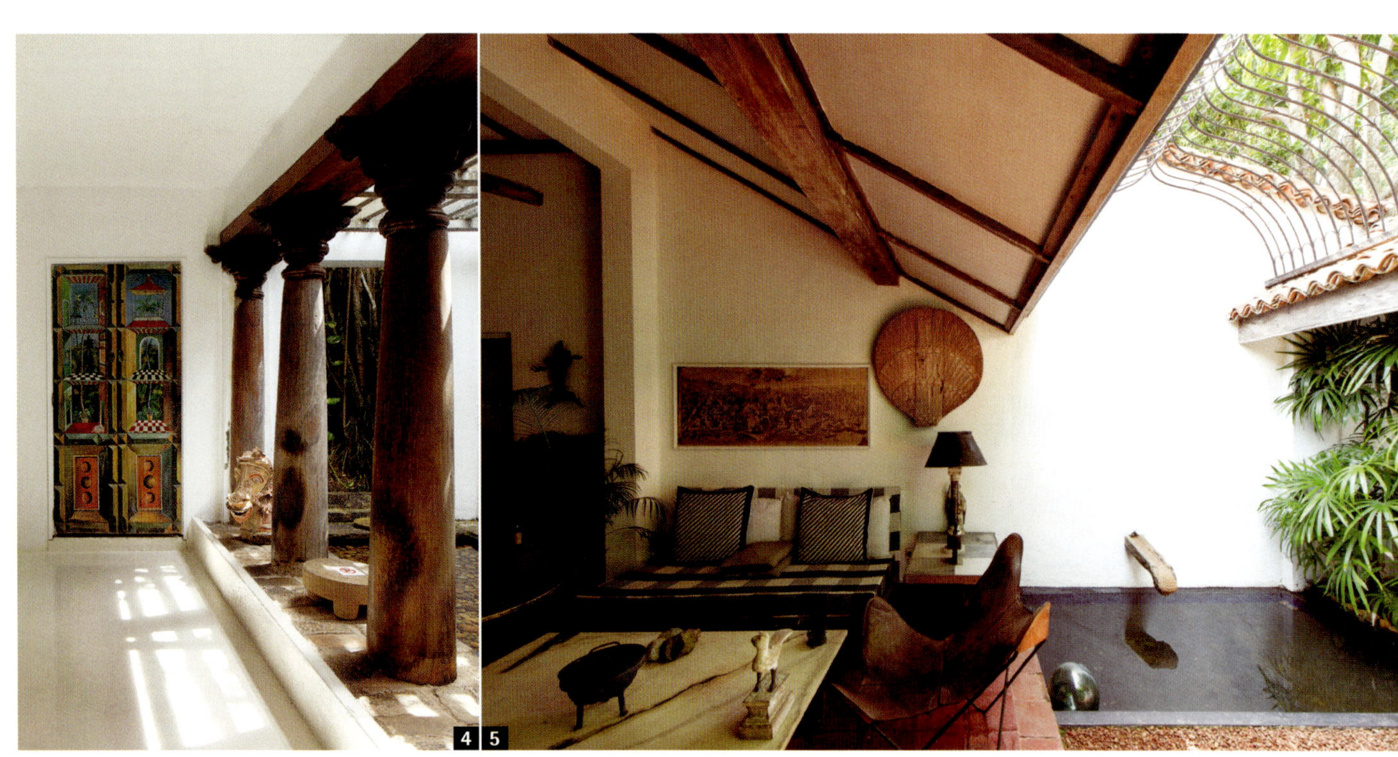

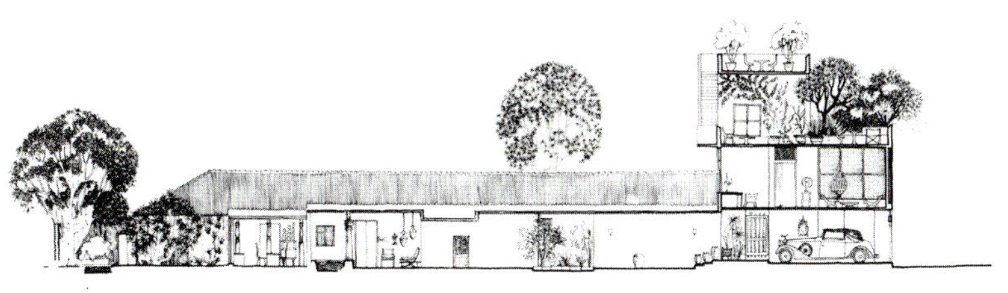

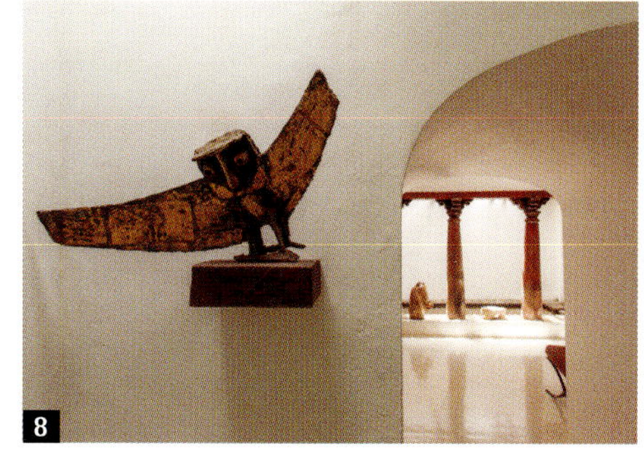

8

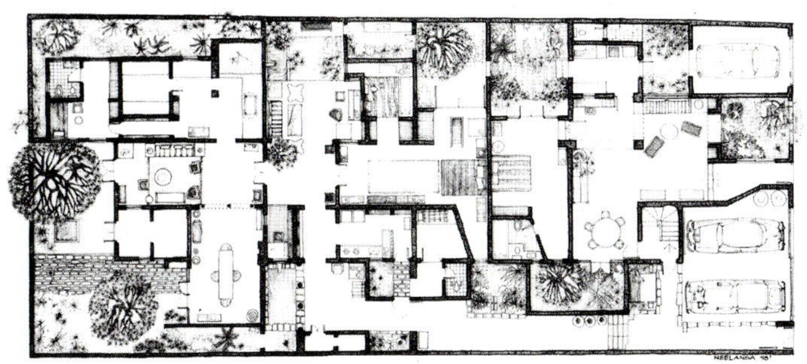

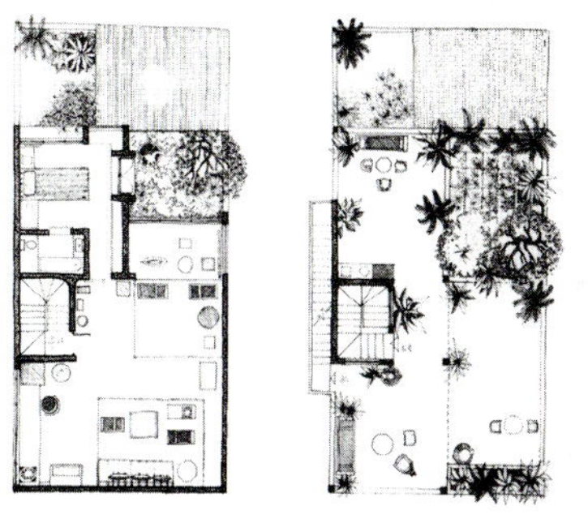

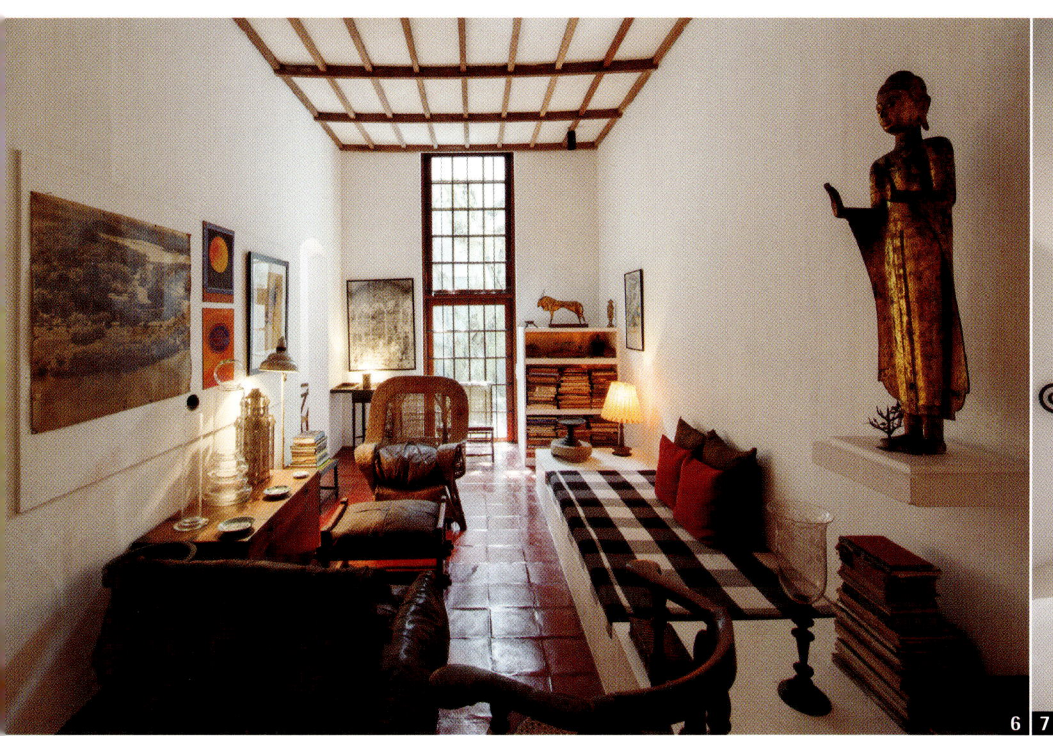

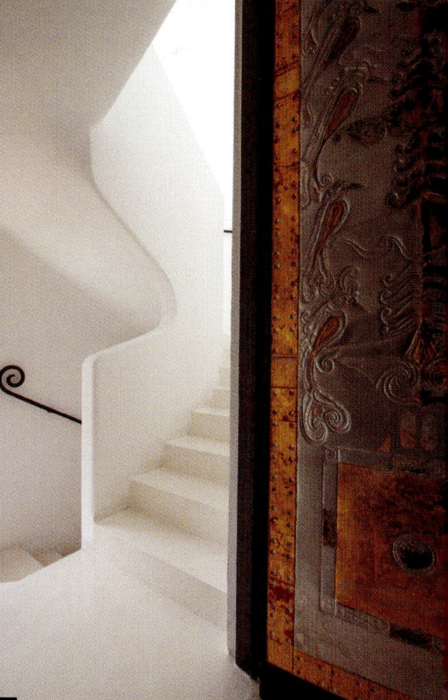

6 | 7

# The Deraniyagala House

## Guildford Crescent
### 1952–1958

In 1952 Paul Deraniyagala, the Director of Colombo Museum, and his wife Prini, persuaded Geoffrey Bawa to design a house for them in Guildford Crescent. Although nominally still a lawyer, Geoffrey had worked briefly as an intern with HH Reid in the rump of Edwards, Reid & Begg during 1951 and was contemplating the possibility of going to London to train to become an architect. As such, this was to become his first independent commission.

Mrs Deraniyagala's family owned the beautiful Ecknelligoda Manor House at Kuruwita and she wanted a contemporary house that would in some way reflect tradition. Geoffrey struggled for months with the design: he wasn't short of ideas, but found that he lacked the necessary skills to put them into effect. In despair he went to Mrs Deraniyagala and advised her to find another architect. She, however, was not to be put off and told him to go to London and complete his studies: she would wait until he returned.

When Bawa returned at the end of 1957 he immediately set about completing the project. The final design, however, embodied too many unresolved ideas. A pair of two-storey pavilions was connected by a single-storey link in a plan which seems to have been developed from an

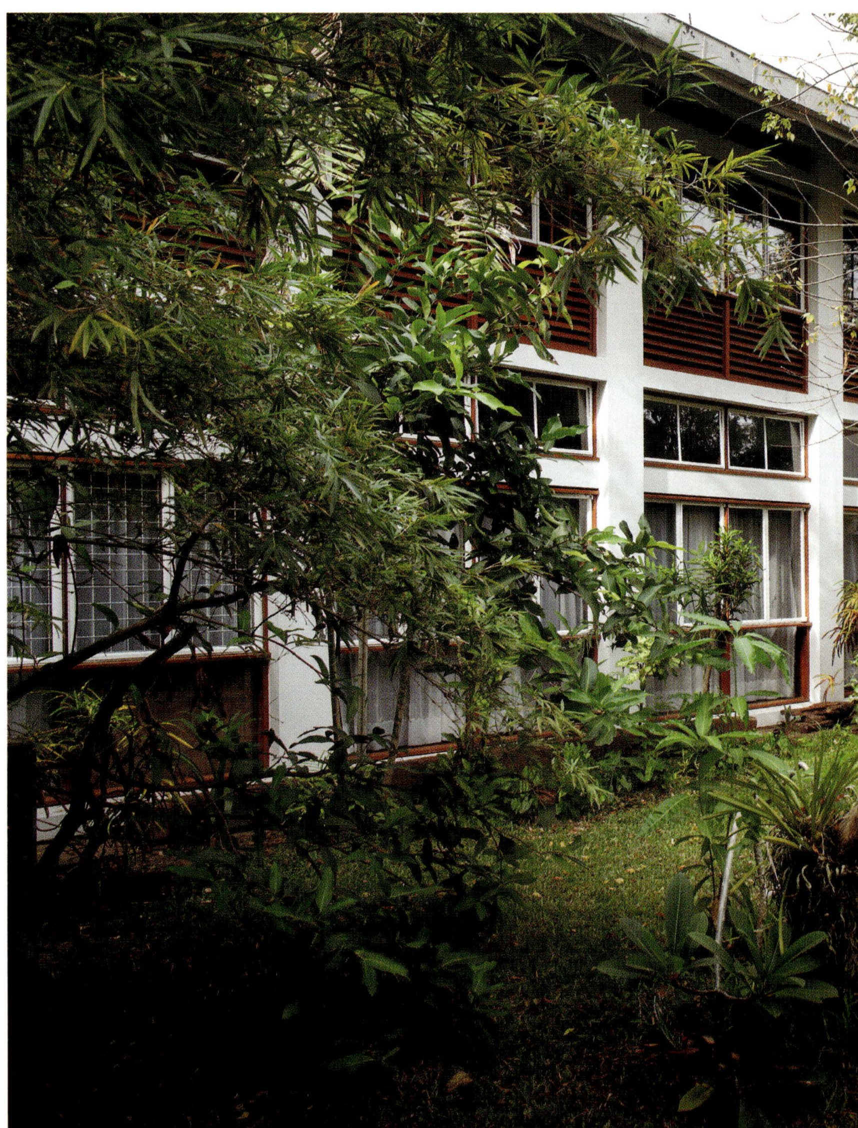

1 The front elevation.
2 The spiral staircase.

unbuilt design of Andrew Boyd. Interestingly it contained a free-standing spiral staircase, regarded at the time as an essential badge of modernity. Bawa later regretted this, believing that a staircase should act as a spatial transition between two levels and not stand as a sculptural object in its own right. His later spiral staircases such as that in the Ena de Silva House were almost always contained within walls.

The house survives in its original condition apart from an extension above the garage that is accessed by a repeat of the spiral staircase.

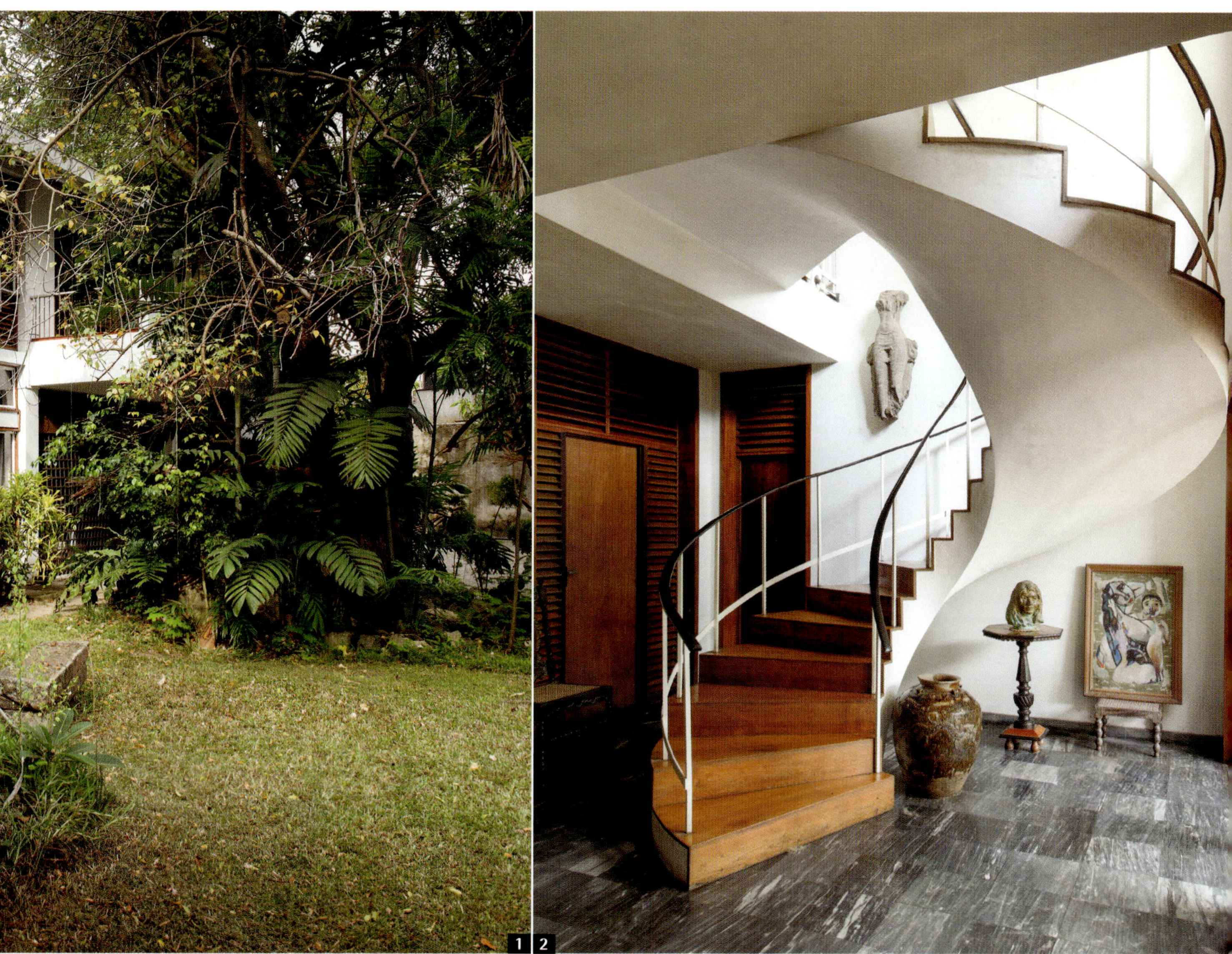

# Ladies' College Classroom Block

Flower Road

1965

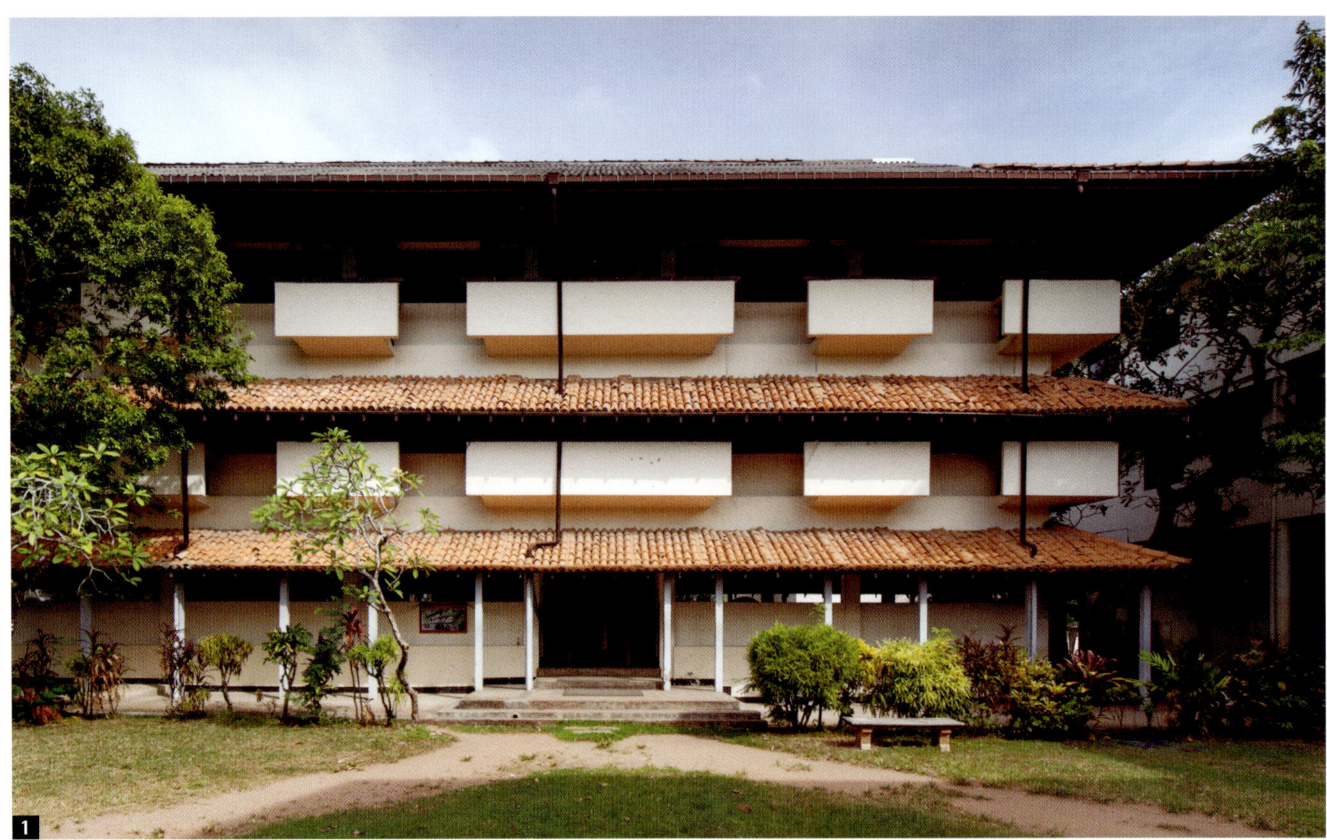

1 The classroom block.

Edwards, Reid & Begg contributed a number of buildings to the Ladies' College Campus during the 1930s, including a range of classrooms and a beautiful chapel designed by HH Reid in a hybrid Kandyan/Arts and Crafts style.

In 1965 Geoffrey added an elegant classroom block to the immediate west of the chapel, thereby creating a shady quadrangle. The three-storey block abandons the perforated grillwork of the earlier classroom designs for St Thomas' Prep School and Bishop's College in favour of overhanging balconies that serve to give shade and exclude rain. It anticipates the outward cantilevering of the Bentota Beach Hotel. The building has survived in its original form, though it now looks somewhat neglected.

# Ladies' College Vocational Training Centre

27th Lane, off Inner Flower Road
1982

The Vocational Training Centre lies on the west side of the Ladies' College Campus and is accessed from 27th Lane. It is planned as a checkerboard arrangement of square classroom pavilions with hipped roofs that create between them a pleasing succession of secluded courtyards. The project architect was Vasantha Jacobsen-Chandraratne.

Over the years the buildings have been well maintained and the Centre has hardly changed since its inauguration.

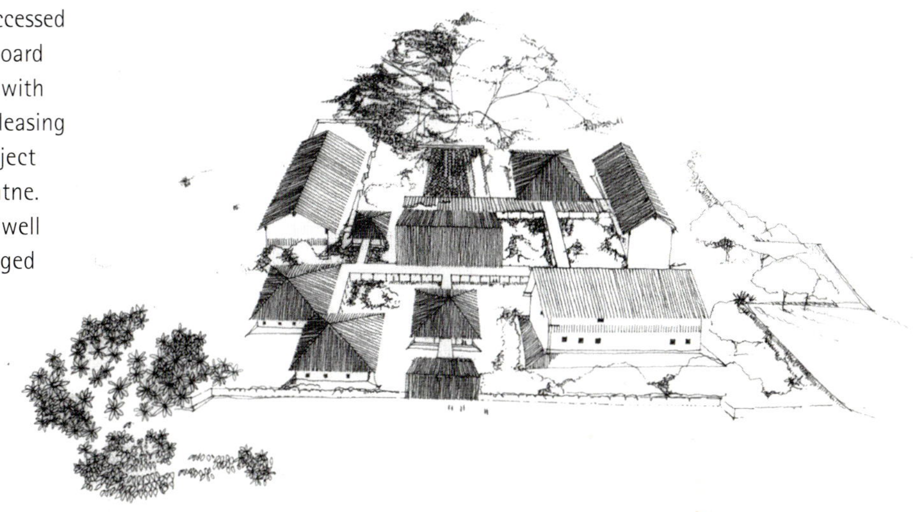

**1** The entrance porch.
**2** A courtyard.
**Right** Bird's-eye view, 1983. Bawa Archive.

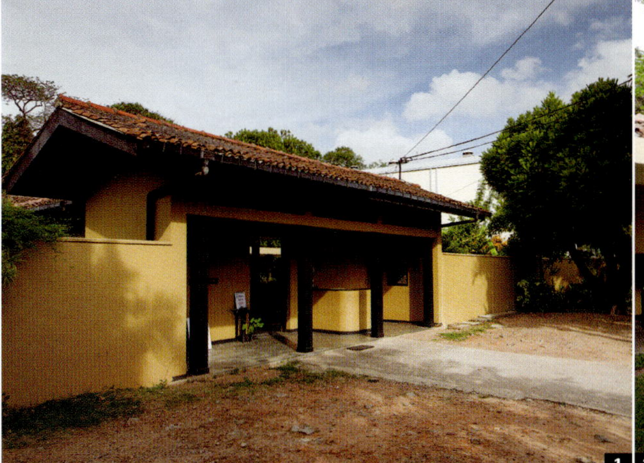
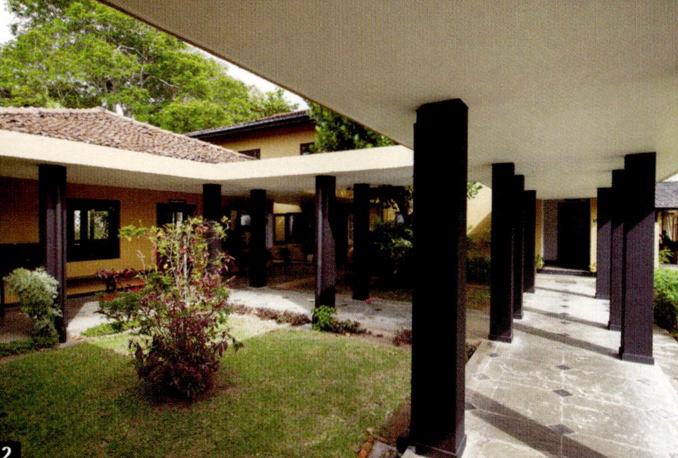

# Stanley de Saram House

## Cambridge Place
## 1971

In his design for the Stanley de Saram House, Bawa pushed the concept of an introspective courtyard house to its limit. The design turned its back on the busy road to create an inner oasis of calm within a high carapace wall of white render. The only openings, the front door and the garage door, were framed in granite, and the only relief to the austerity of the facade came in the form of a decorative wrought iron grille above the entrance.

Within, the reception areas were focused on a central paved court, while the bedrooms were lit from a smaller and more intimate garden court. A hidden staircase gave access to a secluded roof garden above the garage.

Soon after it was completed de Saram sold the house to Bawa associate Pheroze Choksy. Later, when Choksy and Ismeth Raheem set up their own practice, their office occupied one side of the courtyard. The interiors have undergone a number of changes but the façade remains unaltered and makes an intriguing addition to the streetscape.

**1** The front seen from Cambridge Place.
**2** The front door.

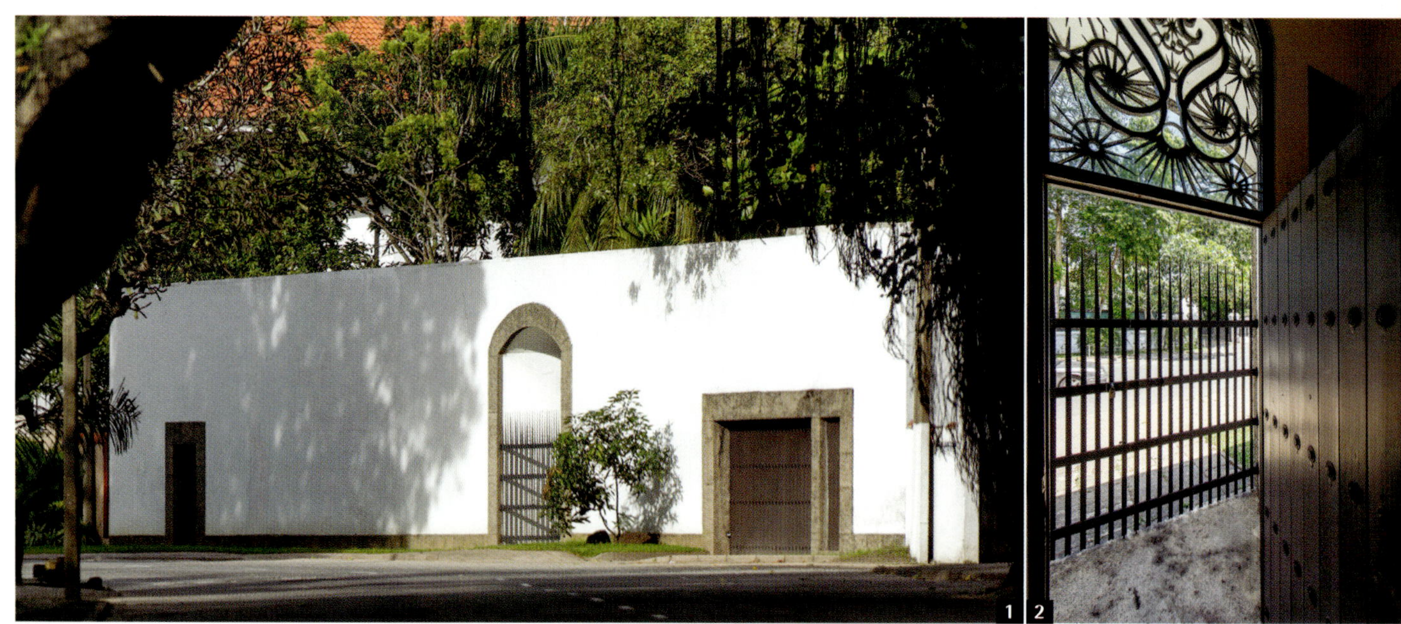

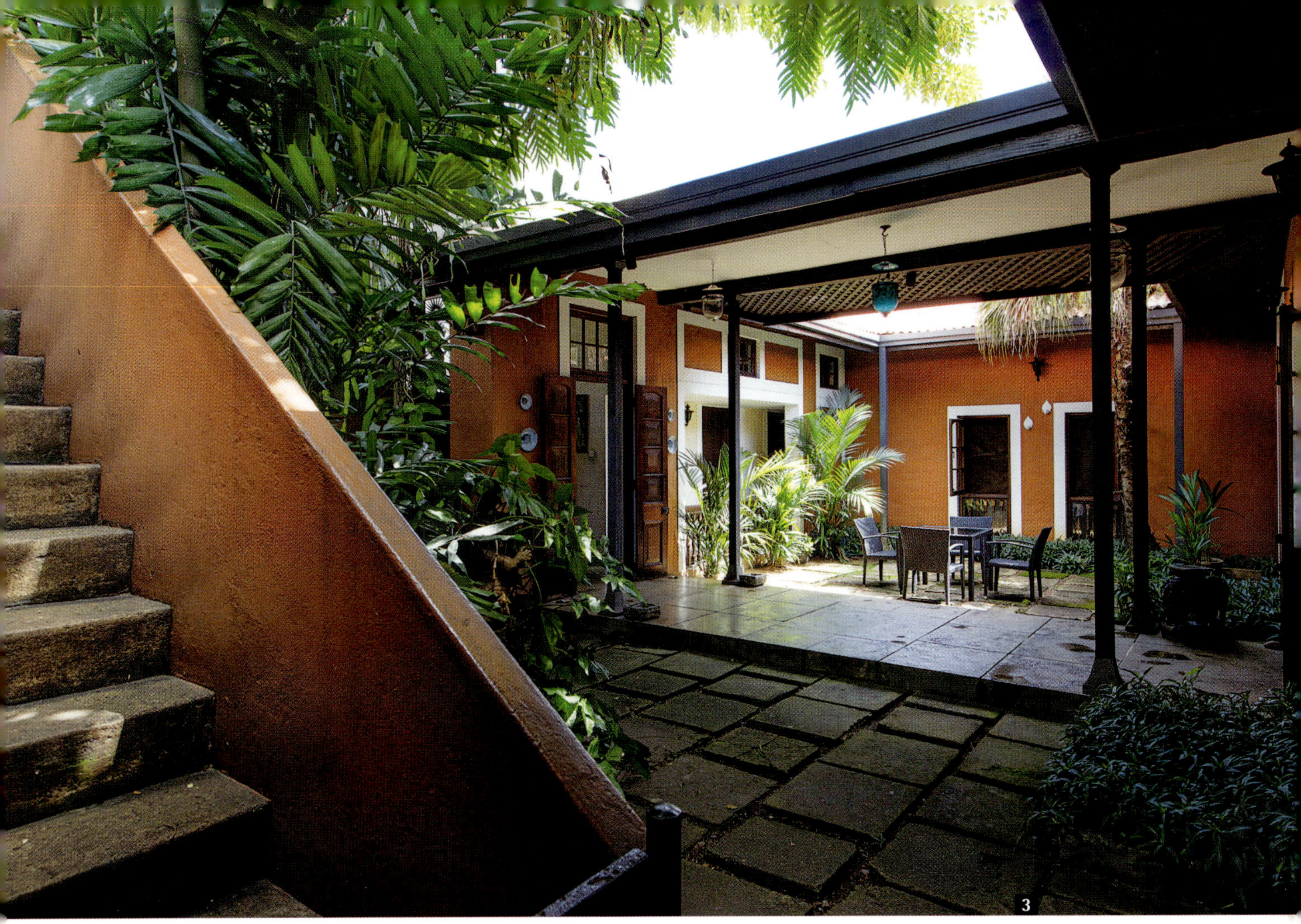

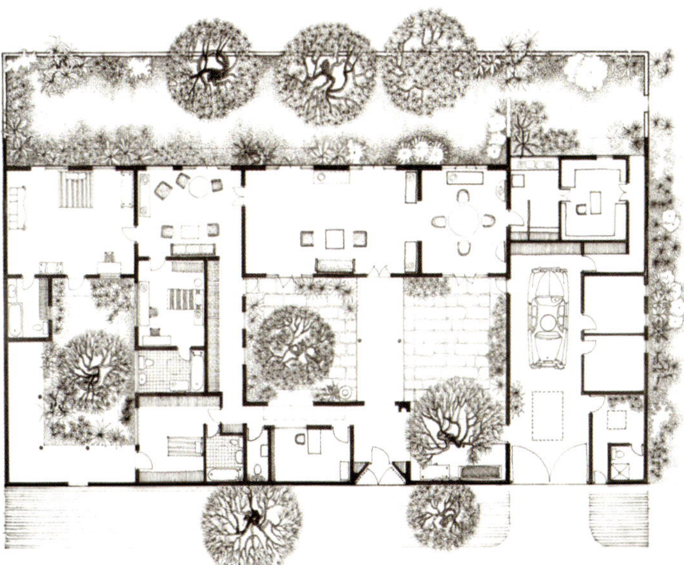



**3** The main courtyard.
**Left** Ground-floor plan,
1972. Bawa Archive.

# Chloé de Soysa House

Dharmapala Mawatha

1987

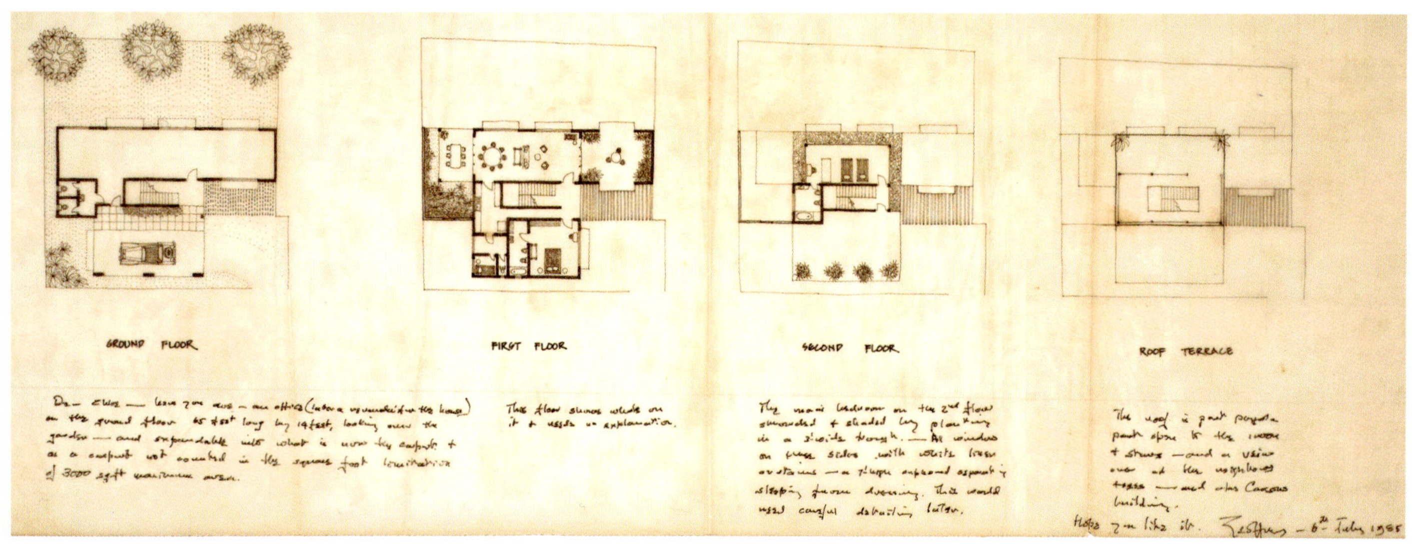


As Chairman of the Hotels Corporation, Cecil de Soysa commissioned Geoffrey Bawa to masterplan the Bentota Beach Resort during the late 1960s. He and his wife Chloé lived in a large Art Deco house on Boyd Place but in 1987, having decided to downsize, they asked Bawa to design a much smaller house on a part of their garden. The project stalled when Cecil died and was only completed in 1991.

The result is one of the series of Bawa tower houses that reach up towards the sky to capture light and air. The ground floor functions as an office and a garage and the main living spaces occupy the first floor alongside generous outside raised terraces. The main bedroom is on the second floor and the top floor serves as a secluded roof terrace. The design employed a stripped down minimalism similar to that found on the Martenstyn House. The large sliding aluminium framed windows seem to colonise the trees of Chloé's former garden.

The project architect was Sumangala Jayatilleke, and Chloé still treasures the print of his plans of the various floors (above). On this Bawa had written her a brief note about the design, ending with the words: "Hope you like it!"

**Above** Drawing by project architect Sumangala Jayatilleke with a message from Bawa to Chloé de Soysa, 1985. Bawa Archive.
**1** View from the street.
**2** The main first-floor sitting room and terrace.
**3** The first-floor landing.

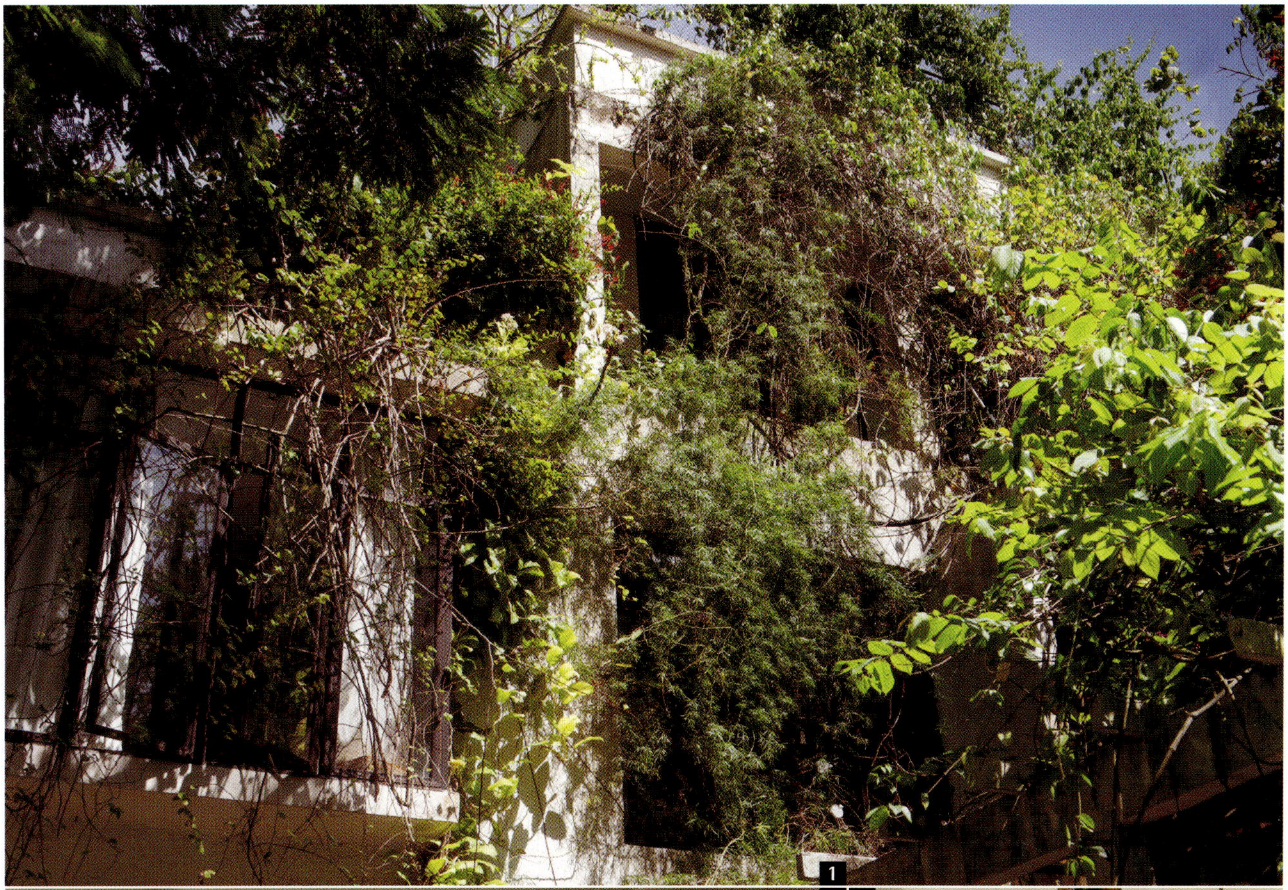

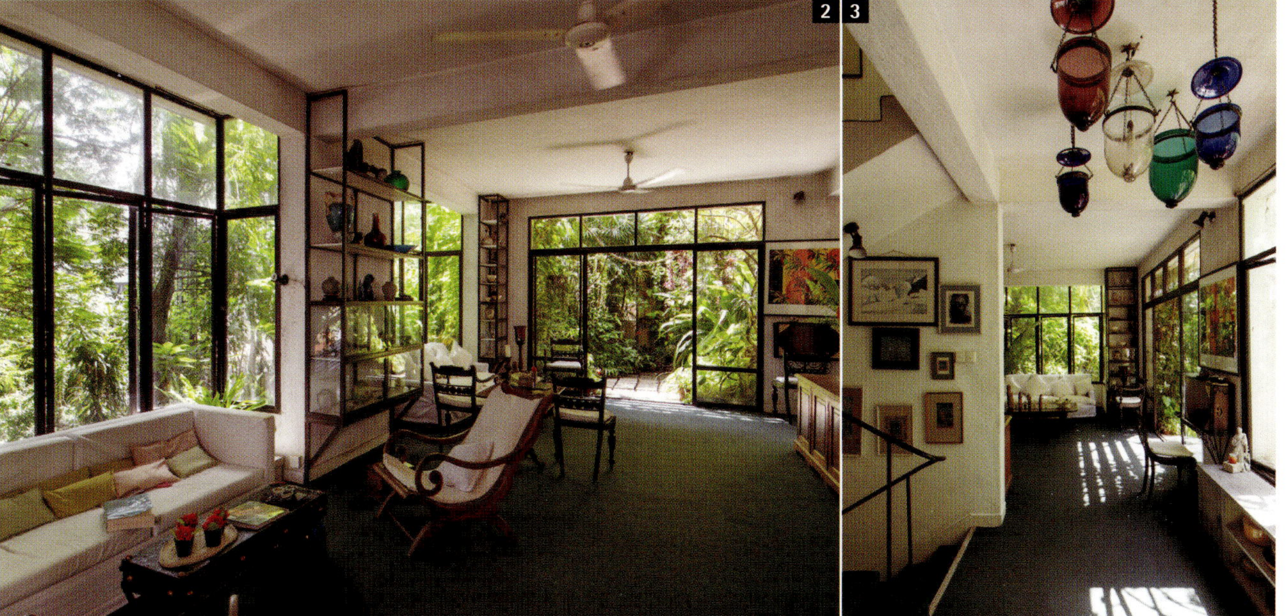

# Wijemanne Flats

## Ananda Coomarswamy Mawatha
## 1962

Hidden away in the Bawa archive, there are some evocative sketches dating from 1960 of a house for a Mrs AF Wijemanne on a site in Coomaraswamy Mawatha. That house was never built, but in 1961 Bawa designed a block of flats on the same site that were completed in 1962. These appeared four years after the iconic Senanayake Flats designed by Minnette de Silva in Gregory's Road and, like them, were originally raised above a line of ground-floor car ports. However, there are only two flats per floor, served by a central dog-leg staircase.

What makes the flats unique is the fact that, following precepts of Tropical Modernism, they are partly clad with geometric screens made up of pre-cast concrete elements. These were intended to minimise the ingress of direct sunlight and rain while maintaining through ventilation. This was an approach that Bawa soon abandoned in favour of a stepped-out section with deep overhanging eaves.

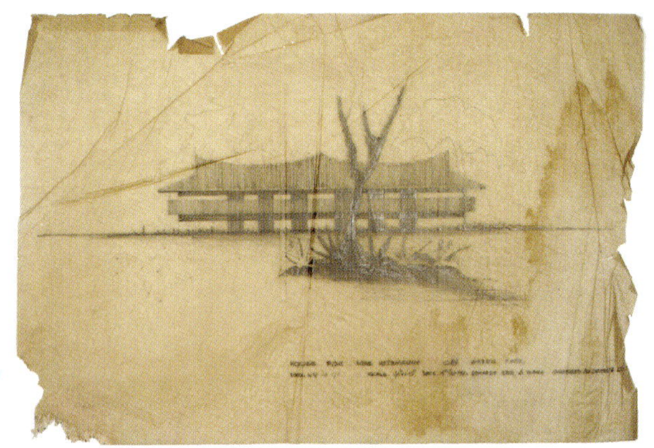

**Top** Drawing of an unbuilt design for the Wijemanne House, 1962. Bawa Archive.
**1** Main elevation of the flats.

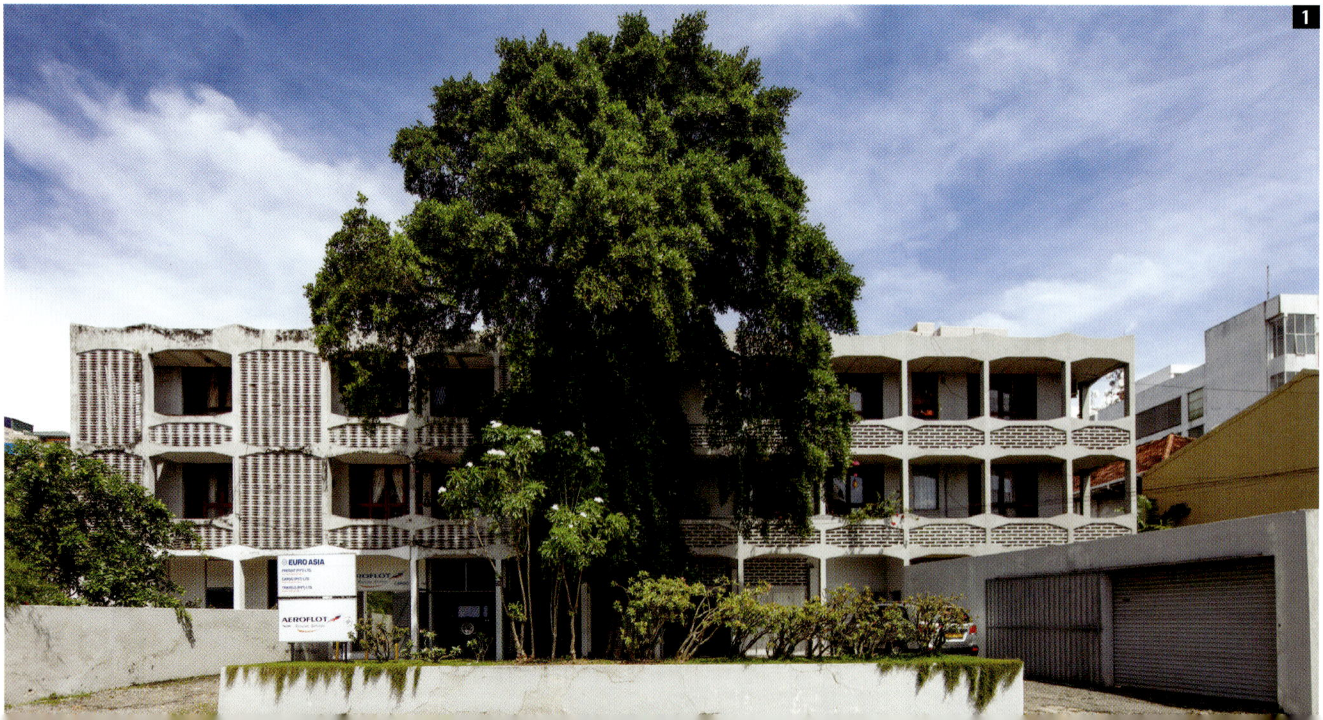

# The YWCA

Rotunda Gardens
1965

The project architect for the YWCA was Ismeth Raheem. It was one of a number of projects that developed the idea of jettying the section in order to create shade and can be seen as a precursor of the Bentota Beach Hotel.

The plan is developed around two internal open-to-the-sky courtyards. The ground floor is given over to the public spaces — reception, offices, kitchen and refectory — and the upper two floors contain the bedrooms. The corridors are single loaded to ensure good cross-ventilation and the windows are screened by lattice shutters.

Though now fairly run-down, the YWCA hostel survives miraculously within a forest of high-rise towers and could easily be restored to its former glory.

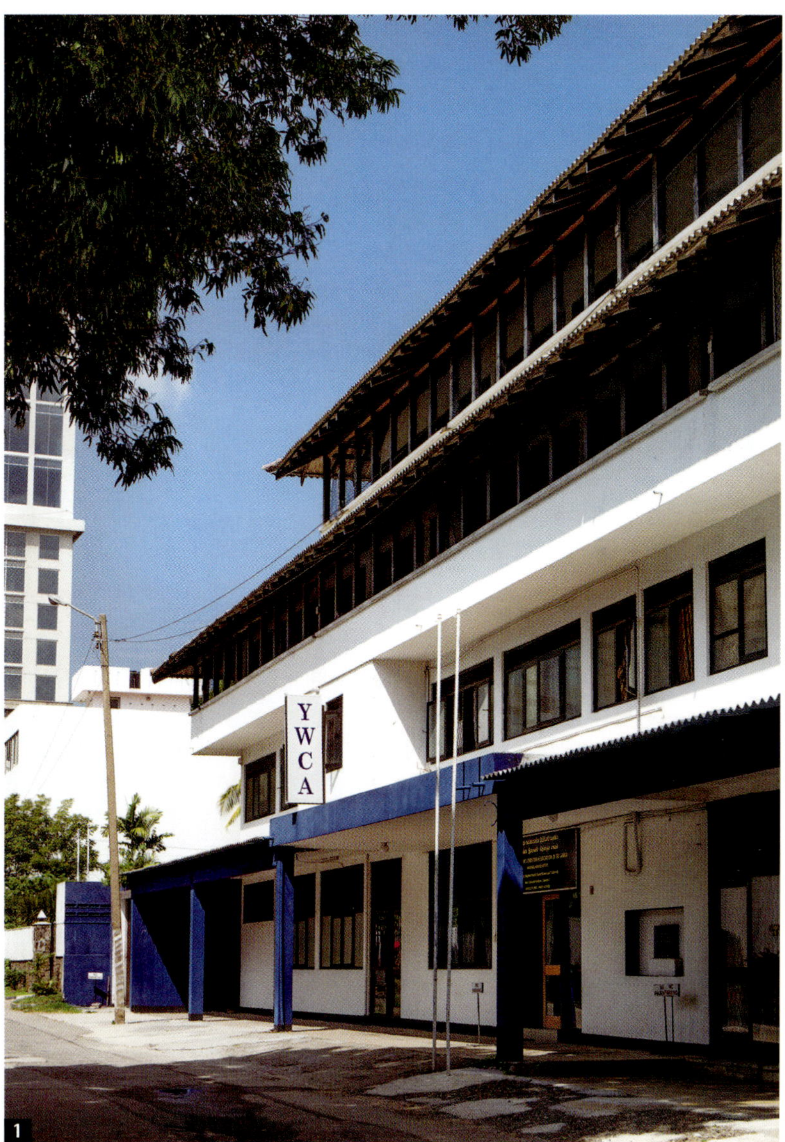


1 The street frontage of the YWCA hostel.

# The Seema Malaka

Beira Lake
1976

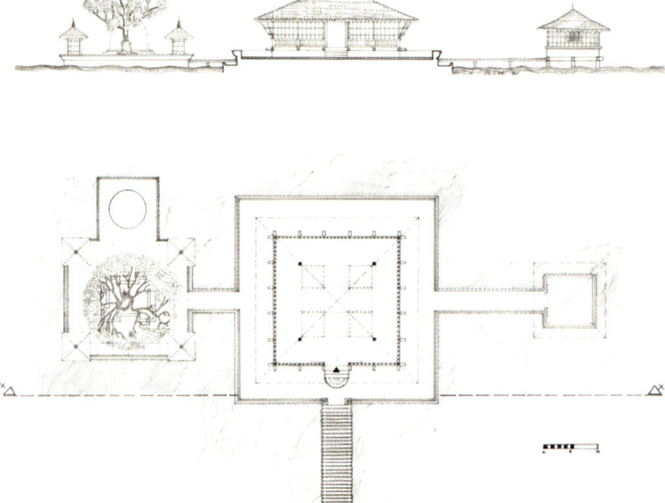

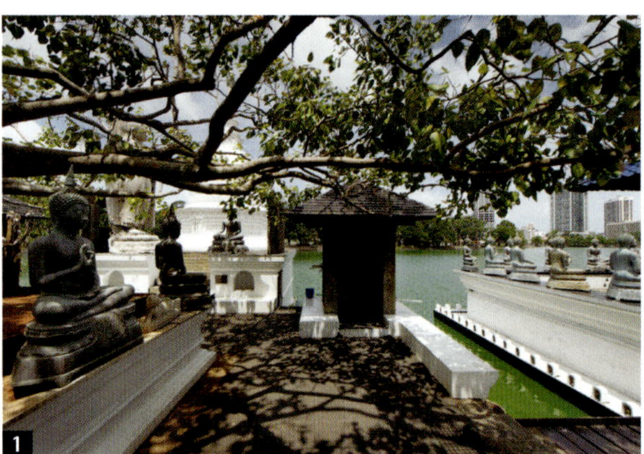

The Seema Malaka is an ordination temple and was commissioned by the *thera* or elder of the nearby Gangaramaya Temple. Geoffrey Bawa, its architect, was nominally Christian, while its main benefactor, Salehbhai Husseinbhai Moosajee, was a leading member of the local Bora community: this could only happen in Sri Lanka!

The ordination of Buddhist monks traditionally takes place on or above water and the temple was built on three platforms in the Beira Lake. A square preaching hall sits on the main platform and is raised up on massive beams in the manner of an ancient *ambalama*. It is enclosed by open screens formed by tilted rafters. The northern platform hovers above the water on stilts and supports the ordination pavilion. The southern platform carries a Bodhi tree at its centre with a quartet of *devale* pavilions devoted to the Gods Kataragama, Saman, Namba and Pattini at its four corners. A fourth platform was added later to support a *stupa*.

The temple has undergone a number of changes over the years – the original clay tiles were replaced with blue-glazed tiles, and a whole platoon of bronze Buddha statutes from Thailand was added to the perimeter of the preaching hall. But it still retains an aura of sanctity and is one of the very few non-traditional Buddhist temples to have been built in Sri Lanka.

**Above** Elevation and plan, 1985. Bawa Archive.
**1** Bodhi tree and *devale* on the southern platform.
**2** View of the main preaching hall and the ordination platform from the northeast.

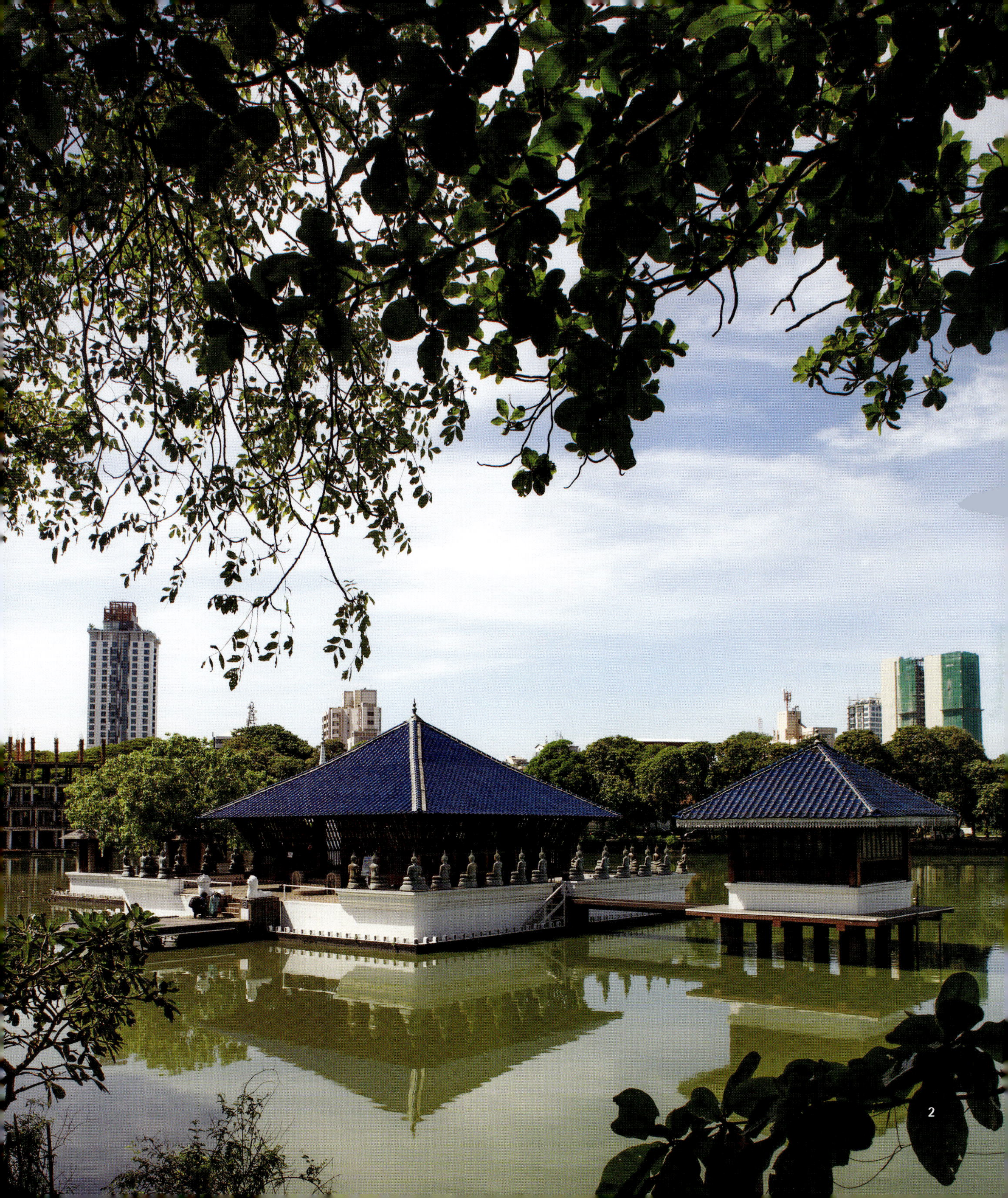

# The Jayakody House

Park Street, Colombo

1991–96

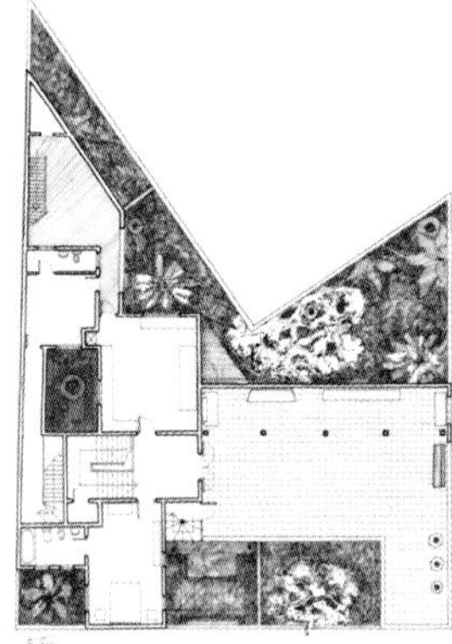

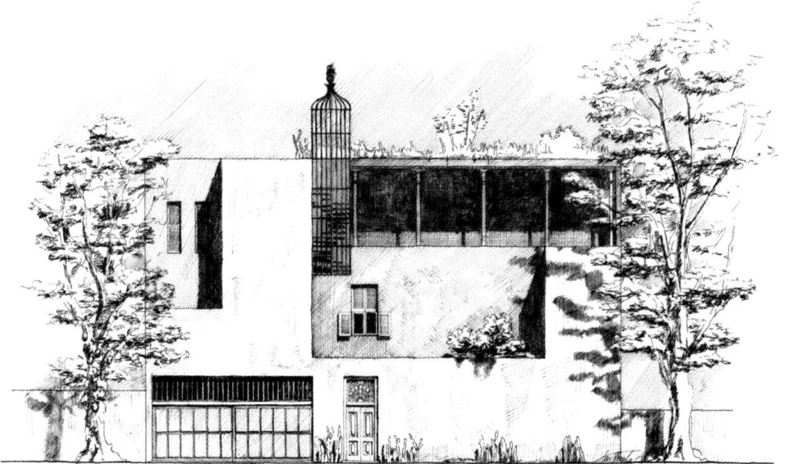

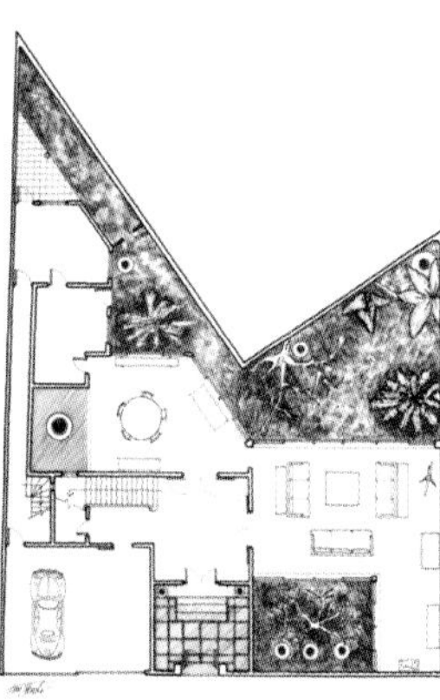

Rohan Jayakody runs a chain of flower shops and exports cut flowers to the Far East. His house occupies an odd-shaped plot in a cul de sac between Union Place and the Viharamahadevi Park. Built on three storeys, it is a cross between a courtyard house and a tower.

The ground floor has a subterranean feel. An understated doorway leads via a small court to the central hallway out of which rises the main staircase. The sitting room is lit from two courtyards, while the dining room abuts a tall blue-painted lightwell that acts as a ventilation chimney. The first floor is occupied by bedrooms, each of which has its own private courtyard. A large part of the second floor is given over to a generous terrace that is partially sheltered by an elegant loggia and a narrow spiral stair leads up, as if within a birdcage, to a rooftop terrace with a small plunge pool.

The project took several years to build and for a time Bawa lost interest in it. Having provided the original sketch design, he delegated its execution to his friend Milroy Perera and only intervened again when it was nearing completion.

**Above** Front elevation, ground-floor plan, second-floor plan, 1994. Bawa Archive.
**1** The entrance lobby.
**2** View from the street.
**3** The stairs up to the top pool terrace.
**4** The spacious terrace and loggia on the second floor.

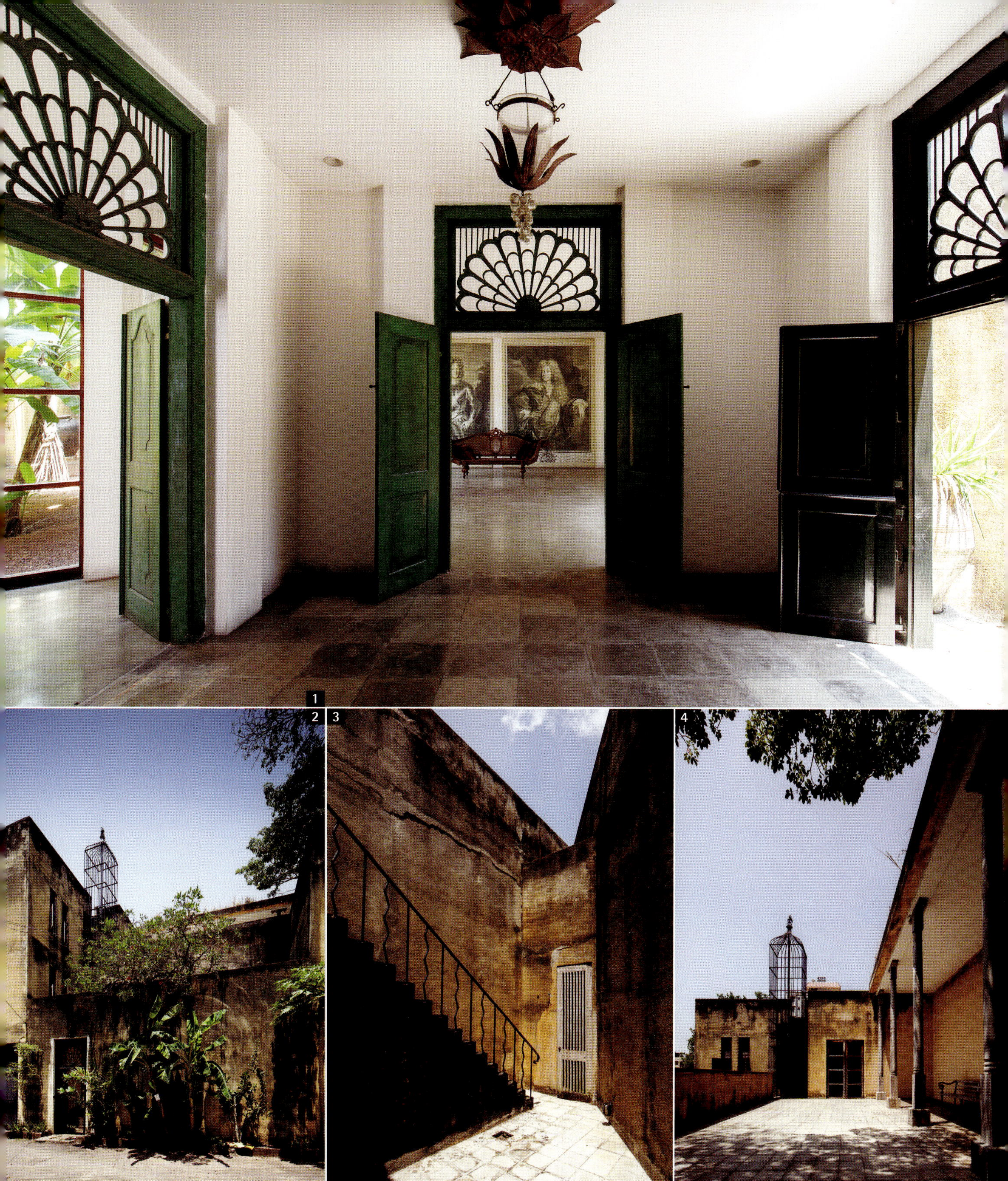

# The State Mortgage Bank

(later known as the Mahaweli Building )
Hyde Park, Darley Road, Colombo

1976–78

Originally this twelve-storey office building was commissioned by the Finance Ministry to house the State Mortgage Bank, but, after the change of government in 1977, it was re-designated as the secretariat of the Mahaweli Development Ministry. For this project Bawa was assisted by Anura Ratnavibushana and together they set out to develop a prototype for a sustainable medium-rise office building in a tropical city that would be economic both to build and to maintain.

The building was aileron-shaped so that its profile varied dramatically according to the viewpoint and it was capped by an open-sided double-height loggia which revealed the geometry of the structure below. The aerodynamic plan was orientated to minimise solar gain and to encourage ventilation from prevailing winds. The windows were set behind deep spandrel panels that were designed as air-intake louvres.

Bawa had intended that the floors be open planned, but the change of client produced an influx of expatriate consultants who demanded partitioned offices and air-conditioning. The air-intake louvres were blocked in and the facade was soon dotted with unsightly compressors. This did not prevent Malaysian architect Ken Yeang from hailing it, some 20 years later, as 'the best example of a bioclimatically responsive tall building to be found anywhere in the world'.

Today, it is surrounded by glass-clad, energy guzzling skyscrapers of twice its height and is in a poor state of repair.

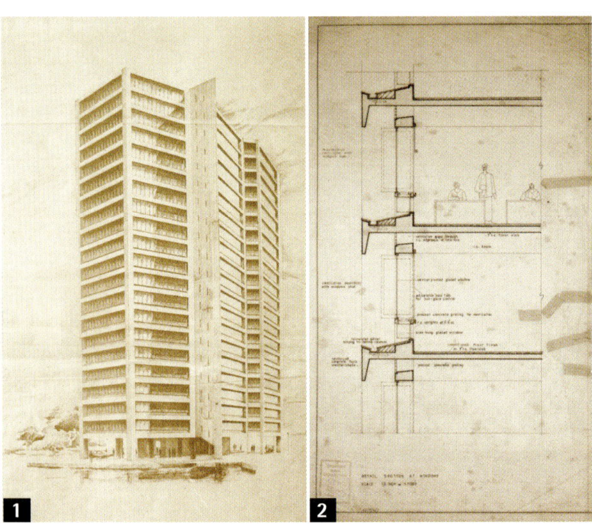

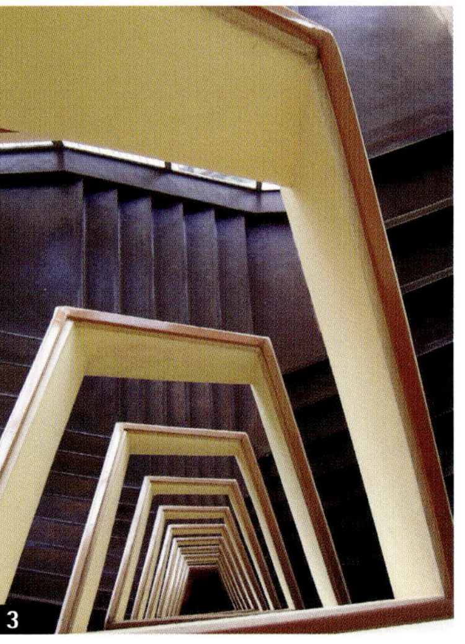

1 Perspective drawing, 1976. Bawa Archive.
2 Section through the external wall showing the air-intake louvres, 1978. Bawa Archive.
3 The staircase.
4 View from Darley Road.

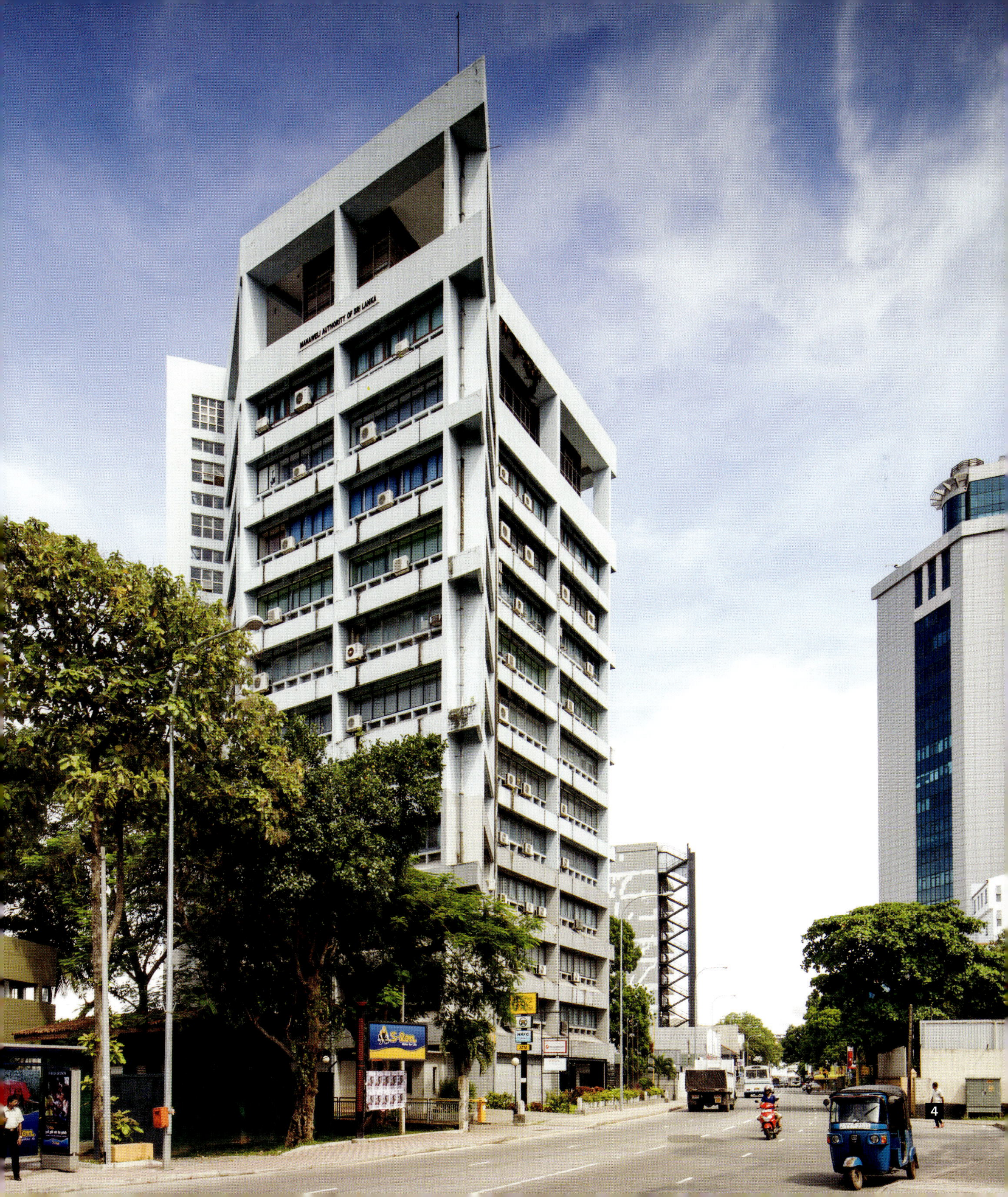
MAHAWELI AUTHORITY OF SRI LANKA

# The Raffel House

Ward Place, Colombo

1962-64

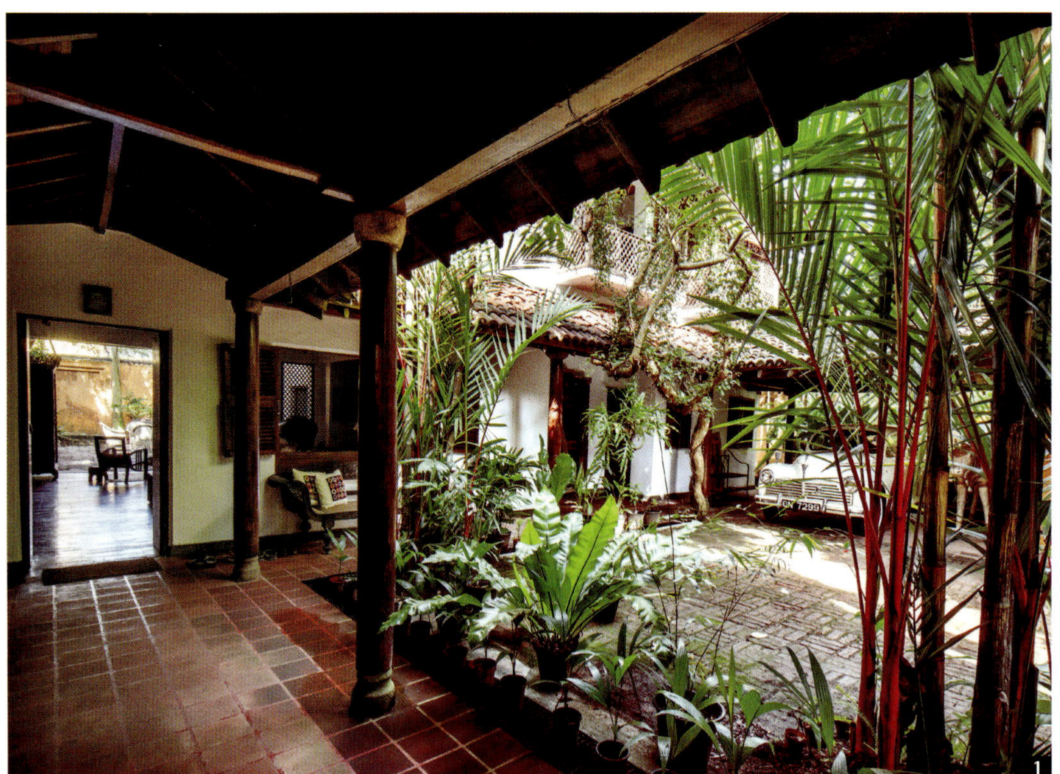

Bawa designed the Raffel house for his doctor friend Chris Raffel and his musician wife Carmen in 1962. It uses the vocabulary of the Ena de Silva house which he had completed in the previous year.

The land-locked site lies off Ward Place at the end of a long, narrow cul-de-sac. It is entered under an archway in a two-storey barbican, which opens into an entrance court with a roofed car port. A narrow staircase gives access to a secret room above the entrance archway that serves as a study and lookout. The car port is linked to the house by a polished terracotta pavement, its tiled roof supported on round timber columns.

The house is on two floors and its 'L'-shaped plan forms a garden courtyard. The original trees have grown to a considerable height and their branches now form a high-level canopy that filters light and creates cooling up-draughts. Before

1 The entrance court with a view through to the sitting room and the garden court just visible beyond.
2 The sitting room seen from the garden court.
3 The first-floor landing of the main staircase.
4 A view of the sitting room with the garden court on right.

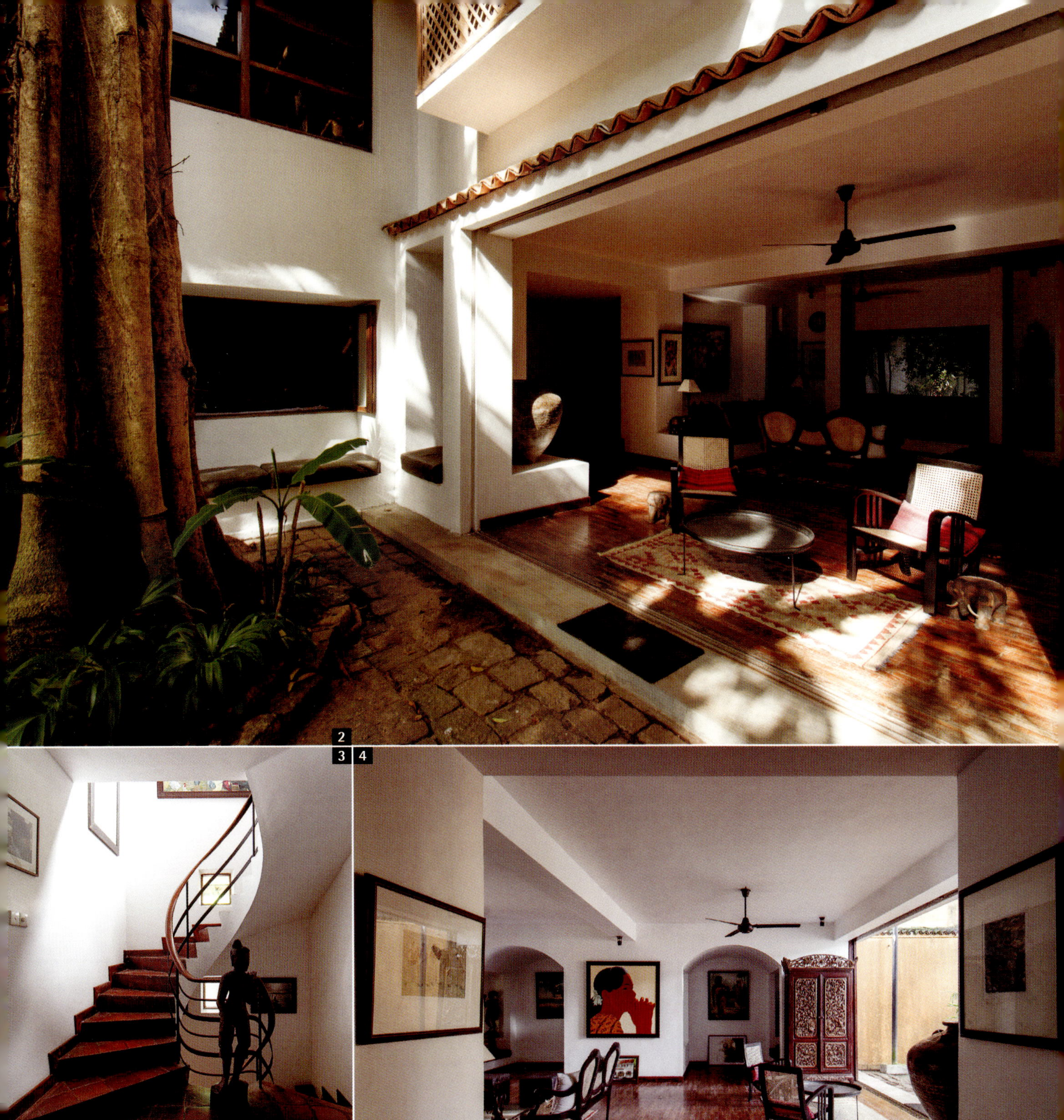

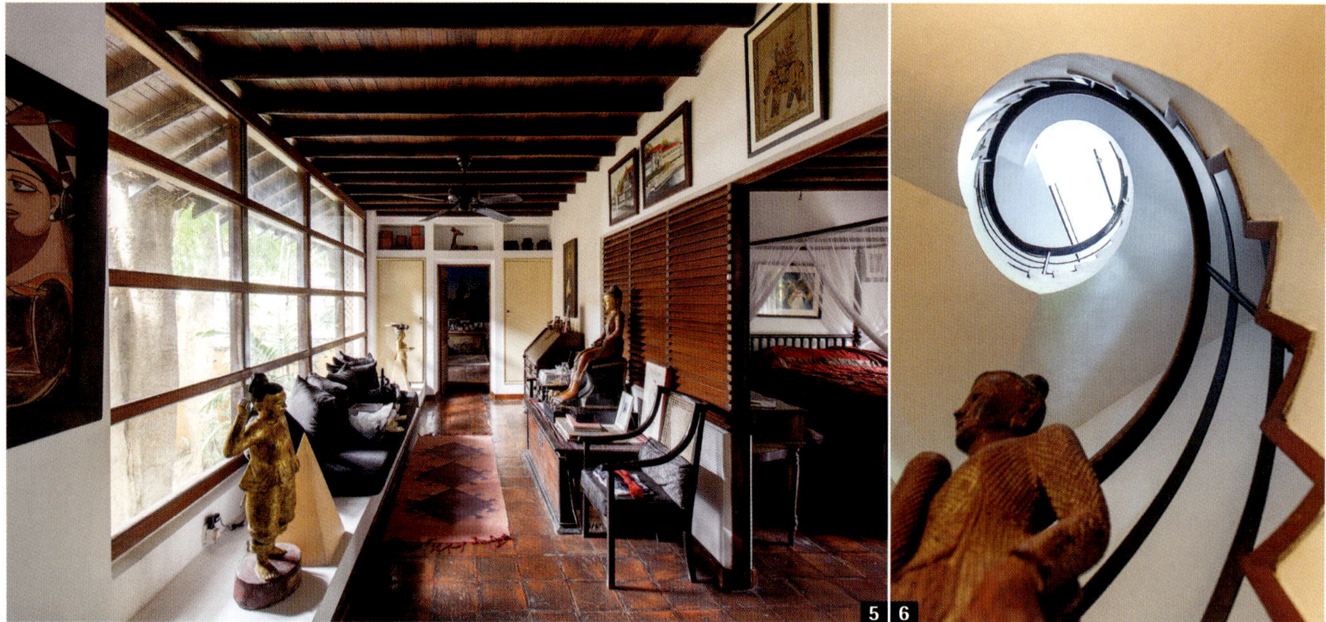

the Raffels emigrated to Australia they used the courtyard for outdoor concerts.

The main sitting room runs between the entrance court and the garden and incorporates top-lit alcoves with built in seats. The main stair-case is a curving dog-leg which snakes up to a generous landing on the first floor. The two principal bedrooms occupy the ends of the wings and each has an exposed timber ceiling with fan rafters supported on a central timber column. The bedrooms all have projecting windows clad in diagonal latticework which can be used as seats. The staircase continues upwards within a tower that houses water tanks at second-floor level to a small belvedere at third-floor level.

The present owners treat the house with exemplary care and it survives as a perfect example of Bawa's 'Contemporary Vernacular' manner.

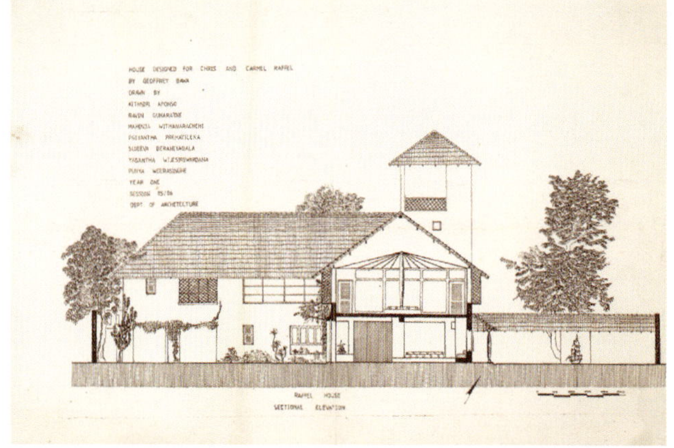

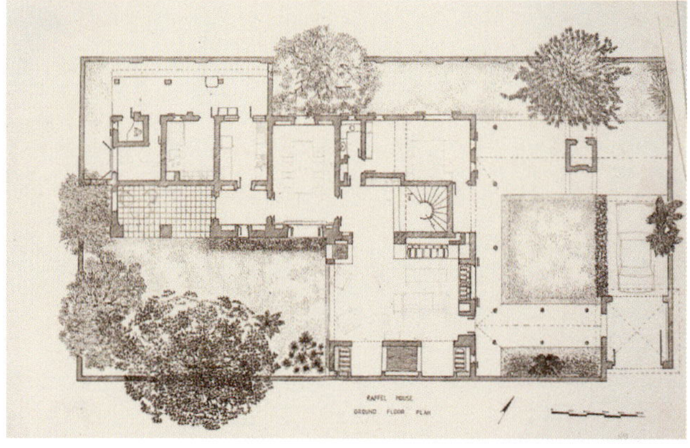

**Right** Sectional elevation and plan. Date unknown. Bawa Archive.

**5** The first-floor gallery.
**6** The spiral stair.
**7** The master bedroom.

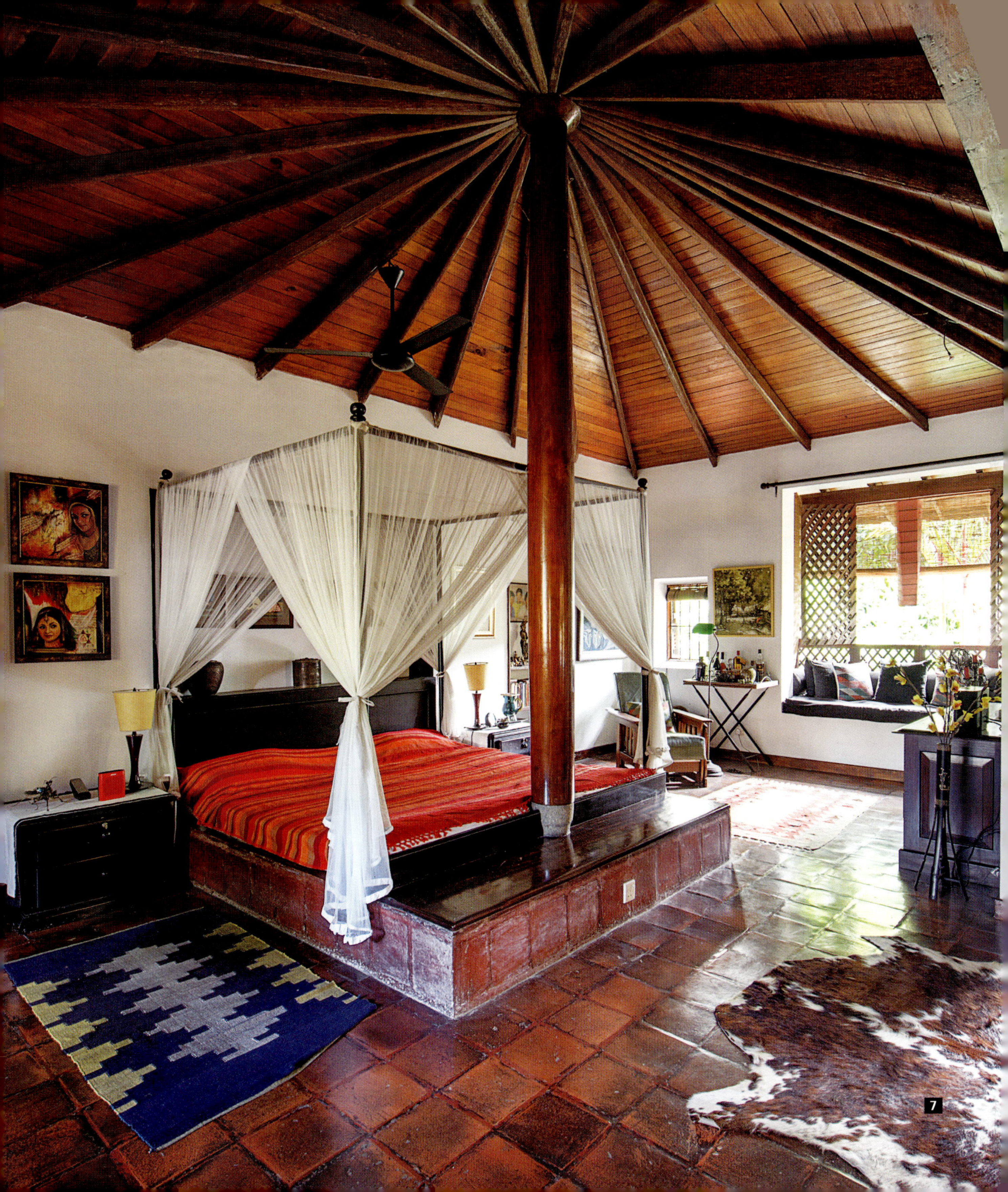

# The David Spenser House

Rosmead Place, Colombo
1997

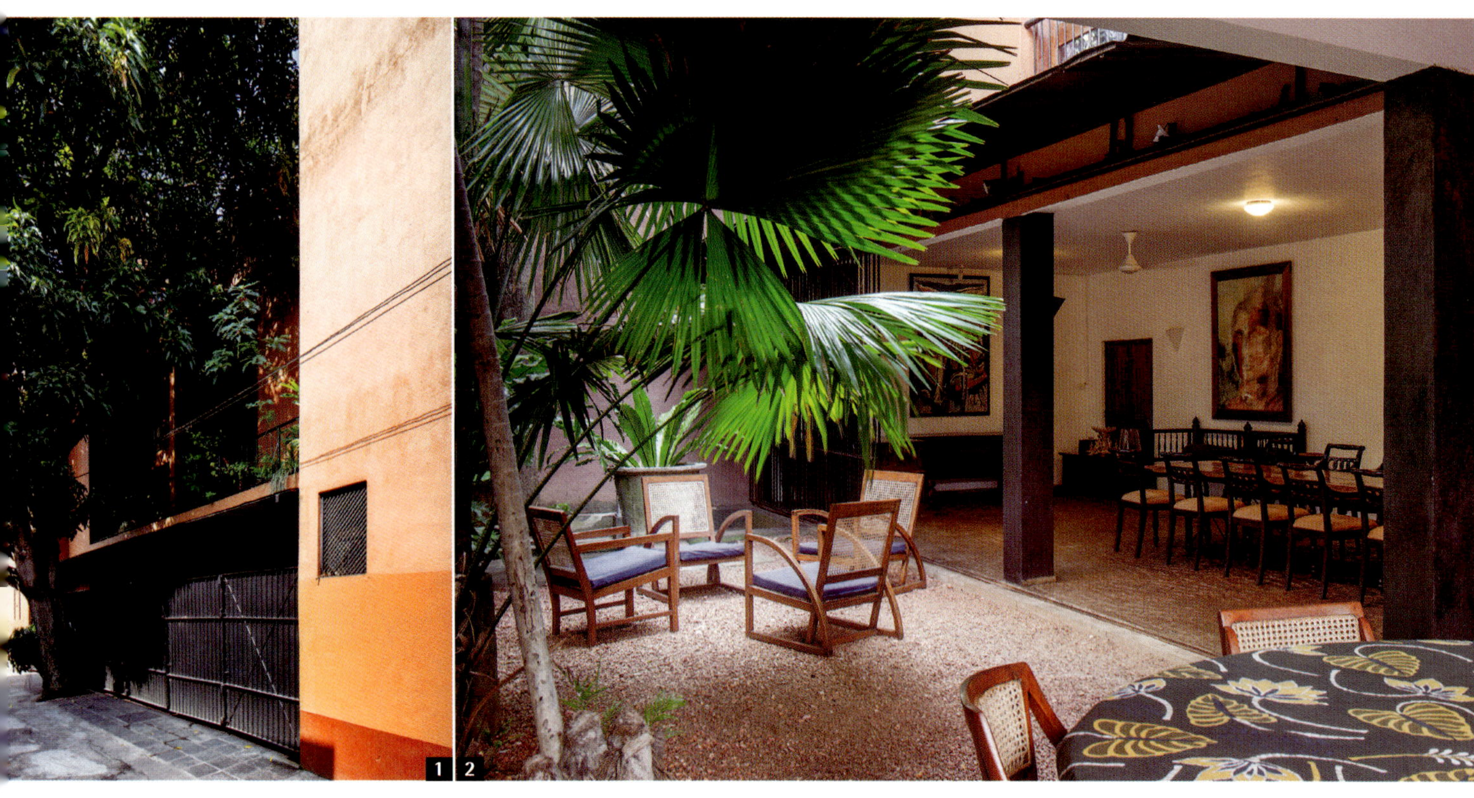

David Spenser was born David de Saram in Colombo in 1934 but spent most of his life in England where he made a name for himself, first as a child radio actor, and later as a film actor and producer. The house lies immediately behind that of Pin and Pam Fernando, to whom he was related, but is accessed from a lane off Rosmead Place. Bawa produced the design in 1997 at a time when his health was failing. The project architect was Murad Ismail. It was the last in a series of tower houses and occupies three floors with a rooftop swimming pool. Designed for a gay couple, the first floor contains two autonomous bedroom suites that share a shared sitting room.

Spenser died in 2013 in Spain. His Colombo house remains in the de Saram family and is still in its original state.

1 View from the street.
2 The ground-floor veranda and court.

# St Bridget's Montessori School

Maitland Crescent, Colombo

1963–64

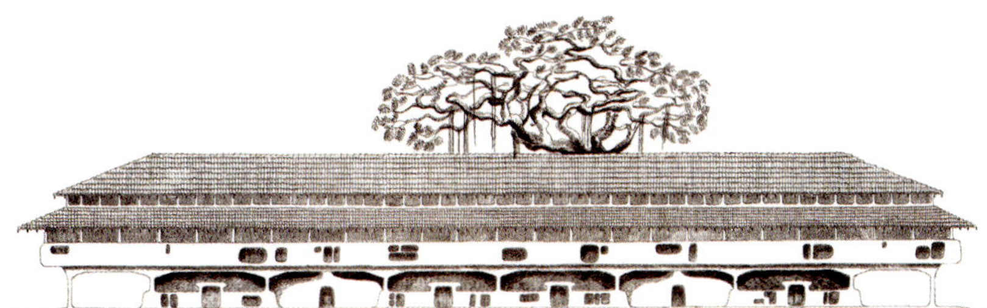

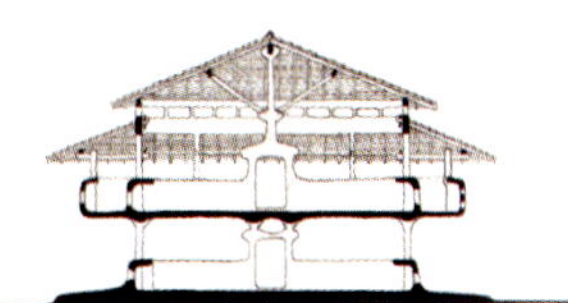

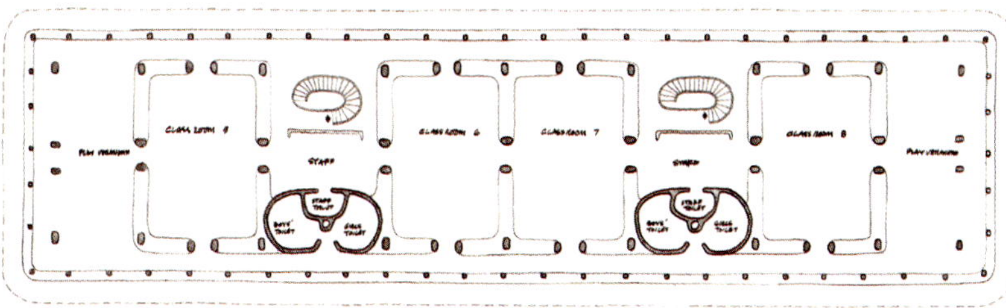

This Montessori School is located on the southern edge of St Bridget's Convent and has independent access from Maitland Crescent. It is run by the Order of the Sisters of the Good Shepherd and was one of a series of commissions that came to Bawa from the Catholic Church.

Bawa was introduced to the Order by his friend Barbara Sansoni who, at the time, was involved in setting up weaving workshops for the nuns. Laki Senanayake was his main collaborator on the project: together they created a witty re-imagining of a traditional village school on two floors with organically rounded walls and deep overhanging roofs suggesting mud walls and thatched roofs.

The upper classrooms were covered by a vast umbrella roof of clay tiles on corrugated cement sheeting that was supported by an elegantly articulated concrete frame and cantilevered out far beyond the building line to provide shelter from sun and rain. The original drawings proposed a raised ridge for ventilation but this was later omitted. The first-floor slab curves upwards around its edge to form the perimeter wall and is supported on mushroom-topped columns, giving the lower floor a cave-like quality. The two levels are linked by curving staircases enclosed by moulded concrete walls, perforated by oval peepholes.

**Above** Plan, long elevation and cross-section, 1964. Bawa Archive.

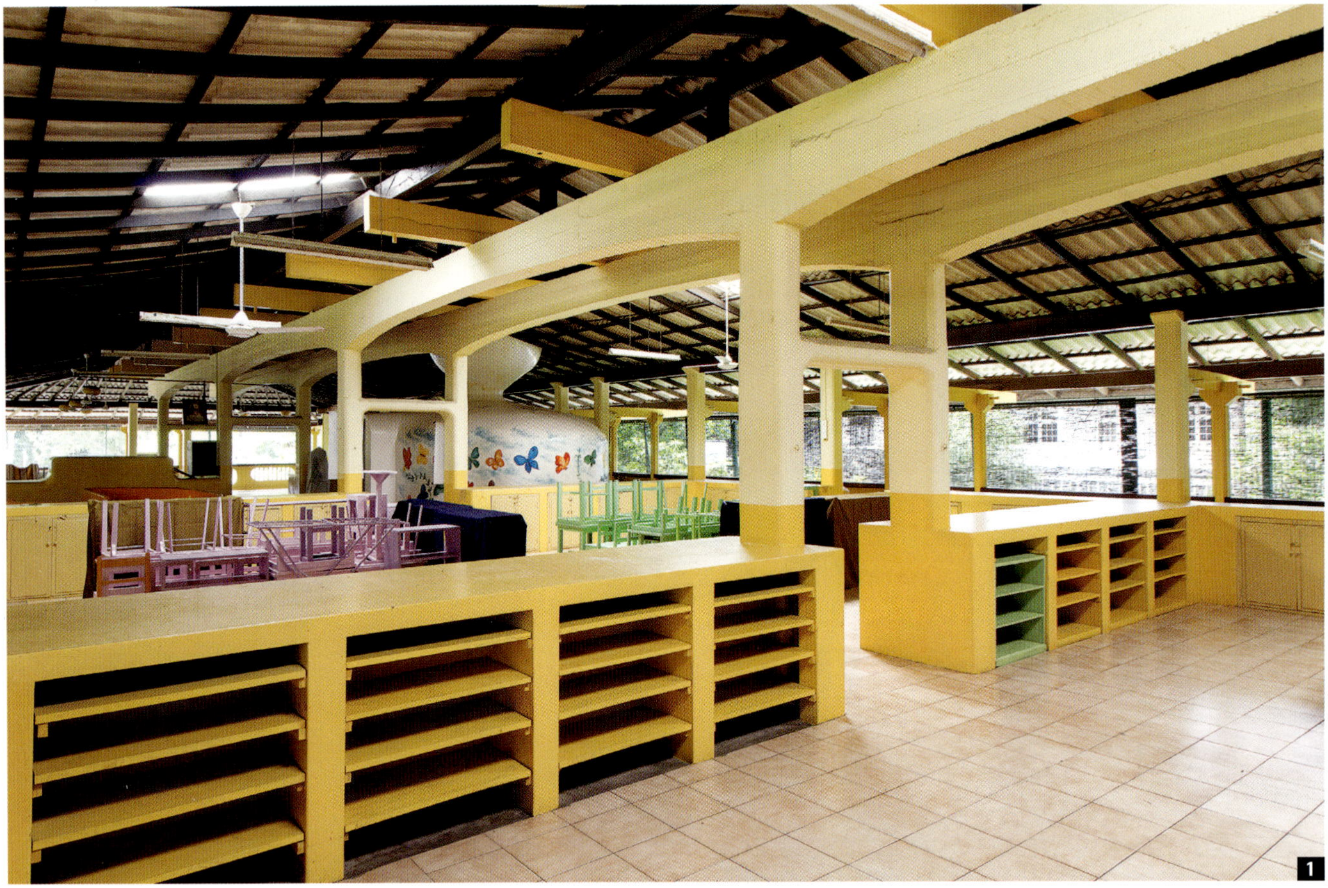

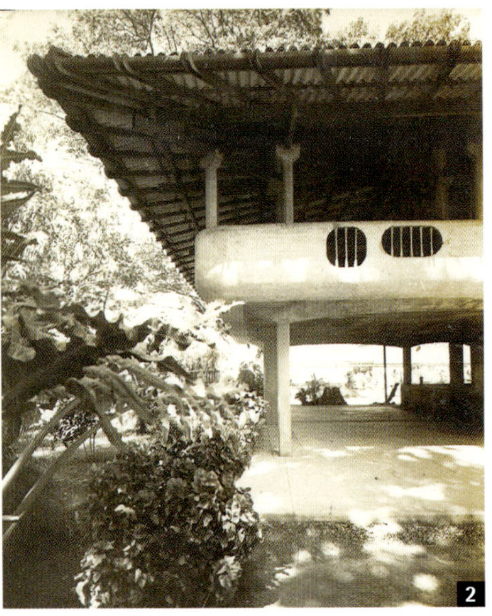

The individual classrooms are defined by low walls incorporating generous cupboards, while toilets and ancillary spaces are located within organically-shaped concrete domes scaled to accommodate small children. The domes and staircase panels were originally decorated with incised coloured drawings by Barabara Sansoni.

The classrooms are still in good condition, though they are now cocooned in netting to keep out marauding crows and successive re-paintings have destroyed the original murals and colour harmonies. Sadly the nuns are now planning partly to demolish and extend the school.

1 First-floor classrooms.
2 External corner, 1964. Bawa Archive.
3 Toilet cubicle.
4 Head of staircase.
5 Staircase at ground-floor level.

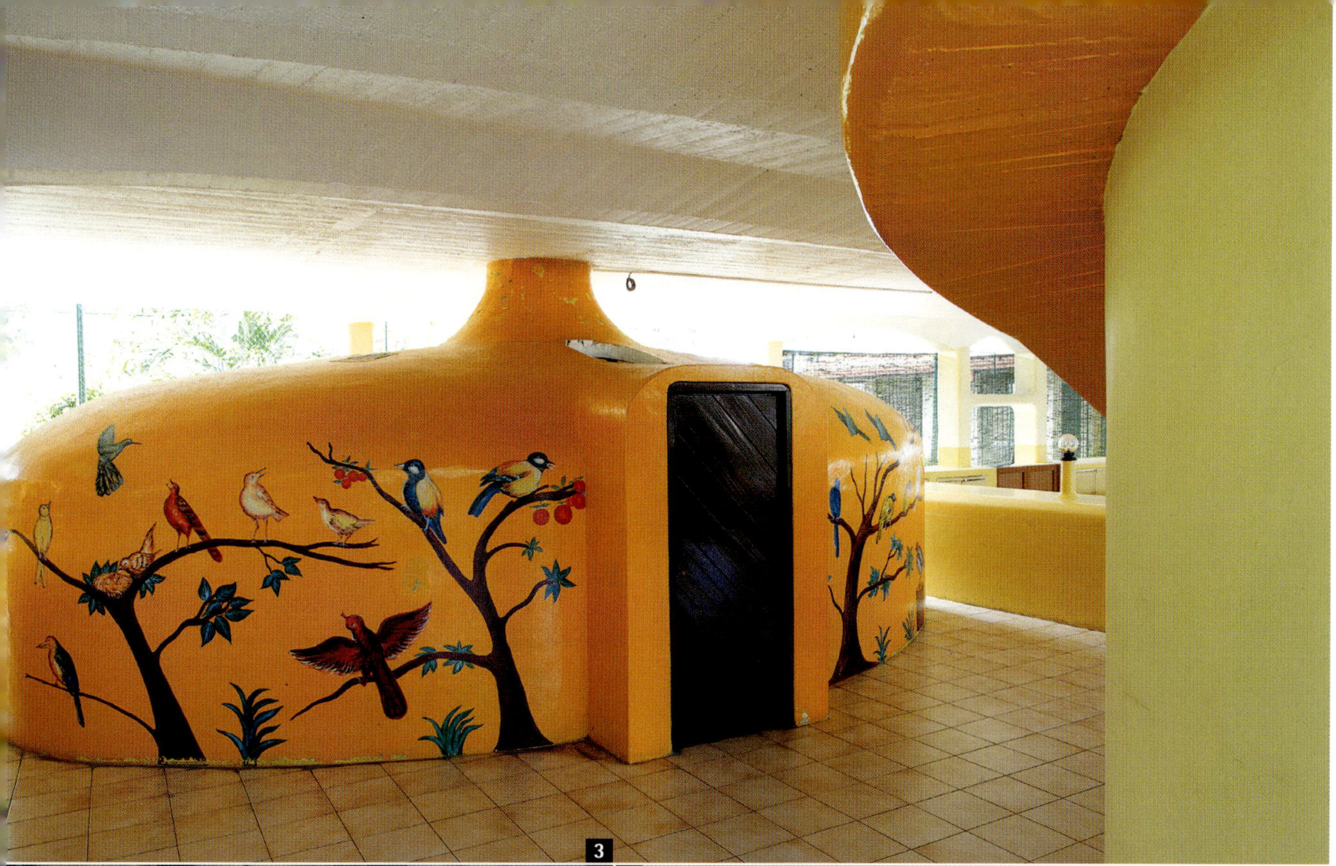

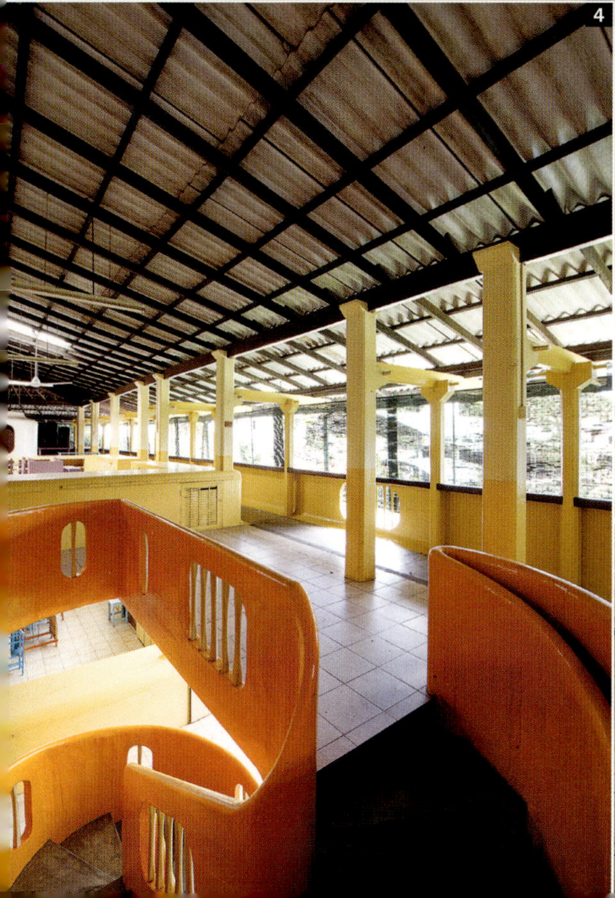

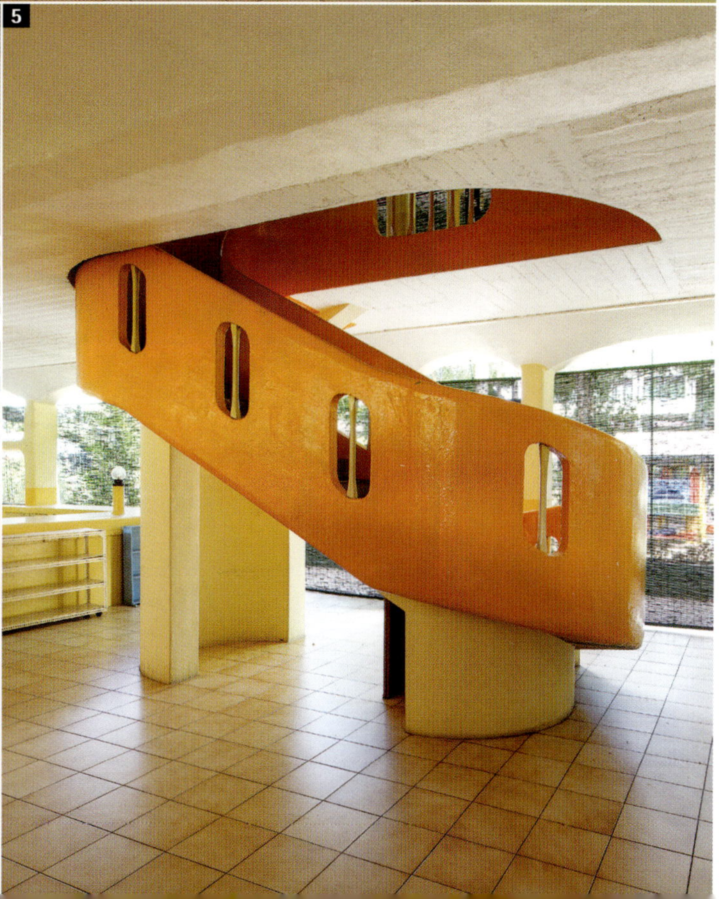

# The Agrarian Research and Training Institute

Wijerama Mawatha, Colombo

1973–1976

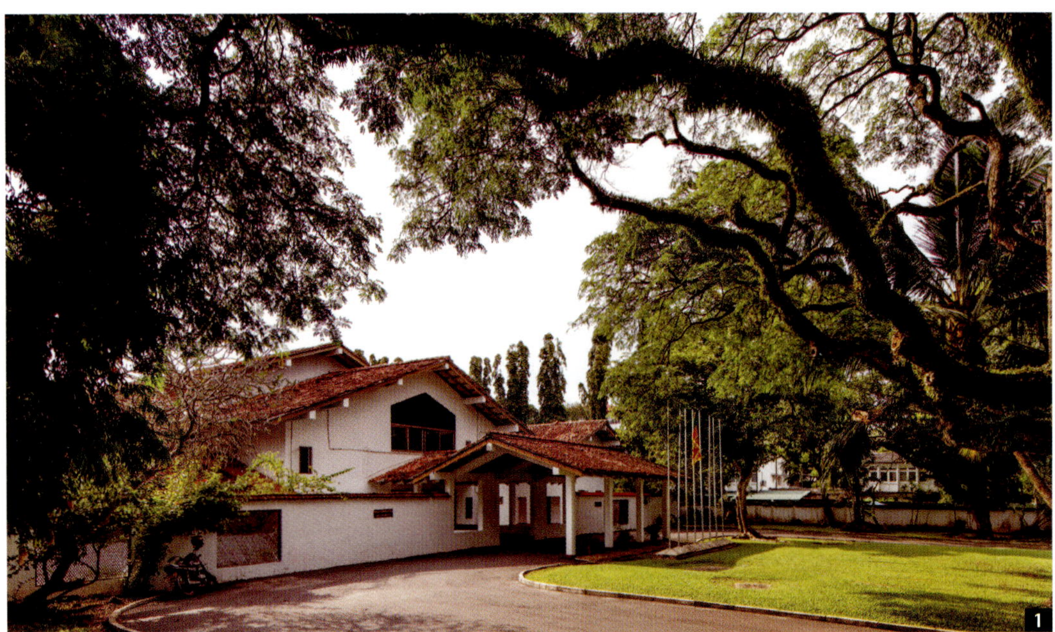



The Agrarian Research and Training Institute (ARTI) was commissioned by the government of Srimavo Bandaranaike during a time of austerity and import control. The brief called for a range of offices of different sizes, a lecture theatre, a library and a residential hostel and challenged Bawa to create a pleasant working environment with a low budget.

The Institute was designed around an informal series of courtyards of different sizes and different degrees of enclosure, dispelling any initial impression of institutional symmetry and introducing variety and surprise. It uses a limited palette of local sourced materials: roofs of clay tile on corrugated cement sheeting, simple hybrid structures of concrete and timber, and terracotta-tiled floors.

The corridors form the edges of the courtyards and are single loaded to encourage cross ventilation and natural lighting. Air-conditioning was provided only for the lecture theatre and the library.

The result offered a low-rise alternative to the Mahaweli Tower and could be considered as a prototype for a sustainable and affordable working environment in a tropical city. After 40 years it still serves its original purpose.

1 The *porte-cochère*.
2 The main courtyard.
3 The long courtyard.
4 First-floor corridor.

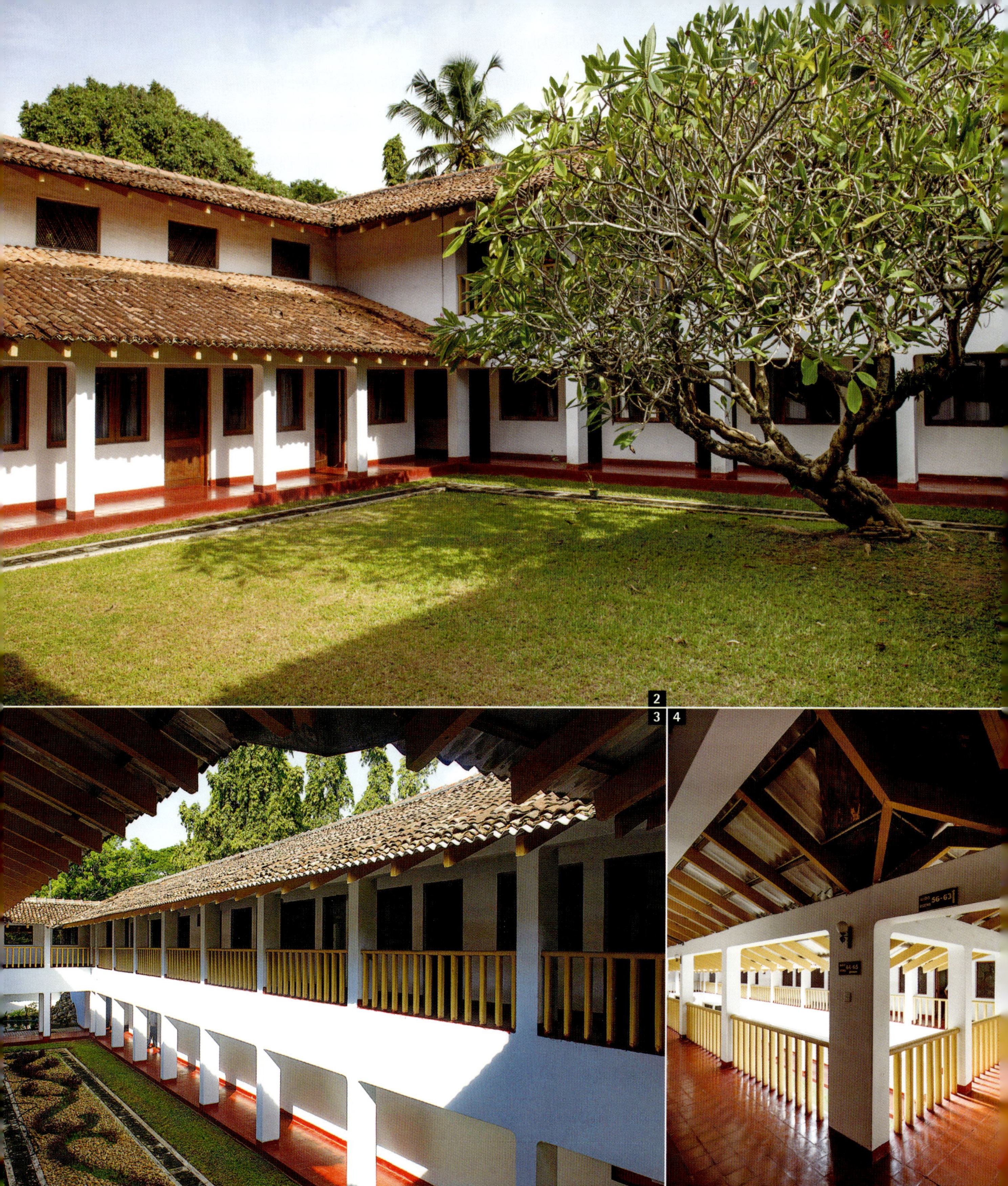
2
3 4
56-63

# The Ratnasivaratnam House

Bhaudaloka Mawatha, Colombo
1979

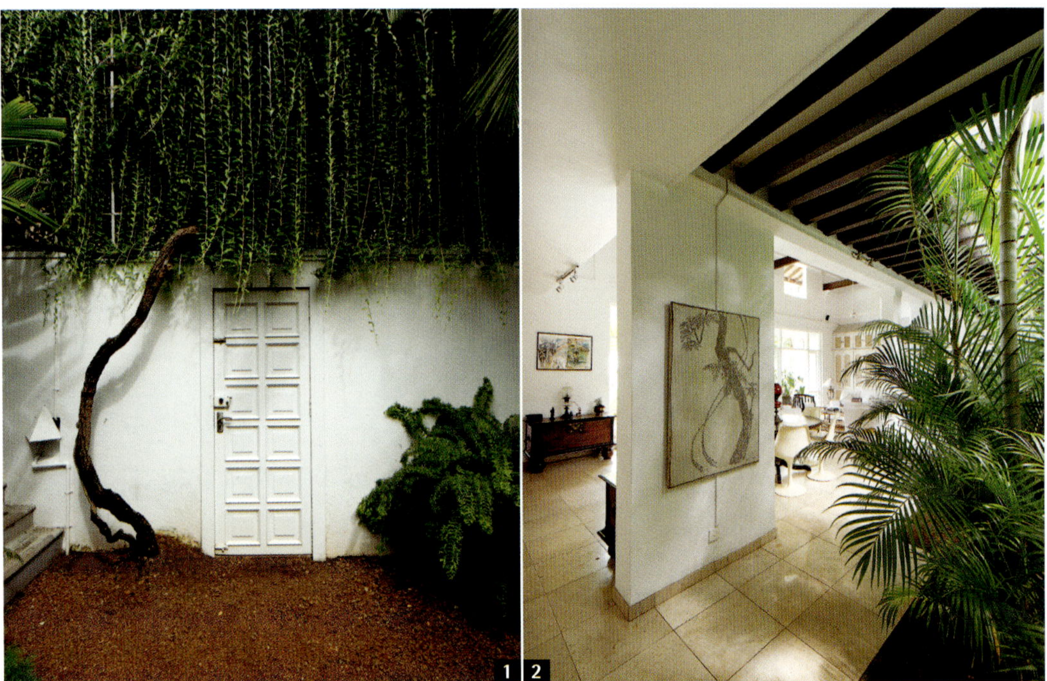

1  2

Bawa designed this house for a director of Aitken Spence at the same time that he was working on the company's Triton Hotel at Ahungalla. The house lies hidden behind a high screen wall which is broken only by the main entrance and the garage.

The entrance opens to a long axial corridor. To its left is a double-height sitting room that is flanked on both sides by open-to-the-sky courtyards. The furthermost court is covered by what came to be known as a 'Burglar Pergola' — parallel pre-cast concrete rafters that provide security while admitting light and air. An undulating wall separates this from a third court, beyond which are a pair of bedrooms.

The garage and kitchen are situated to the right of the main corridor. Beyond lies a small court and the master bedroom that incorporates a mezzanine study. A narrow staircase rises up beside the garage to a roof terrace and an independent studio bedroom.

The house was neglected for a time, but has recently been carefully restored by the original owner's son.

1 The street entrance.
2 View from the pergola court towards the sitting room.
3 A fuller view of the pergola court with the sitting room.
4 The sitting room.

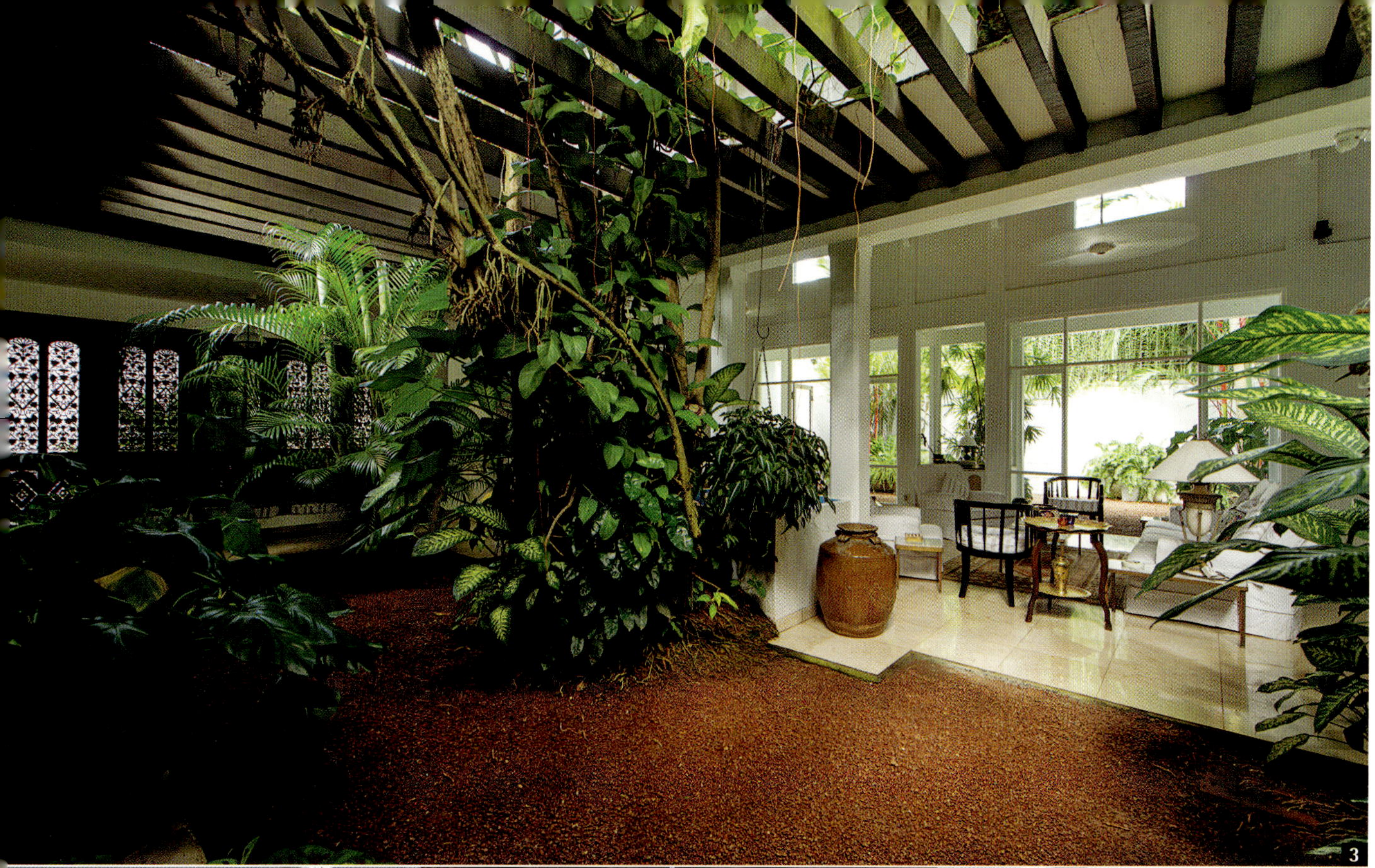

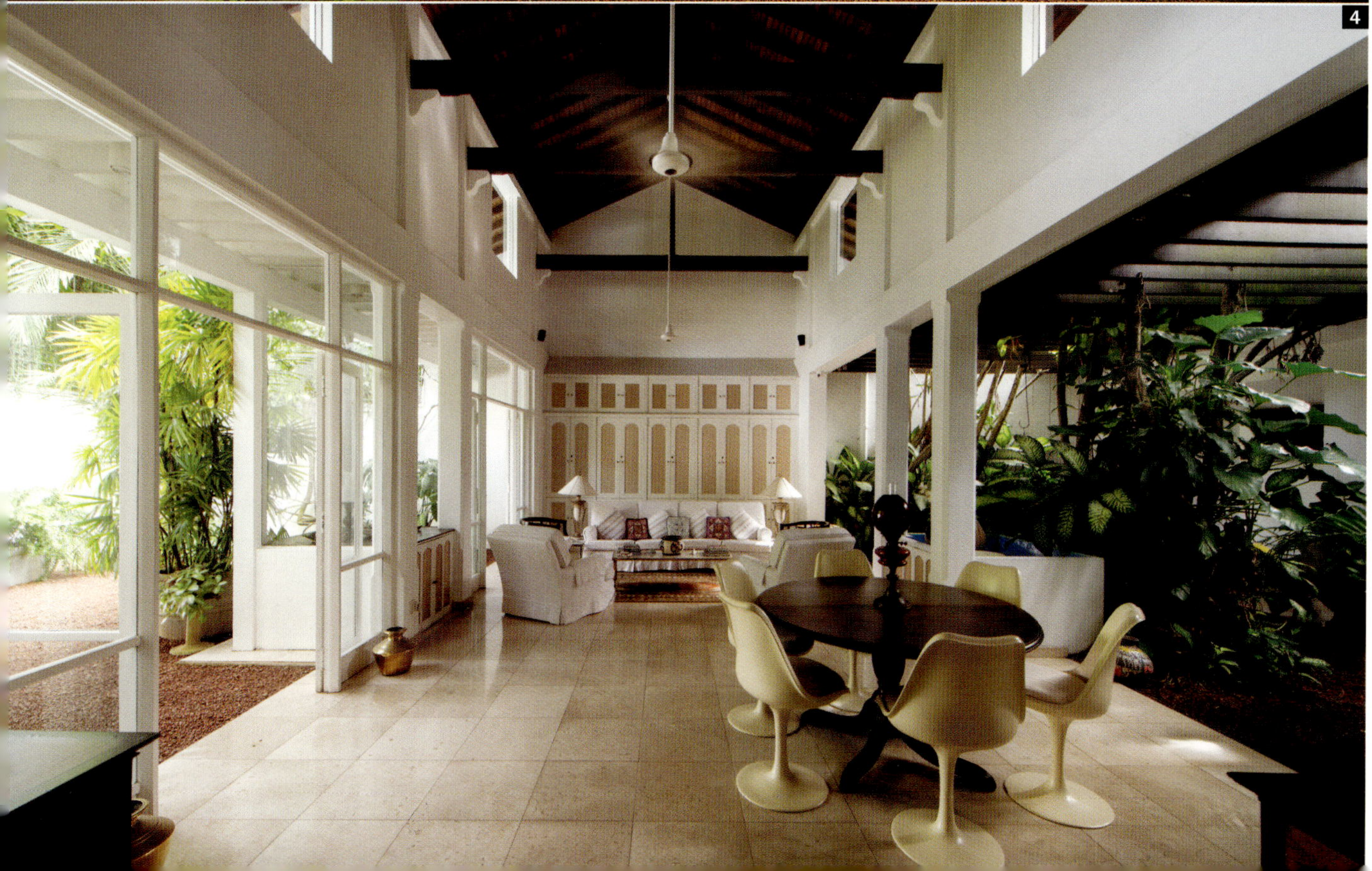

# The New Sri Lanka Parliament

## Kotte

### 1979-1982

Early in 1979, Geoffrey Bawa was summoned out of the blue to a meeting with President JR Jayawardene who commissioned him, there and then, to design a new Parliament. The proposed location was at Kotte, the site of a former medieval capital of Ceylon that lay in marshland some eight kilometres east of Colombo. Jayawardene gave him a free hand with the one proviso that the building had to be ready within three years. According to anecdotal evidence, Bawa then sketched out his design concept in a matter of hours and presented it to the President for his approval.

The truth is more complicated, however. Five years earlier, at the behest of prime minister Sirimavo Bandaranaike, Bawa had already produced detailed plans for a new Parliament next to the old one on the Galle Face in Colombo — and he used these as his starting point for the new design.

The choice of the new location seems to have been Jayawardene's alone and was not anticipated in any development plan for the city. It had been the seat of the Alakonderas — a clan of south Indian mercenaries who ruled the whole of the island during the 15th century and it had been known, fortuitously, as Sri Jayawardenepura, the City of Victories. This symbolic move took the Parliament away from the Fort, which had been the centre of colonial rule, and shifted it towards the interior of the island. It was also a clever move in planning terms — Colombo was constrained by a cordon of marshes to the east and its growth had been limited to a north-south axis. The new location of the Parliament created

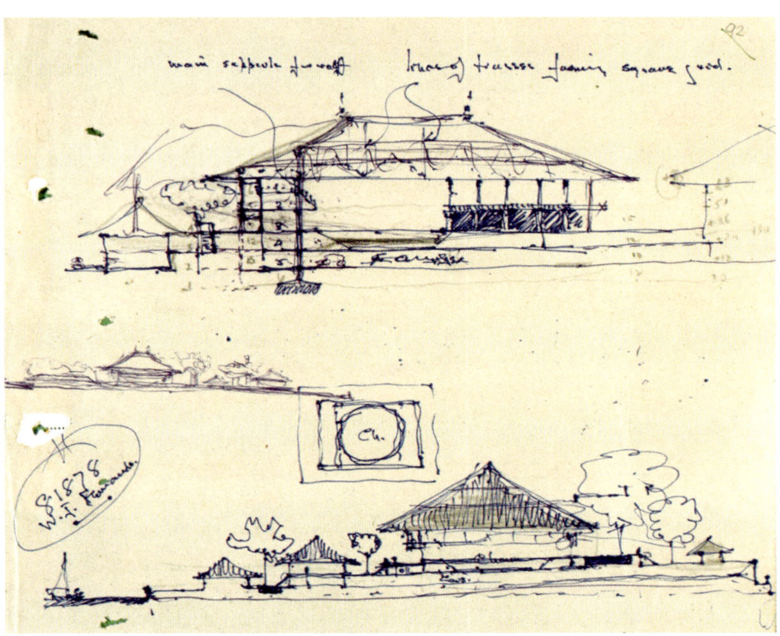

an opportunity for expansion towards the interior and the Urban Development Authority quickly drew up impressive plans for a new capital city to be built around it.

Bawa proposed to drain the marshes and site the new Parliament on a strict north-south axis atop an island in the middle of an artificial lake. A detailed design was drawn up and the construction was entrusted to a Japanese company by the name of Mitsui.

The original Parliament of 1926 was housed in a pompous neo-classical building that turned its back on Ceylon and faced towards Britain and

**Above** An early sketch of the Parliament by Geoffrey Bawa, 1979. Bawa Archive.
**1** The view across the lake towards the island Parliament.

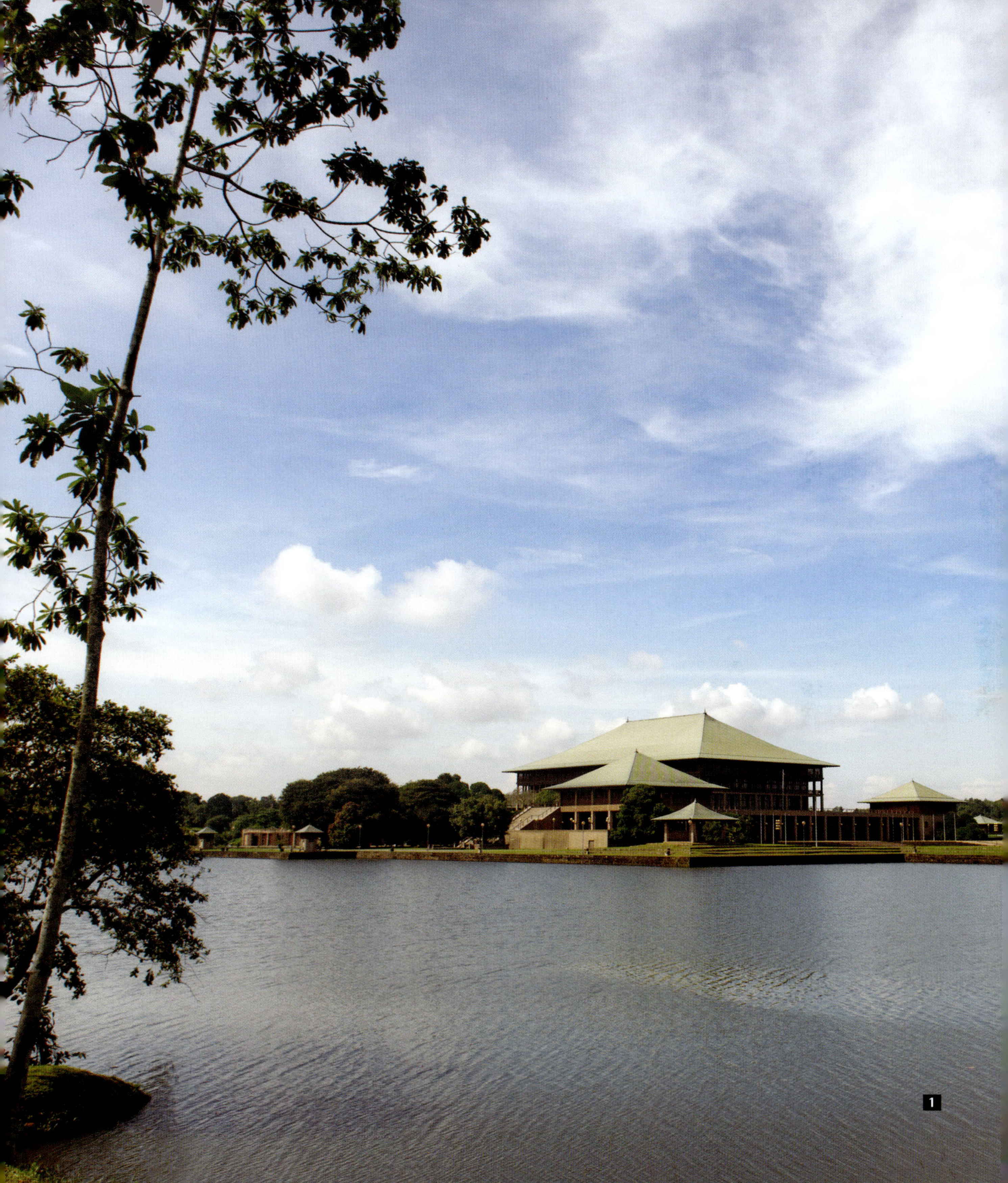
1

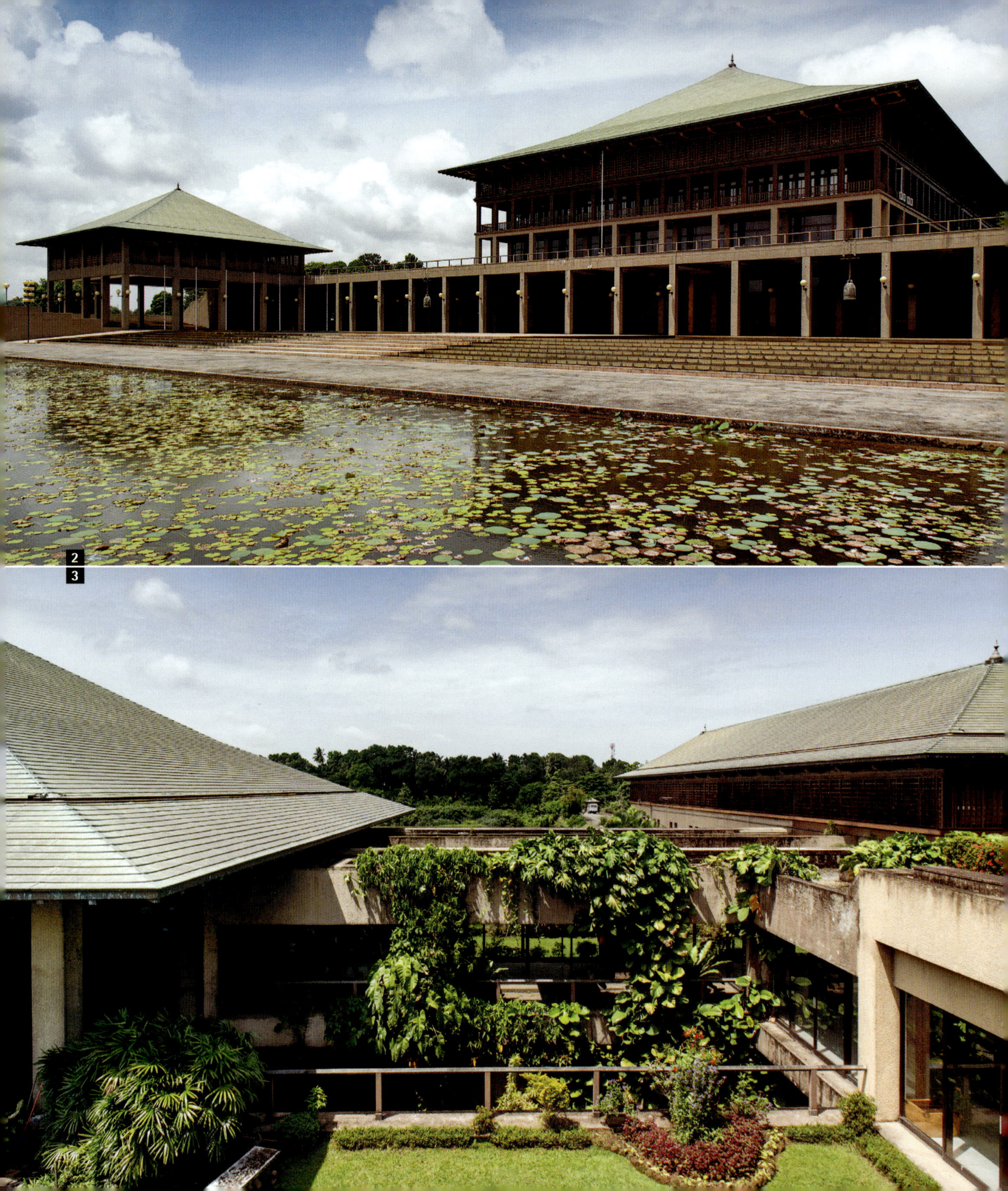
2
3

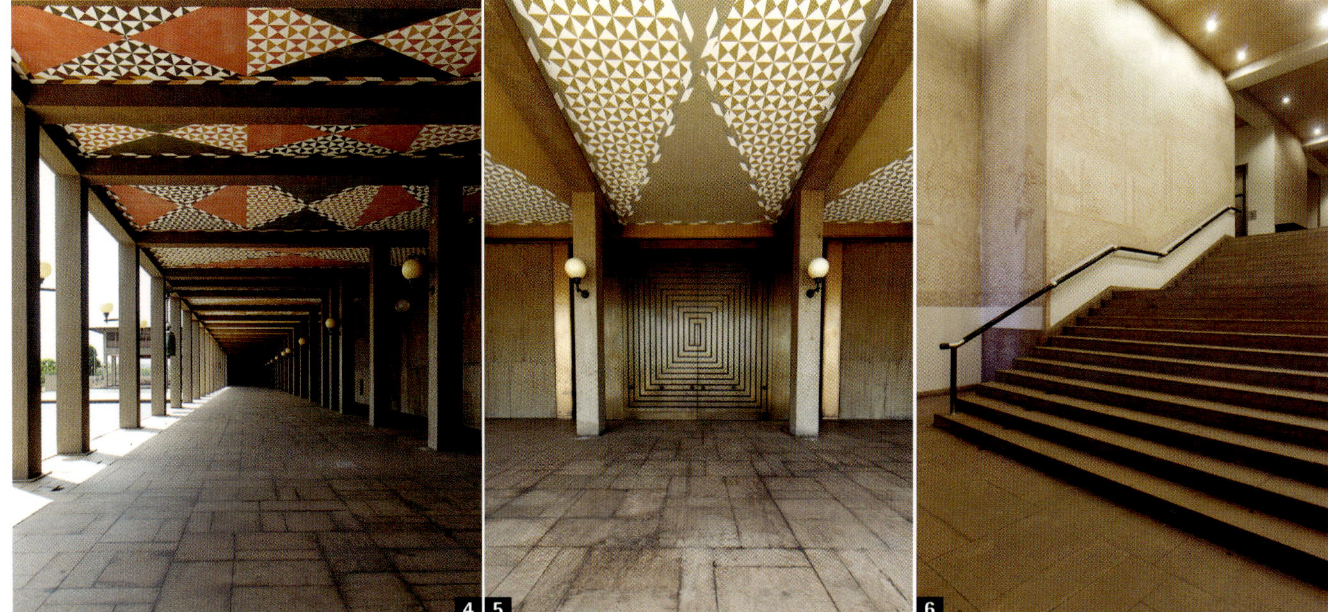

the setting sun. However, its debating chamber was planned as a hemicycle, which suited the structure of the legislature. Bizarrely both of Bawa's designs incorporated a symmetrical debating chamber similar to that of the Palace of Westminster, ignoring the fact that Sri Lankans rarely elected two opposing parties of equal size. Bawa later justified the design by pointing to traditional audience halls such as those at Polonnaruwa and Kandy.

The central pavilion contained the debating chamber under a sweeping copper roof, but the symmetry was broken deliberately by the five ancillary pavilions, each with its own roof, that were added in a seemingly random fashion around its perimeter, creating a succession of open-sided courts. The ancillary pavilions included the MPs' dining room and a massive loggia for staging public meetings.

Bawa had intended the debating chamber to open directly into glass-sided lobbies with panoramic views out across the lake, but he had under-estimated the need for committee rooms and the idea had to be dropped. It was

planned symmetrically with opposing lines of seats facing each other across the central axis of the Speaker's chair. At the official opening of Parliament the President would proceed in state from his official residence in the city, cross the causeway to the island and arrive at the front piazza. Here a pair of vast silver doors opened to reveal a grand staircase rising up to the floor of the House. Bawa knew all the politicians of the day — Jayawardene was his brother's school friend — and it amused him that the President would appear head-first from between the serried ranks of parliamentarians.

The furnishings of the chamber were of dark calamander wood and the suspended ceiling was formed by catenaries of small aluminium bars that glittered like a tent of gold, inspired by a metal handbag that had belonged to Bawa's mother. A huge chandelier of silver coconut fronds made by artist Laki Senanayake hung above the centre of the chamber and silver *korale* flags lined the galleries, reflecting the concealed lighting upwards towards the ceiling.

**2** The front piazza.
**3** Terraces beside the members' dining room.
**4** The front loggia looking east.
**5** The ceremonial doorway leading to the chamber.
**6** The ceremonial staircase leading up to the chamber.

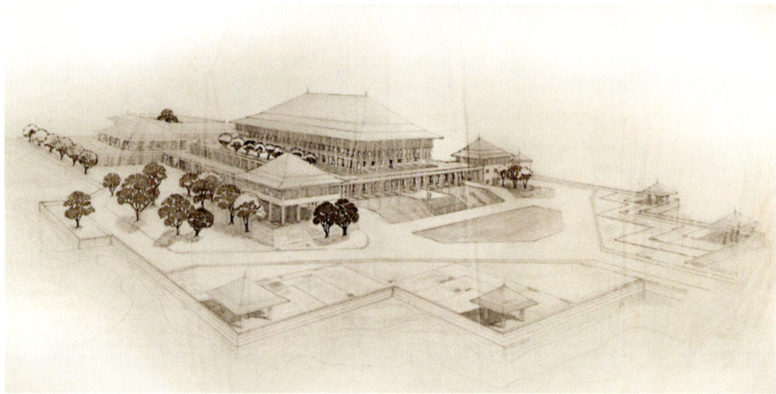

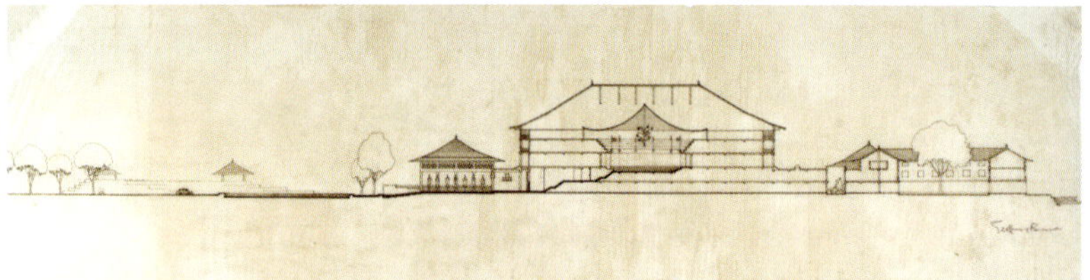

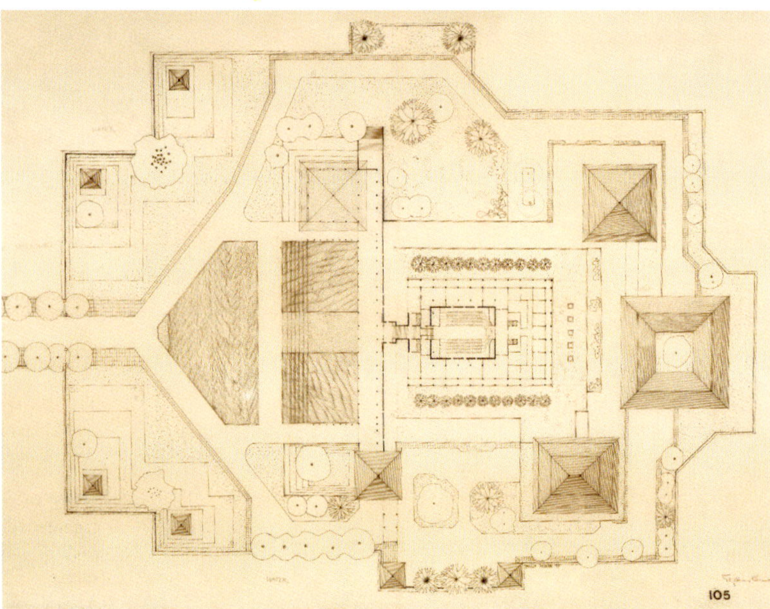

Tragically the new capital city failed to materialise: speculators bought up the available land and chaotic unplanned suburbs grew up around Kotte and Battaramulla. One of Bawa's last commissions in 1997 was to design a new presidential residence and secretariat for Chandrika Kumaratunga on the southern shore of the great lake, but this was cancelled when she fell from power.

Some critics have suggested that Bawa's concept drew exclusively from Buddhist Sinhalese traditions and ignored Sri Lanka's minority communities. Whilst it is true that the sweeping copper roofs hark back to Anuradhapura's legendary Brazen Palace and the asymmetrical plan was in part inspired by the Western Monasteries of Anuradhapura, Bawa himself cited the Padmanabhapuram Palace in Tamil Nadu as a source and suggested that the design was an abstraction of a number of traditions which reflected the cultural complexity of Sri Lanka. To support this, the foundation stone records that the building was built by Japanese contractors and designed by the ghosts of Edwards, Reid & Begg, with Geoffrey Bawa (Christian-Moslem-Burgher), Dr K Poologasundram (Tamil-Hindu) and Vasantha Jacobsen-Chandraratne

**Left** A perspective sketch; a section through the chamber; plan at the level of the chamber. All 1980. Bawa Archive.
**7** The main chamber with palm frond chandelier and silver *korale* flags lining the galleries.
**8** An upper corner of the public forum.
**9** The Japanese bell donated by the contractor.

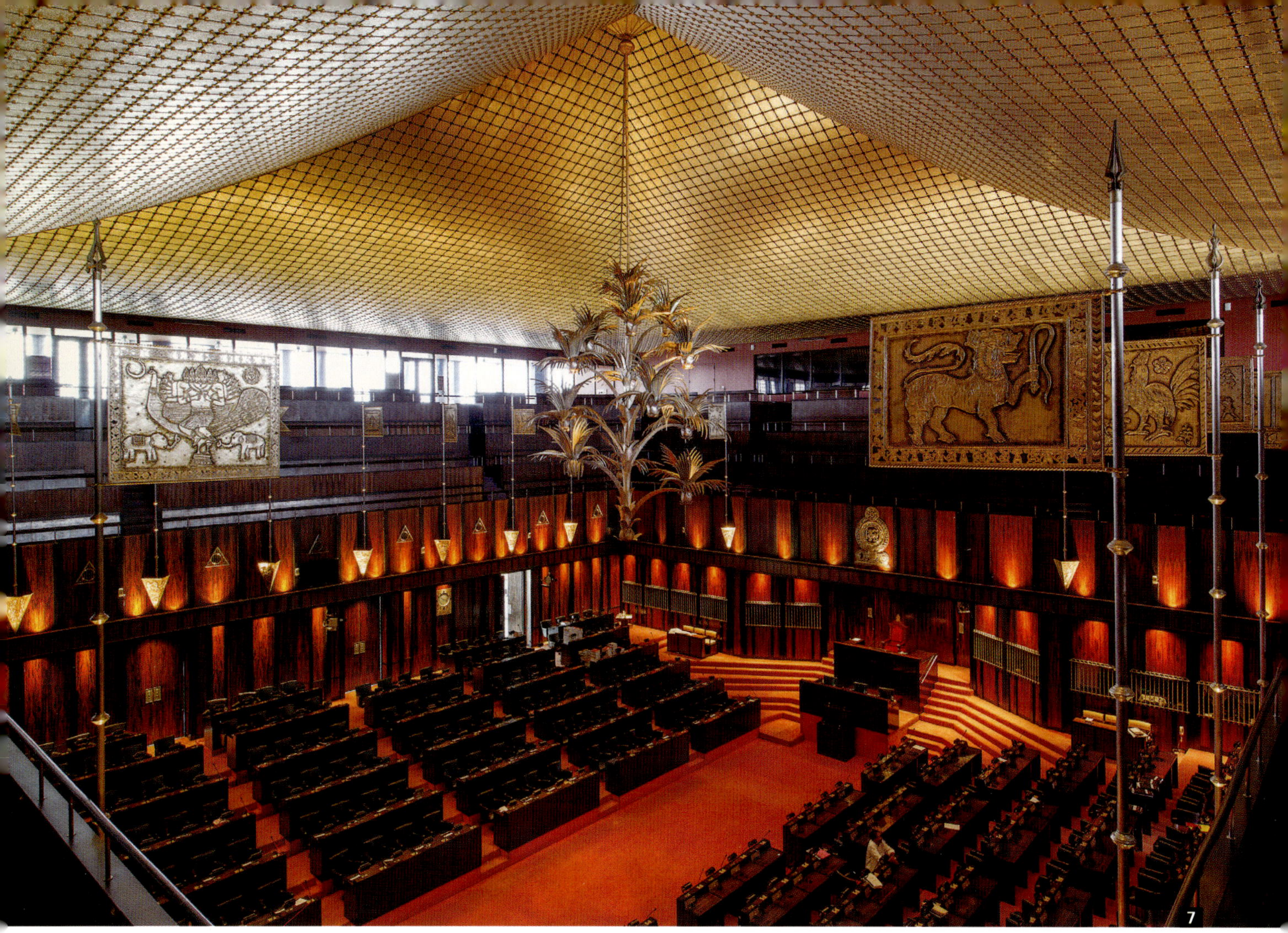

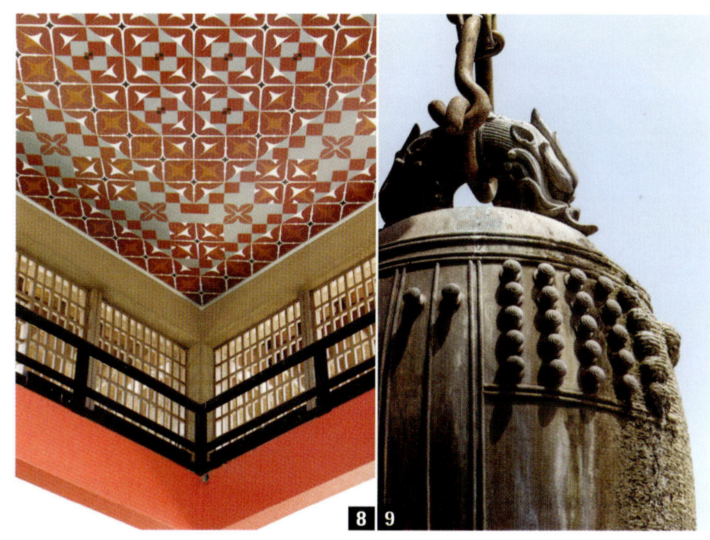


(Sinhalese-Buddhist). Vasantha, whose hair turned from jet black to snow white during the project, quit Bawa's office after the Parliament was completed and entered a Buddhist monastery.

Bawa dreamed of creating a friendly monument where people would meet their elected representatives in the *amabalamas* that were dotted around the landscaped lakeside gardens and would flock to public meetings in the great open-sided hall. But soon after its completion Sri Lanka was torn apart by civil war. The *amabalamas* became machine-gun posts and the island parliament took on the air of an institution under siege.

# The Sunethra Bandaranaike House

## Horagolla
### 1984-1986

Sunethra Bandaranaike, daughter of two prime ministers, was Bawa's close friend and to this day remains a leading member of the Geoffrey Bawa Trust. When she first approached him to remodel an old stable block behind the family home at Horagolla, he was initially reluctant to take on the project, but all of his misgivings evaporated when they visited the site together. Having set out her requirements, Sunethra gave him a free hand and he worked on the project for four years with his assistant Philip Fowler. The main house at Horagolla was built by Sunethra's great-grandfather and the rather grand stables occupied what had been a previous home of the Bandaranaikes.

Bawa established generous garden courts to either side of the stable block, enclosing them within high screen walls. A new wing containing the dining veranda, the kitchens and a guest suite was projected from the corner of the stables along the edge of the rear lawn. A new neo-classical *porte-cochère* was then inserted at the elbow between the two wings. Finally a line of garages and staff rooms was placed along the far edge of the lawn to form a foil against the backdrop of *hora* trees that gave the estate its name. All of these changes allowed Bawa to sidestep an obvious full-frontal entrance sequence. Instead he smuggled visitors past the side of the main house and along a walled alley to the new *porte-cochère*. There they encountered the long veranda that runs beside the rear lawn and to the entrance of the former stables.

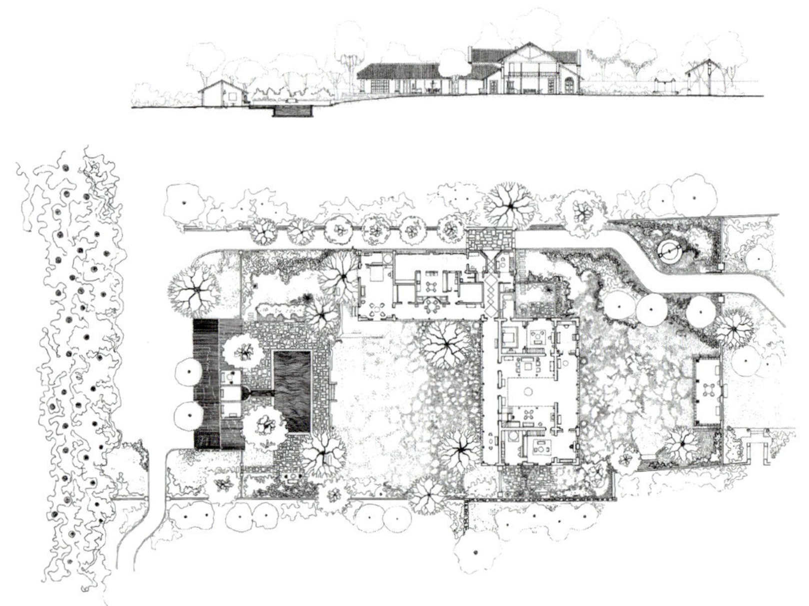

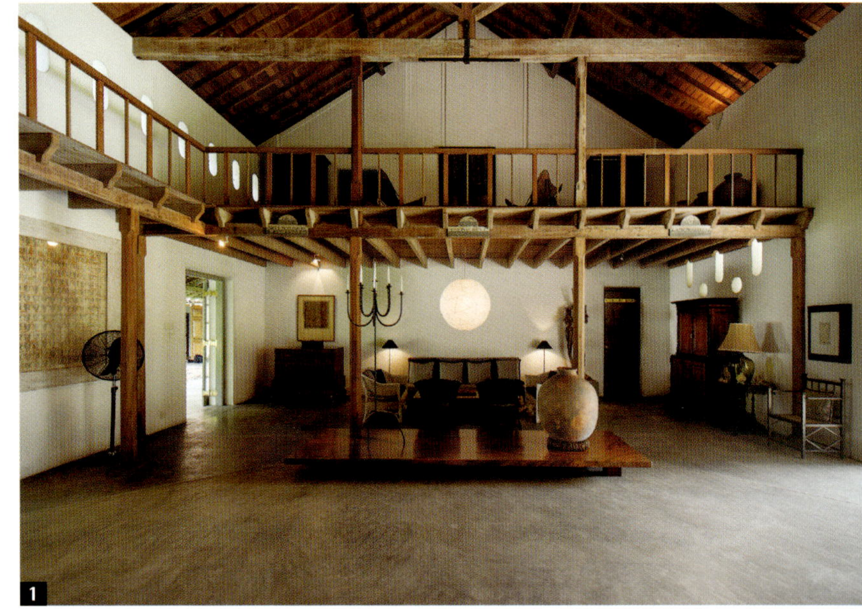

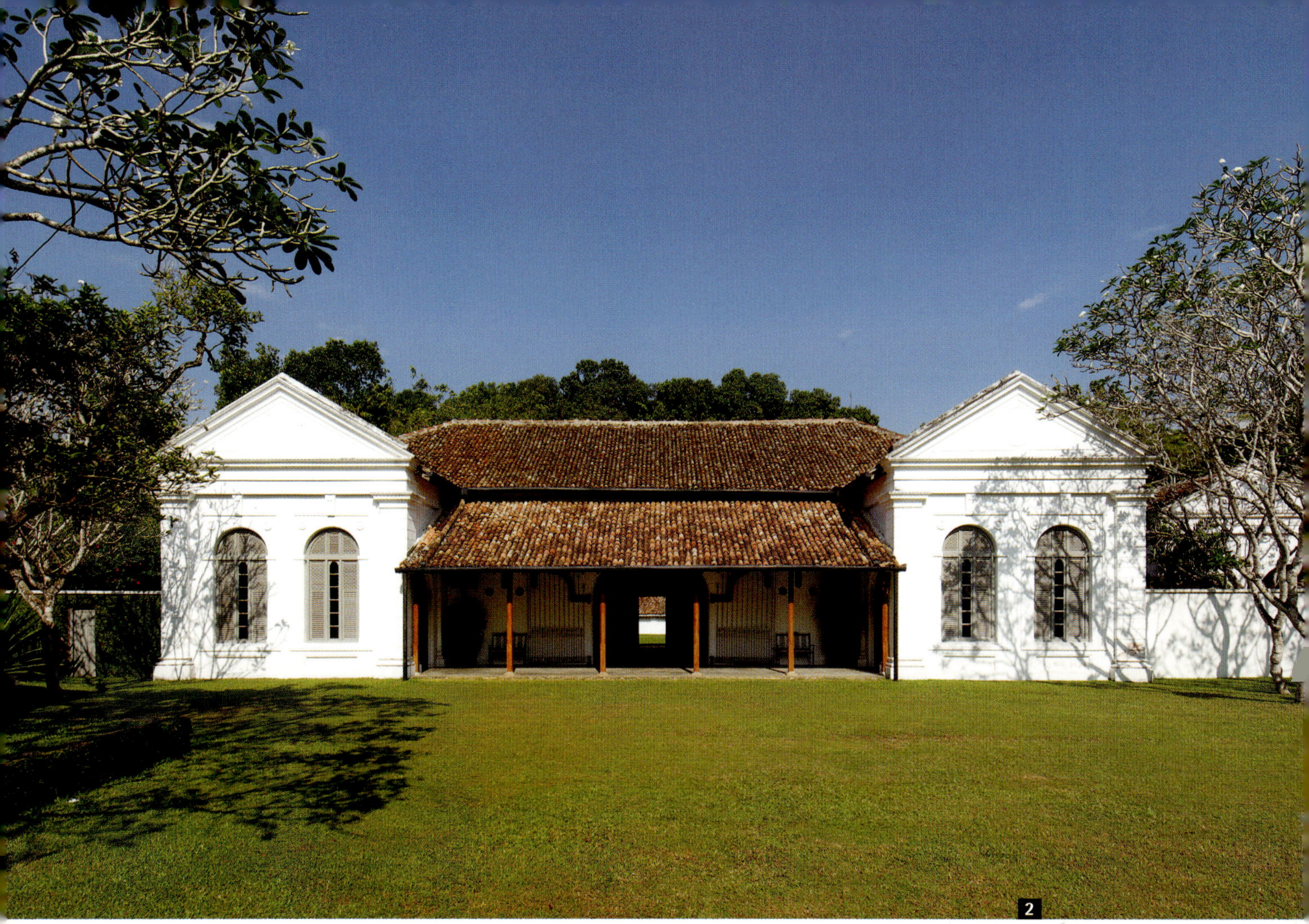

The stable hall has been fashioned into a double-height living space with a timber mezzanine added to give scale and articulation. Its two flanks are then given over to the principle bedrooms and the library. Beyond, like a secret garden, lies the front lawn.

The two garden courts function like a pair of grand open-to-the-sky rooms and the life of the house takes place on the various verandas that line their edges, making the magnificent stable hall almost superfluous.

The conversion was achieved with great restraint, but Bawa could not resist adding in a few witticisms — the two occuli which mark the ends of the long veranda, the ancient fan which hangs from a gallows' bracket above the dining table, the name boards of long-deceased horses, the small pavilion on the front lawn with the door which leads nowhere, and the Art Deco bathrooms which seem to have escaped from a Hollywood movie.

Bawa treated an ancient building with respect, adding a new chapter to its unfolding story, and created an elegant pleasure pavilion for a cherished friend.

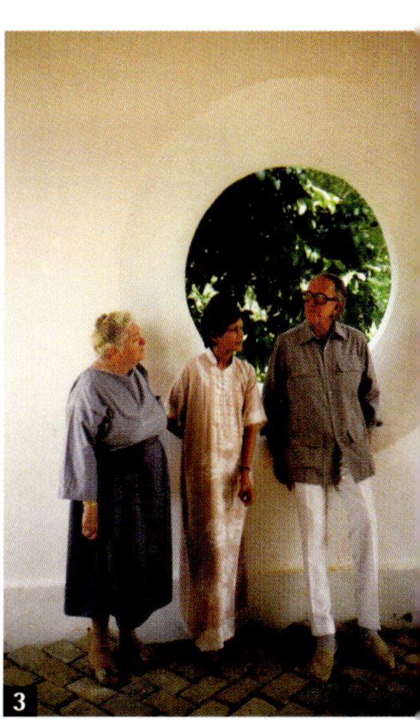

**Opposite** Site plan and section, 1986. Bawa Archive.
**1** The sitting room, in what were former stables.
**2** The garden façade of the stable block.

**3** Left to right: Jean Chamberlin and Sunethra Bandaranaike with Geoffrey Bawa in the *porte-cochère*. 1986.

# Steel Corporation Offices and Housing

Oruwela

1966-1969

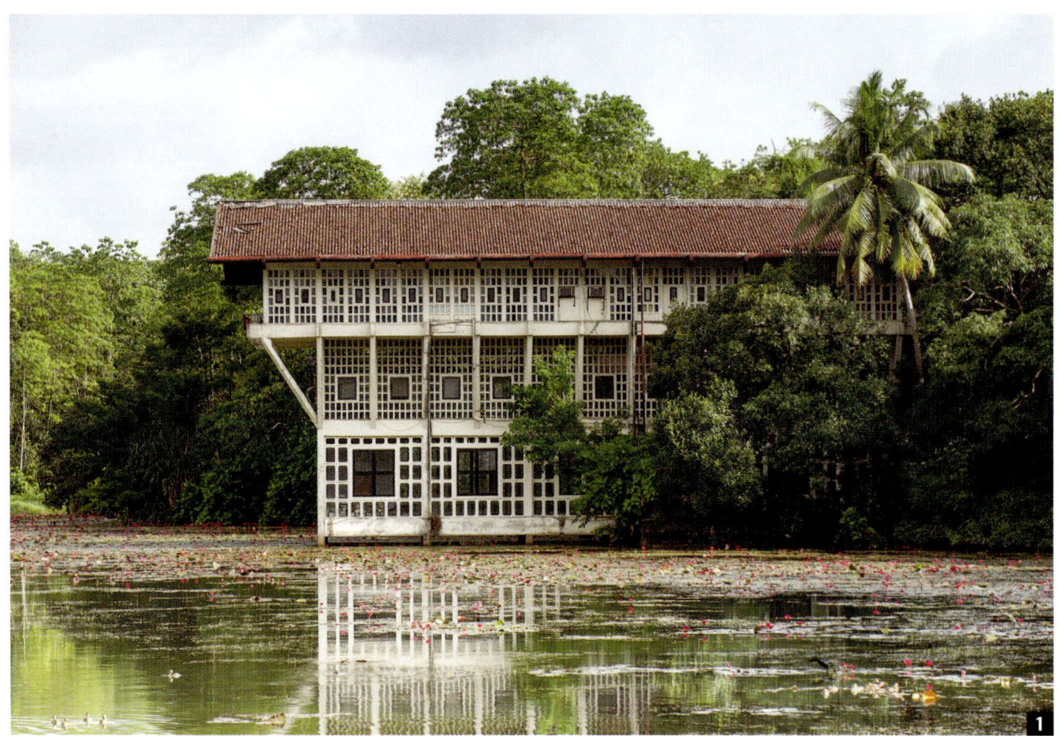

The steel mills at Oruwela were built with
Soviet aid to manufacture steel sections from
imported billets. Bizarrely, following the whim
of a government minister, they were located far
from the Colombo port in the midst of rubber
and coconut plantations where a large reservoir
was created to store water for cooling. Bawa was
commissioned to design the main office building
along with various staff and ancillary buildings
and he advised on the design of the cladding
of the main production buildings. The project
architect was Anura Ratnavibushana.

The three-storey office building projects into
the reservoir with an outward-stepping section
to provide shade and rain-shelter. The walls are
formed from a matrix of pre-cast concrete units,
some glazed and some open. As a result the
interiors are protected from direct sunshine
and filled with light and air. Seen from the
reservoir bund the building looks like an

1 View across the reservoir
towards the main office block.
2 The main office block and
the reservoir.
3 Detail of the end gable.
4 An abandoned office.

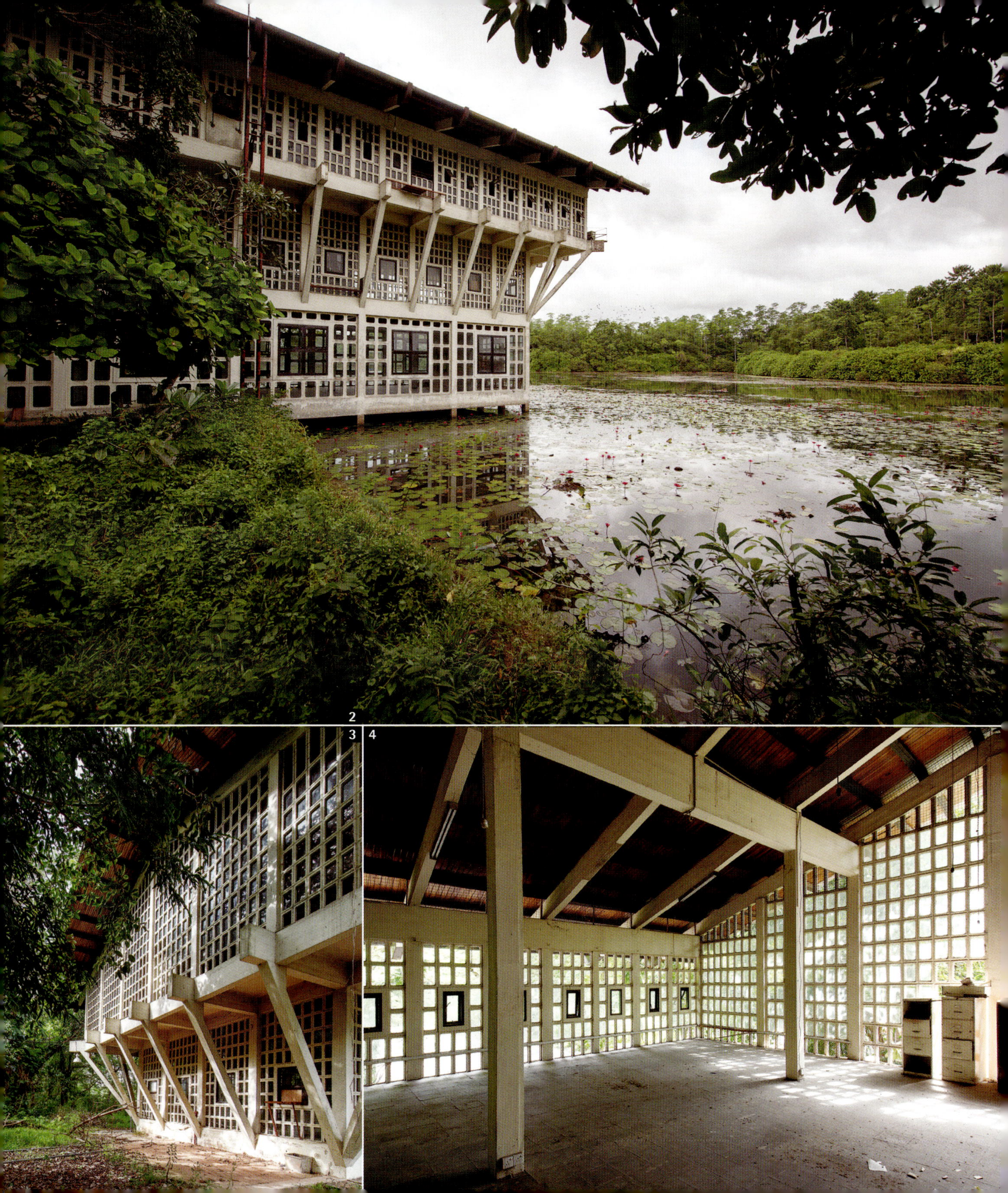

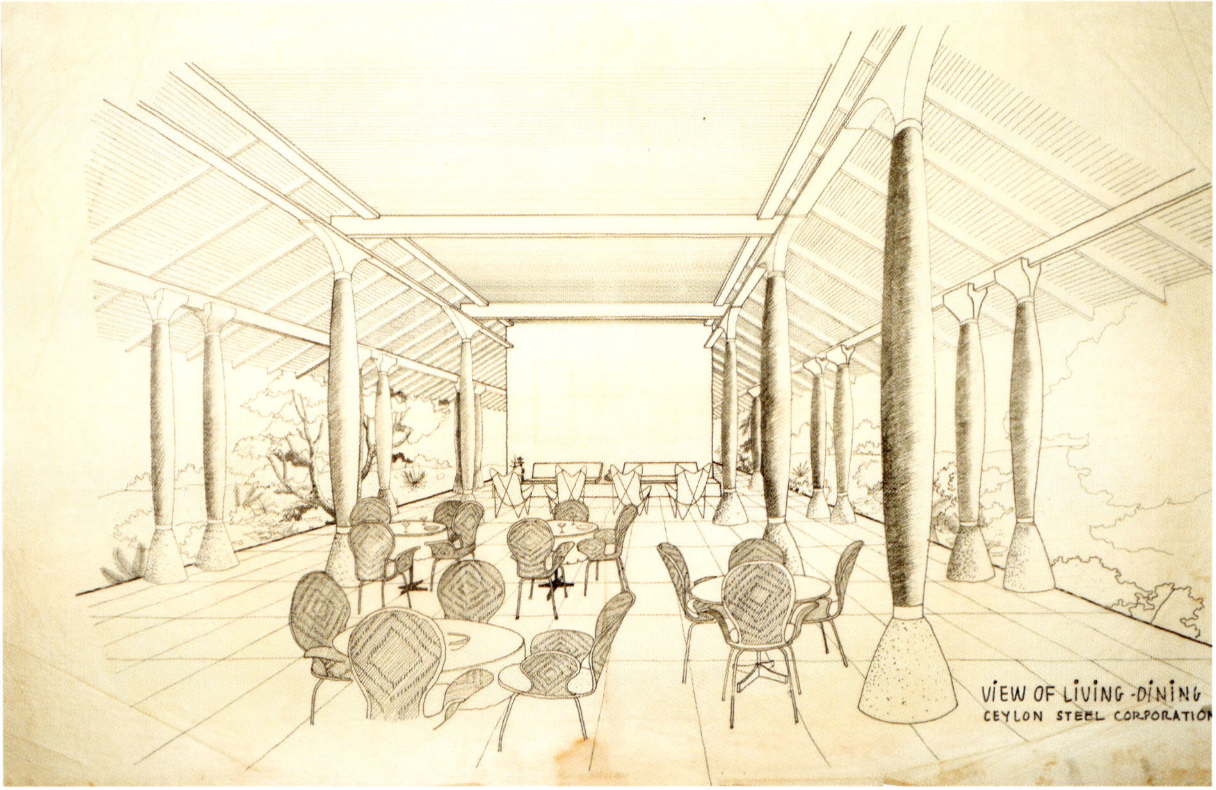

elegant Mississippi river boat moored to the shore.

The factory entrance was recently shifted from the west to the east of the site where a new and predictably ugly office building has been erected, leaving the original building empty and forlorn. One hopes that it will be saved from destruction and that a new use will be found for it.

Bawa also designed a staff housing scheme and a guest house to the west of the steel mills. The elegant housing is arranged in rows along the contours. Each house is entered via a projecting *porte-cochère* and opens into a walled courtyard garden. The long guest house is raised off the ground on a plinth and its roof tips upwards at the gables in the manner of Bawa's earlier design

for the Shell Bungalow in Anuradhapura. The neighbouring kitchen block is square in plan with a stepped roof rising to a clerestory. Both the housing and the guest house are still in use.

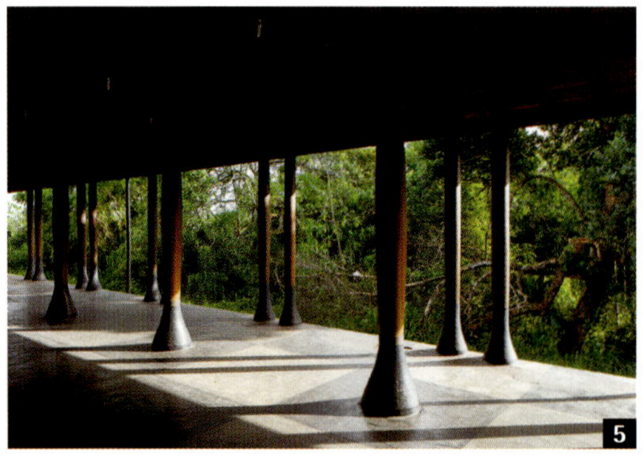

**Above** Sketch perspective of the guest house lounge, 1968. Bawa Archive.
**5** The guest house lounge.

# The Leela Dias Bandaranayake House

## Mount Lavinia

## 1963-1965

Ulrik Plesner's design for the Baur Office Building in Grand Pass incorporated a long spandrel panel on the main façade to carry a relief mural in coloured glass by the Australian artist Donald Friend. Friend quit Sri Lanka before the mural could be executed and the commission was passed to Leela Dias Bandaranayake who had trained as an artist in London and who later became a much admired sculptor. Sadly, government restrictions prevented the import of the necessary coloured glass from Italy and the mural was abandoned.

Having made their acquaintance, Leela invited Bawa and Plesner to design a house for her on land that she had inherited at Mount Lavinia. The result was a strange hybrid: the main pavilion was a simple prism under a tiled roof and incorporated a double-height living room in the manner of Plesner's design for the Sansoni Annexe, but the ancillary accommodation was organised around a courtyard in the manner of Bawa's design for Ena de Silva.

The house has hardly changed since it was built though it is looking a little tired nowadays.

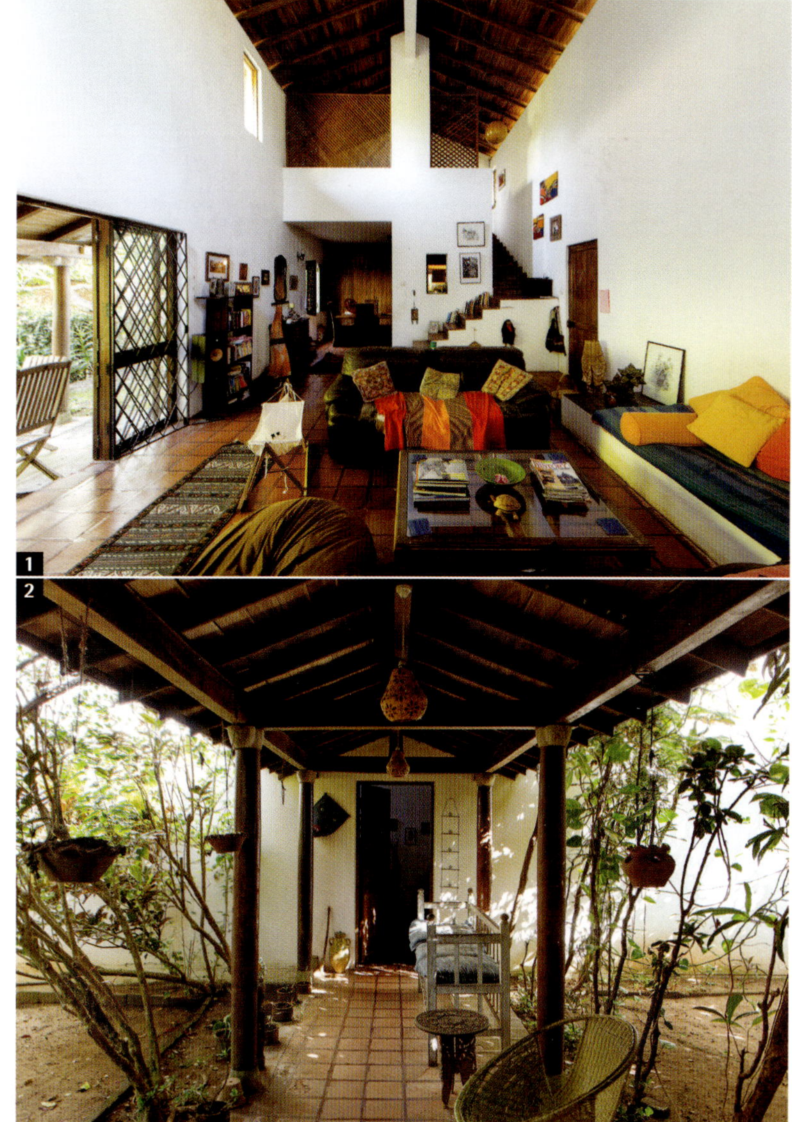

**1** A view along the sitting room towards the mezzanine.
**2** The covered entrance link.

# The Polontalawa Estate Bungalow

Northeast of Chilaw on the road from Palame to Nikarawetiya

1964

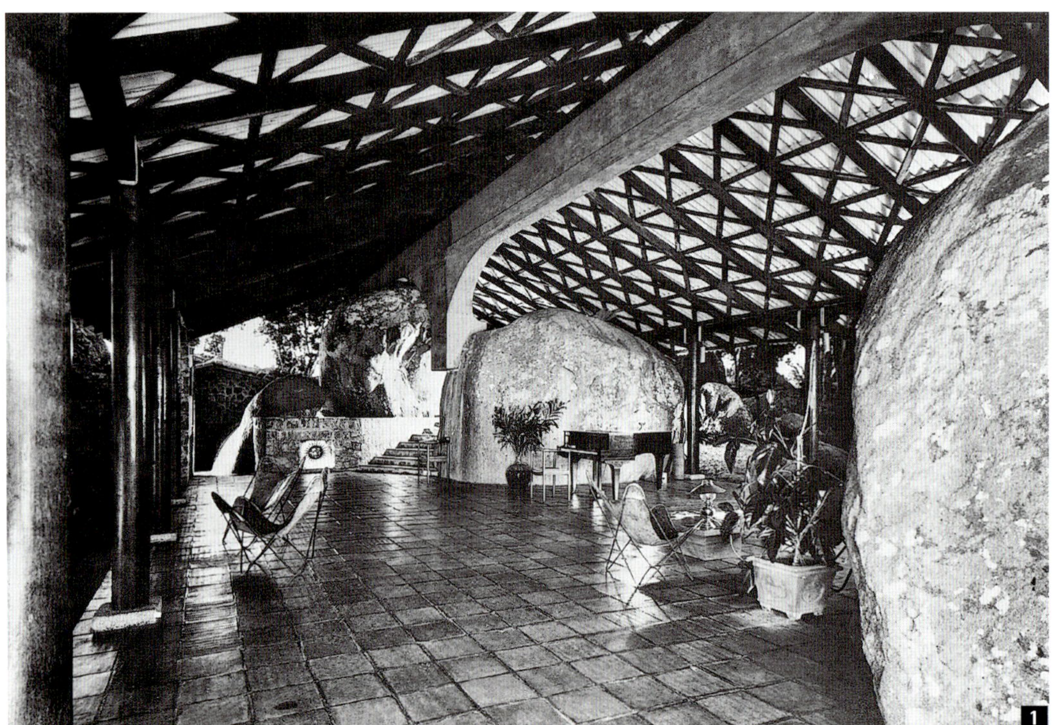

1 The main pavilion soon after completion. 1964.

The design for the Polontalawa Estate Bungalow was one of the most startling and original to emerge during Bawa's first decade in practice. The client was a Swiss trading company that owned a number of tea and coconut estates. Its director, Thilo Hoffmann, a friend of Geoffrey Bawa and a neighbour of Ulrik Plesner, commissioned them to build a new estate bungalow on a remote coconut estate that lay about 30 kilometres north east of Chilaw.

Hoffmann has given a clear account of how the design evolved: "Geoffrey produced the big idea, while Ulrik was the technician who turned it into reality." Hoffmann had identified a flat piece of land near the meeting of two estate roads and Plesner proposed a design based on a circuit bungalow in Anuradhapura that the practice had recently built for Shell. At this point Bawa intervened and insisted that all three of them should visit the site together before putting

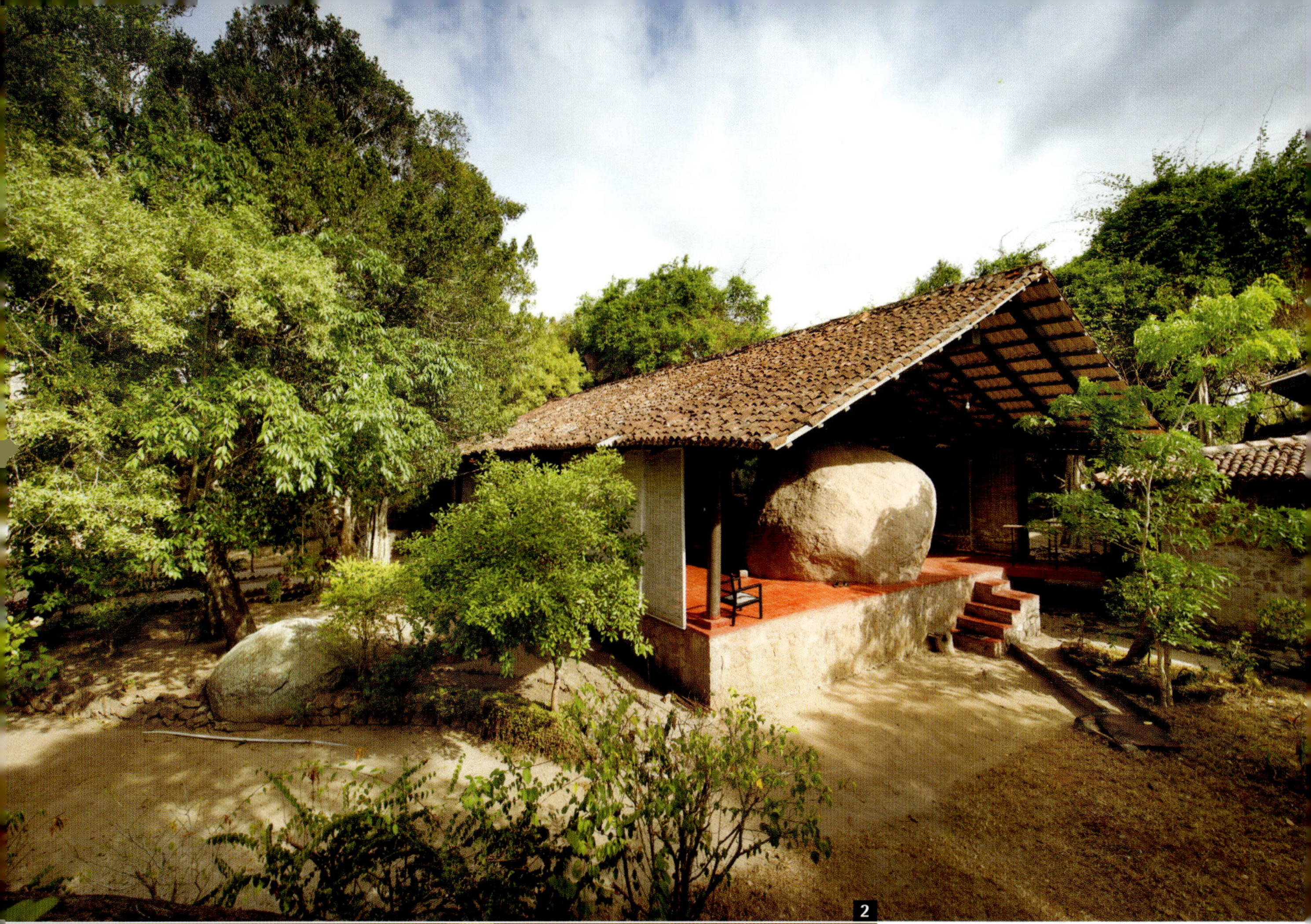

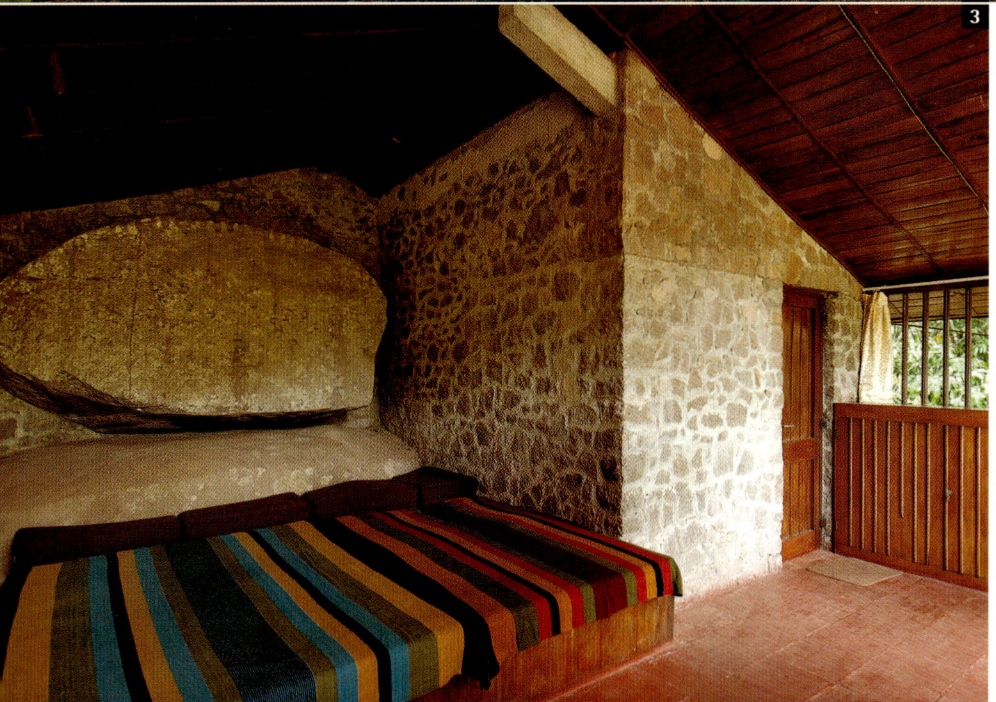

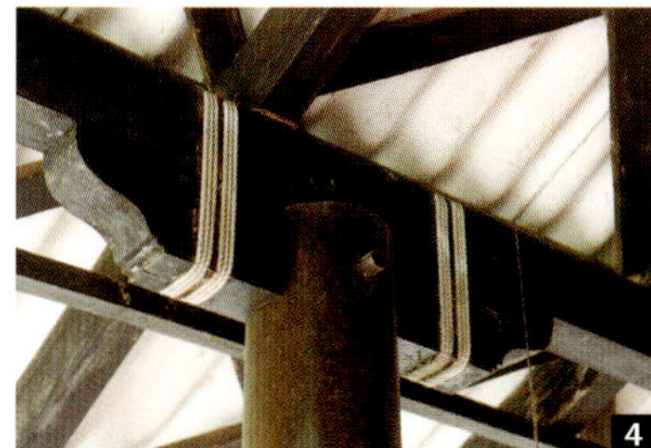

**2** The east end of the main pavilion with massive boulder.
**3** Between a rock and hard place – the guest bedroom.
**4** Column head detail.

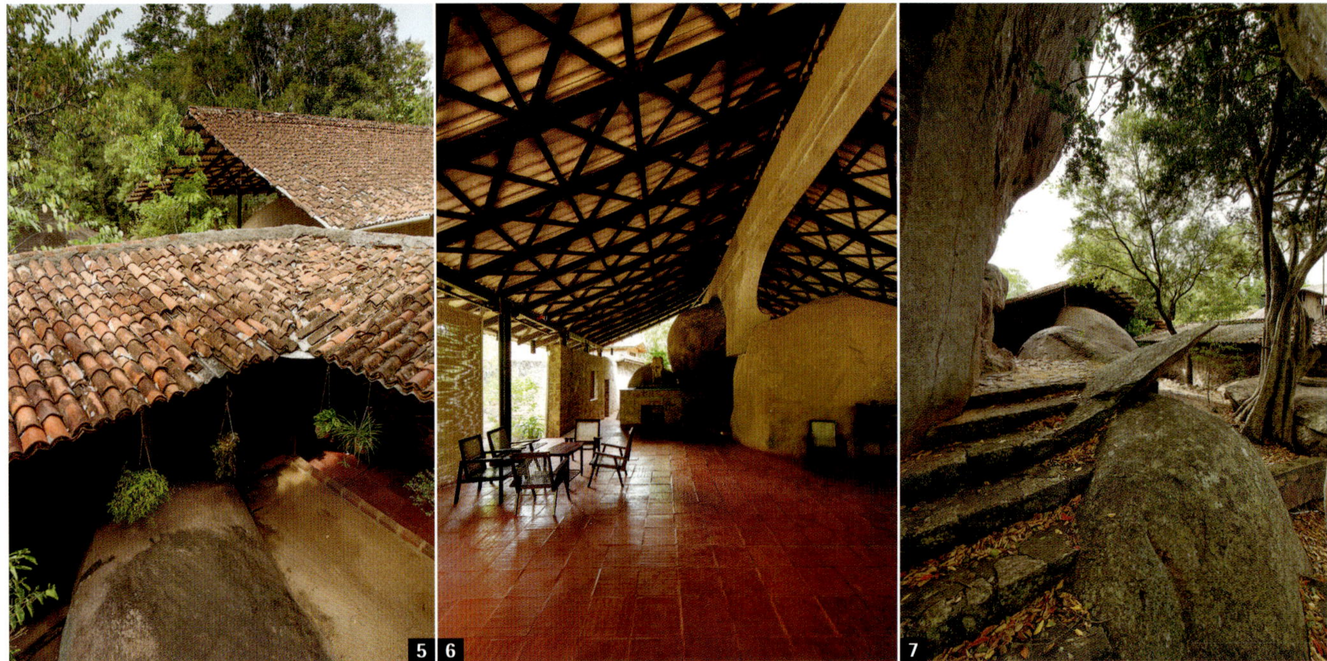

pen to paper. The estate lay within an area of strange rocky outcrops and close to a group of cave temples that overlooked the Kadiyagawa Tank. Bawa was critical of the choice of site and persuaded Hoffmann to shift his attention to a group of large boulders which lay a few hundred metres away to the south east. He then called for 'sticks and string' and proceeded to lay out the bungalow in amongst the boulders. This full-scale mock-up formed the basis of the design that Plesner then developed and detailed.

A high wall of rubble was thrown up around the boulders, as if this were a fortified outpost on some far-flung frontier, and was broken by an elegant lych-gate. The gate opens to a tight corridor that snakes between the rocks before reaching the main living area. This is defined by a great umbrella roof, supported on a massive

concrete ridge beam that spans between three boulders and is open on both its sides to the petrified landscape of the compound.

Beyond lies a pair of linked pavilions. The first, reached by a narrow staircase rising out of a small courtyard, contains the main guest room, its gable wall filled by a single boulder that forms the head of the bed. The second contains the sleeping quarters of the estate manager.

The estate bungalow was built entirely from materials gleaned from the surrounding area and seems to grow out of its site. It belongs to a long tradition of temples and hermitages that were built in caves and between boulders. It also affirms that the roof is the prime element of a tropical house.

The estate was confiscated during the 1970s and is now run by the National Livestock Board. The bungalow is reasonably well-maintained.

**5** The courtyard below the guest bedroom.
**6** Within the main pavilion.
**7** The approach from the lych-gate.

# The Anuradhapura Pilgrims' Rest House

Jayanthi Mawatha, Anuradhapura New Town
1982

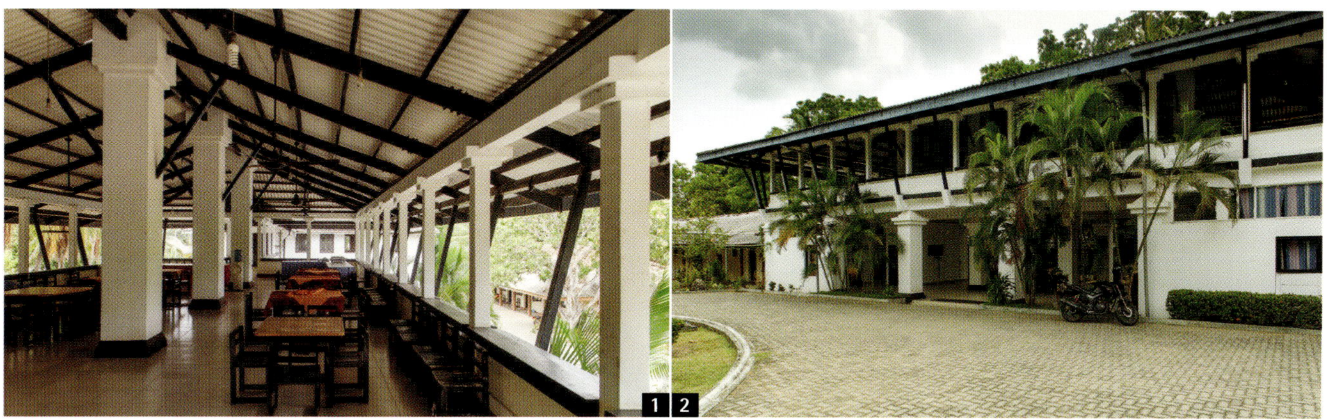

The Anuradhapura Pilgrims' Rest House was commissioned by the Hotels Corporation to provide affordable accommodation for Sri Lankan pilgrims visiting Anuradhapura's Sacred Area. The project architect was Vasantha Jacobsen-Chandraratne.

A five-bayed pavilion contains an open reception area on its ground floor and a restaurant on its upper floor. The ground floor is supported on massive square Tuscan columns in a parody of British colonial buildings found within the Sacred Area. The Tuscan columns are repeated along the spine of the upper floor to support the roof ridge, but the overhanging eaves are carried on elegantly splayed rafters.

The hostel rooms were built in single-storey lines served by veranda corridors and laid out around a series of pleasant landscaped courtyards. Today, although the main reception building is still well-maintained, the rooms have fallen into disrepair.

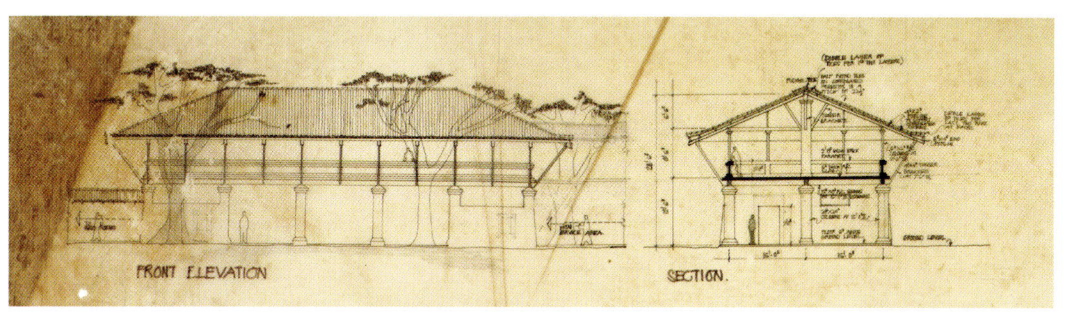

**Left** Elevation and section of the reception building, 1982. Bawa Archive.
**1** The first floor of the reception building.
**2** The driveway and front of the reception building.

# The Kandalama Hotel

Due east of Dambulla

1992

The Kandalama Hotel was the first of Bawa's designs to be carried through to completion after he withdrew from Edwards, Reid & Begg and set up his own design studio. He worked on it with a young and inexperienced team of assistants that included Sumangala Jayatillike, Channa Daswatte and Amila de Mel, while Milroy Perera and Deepal Wickremasinghe acted as executive consultants.

The commission came from Aitken Spence who, with government support, wanted to create a new hotel within Sri Lanka's 'Cultural Triangle' to complement their popular Triton Hotel at Ahungalla. When Bawa was taken to look at a proposed site near to the foot of Sigiriya Rock he rejected it out of hand, and suggested instead that the hotel be built on land overlooking the beautiful and ancient Kandalama reservoir some miles away to the south that would give distant views of the Rock. Surprisingly, his clients were willing to listen and, with some difficulty, the party drove to the north side of the reservoir and looked across the water to the cliffs where Bawa proposed to build. After overflying the site in a helicopter, the proposal was accepted.

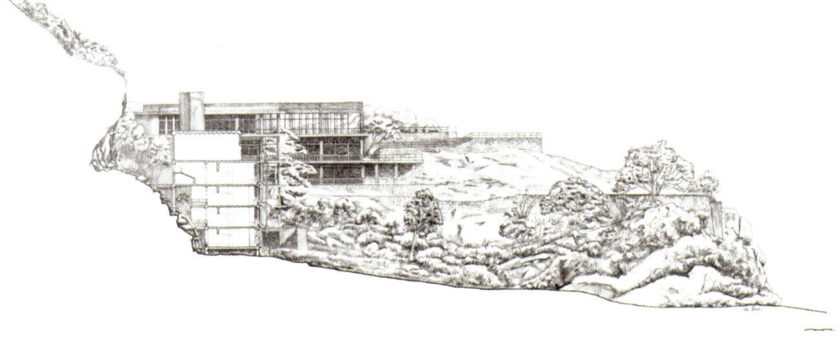

**Above** Section through the cliff and the Sigiriya Wing,1 1992. Bawa Archive.
**1** The link to the Dambulla Wing.
**2** The upper pools.
**3** View of the Sigiriya Wing showing the roof garden and the dining room.

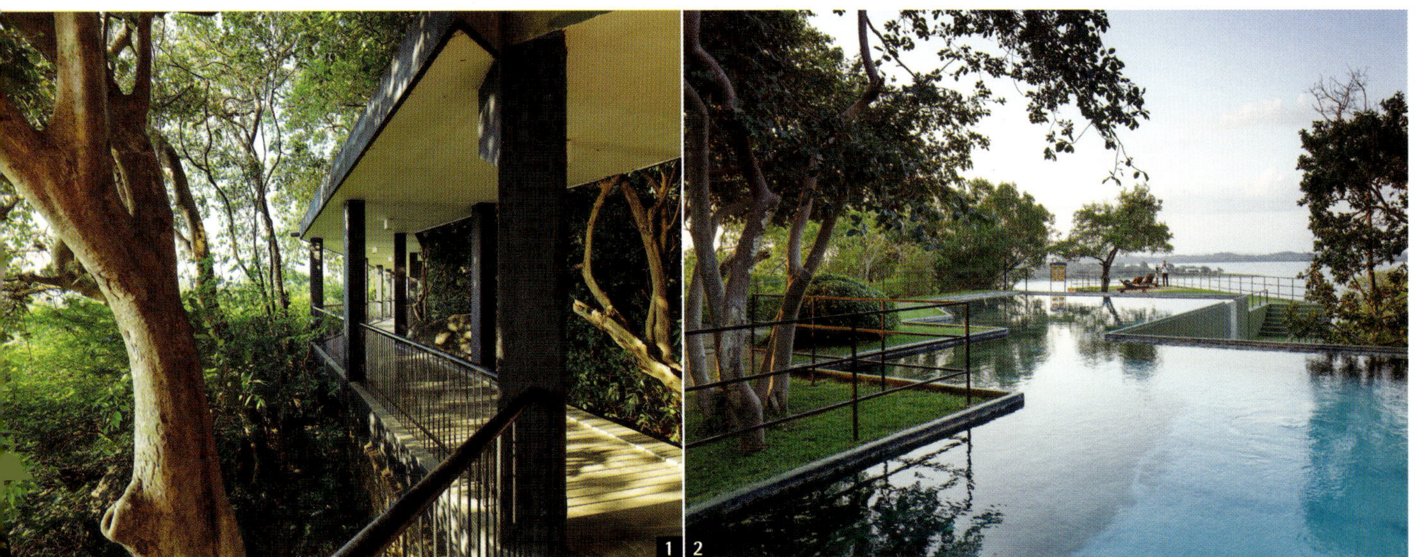

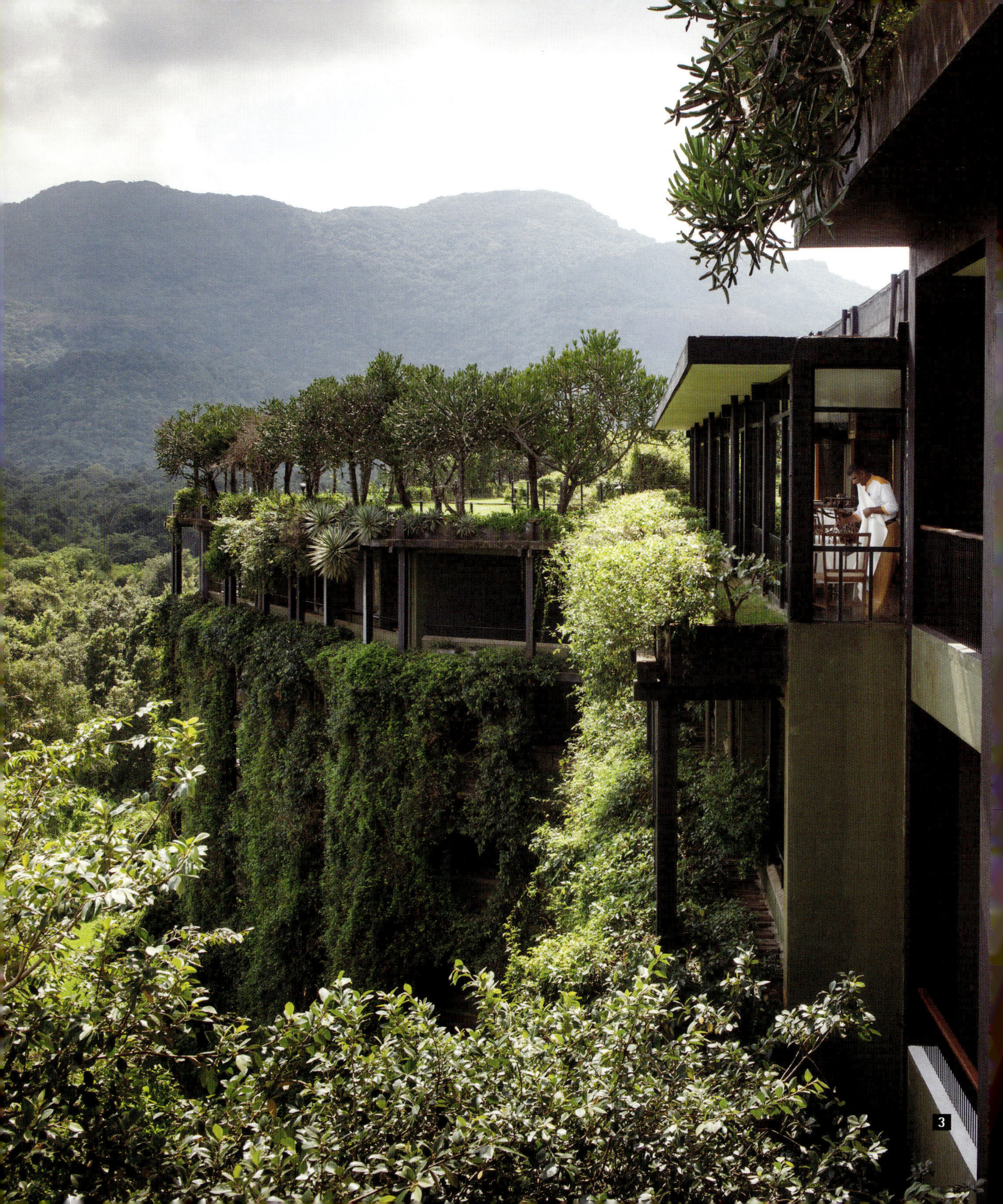
3

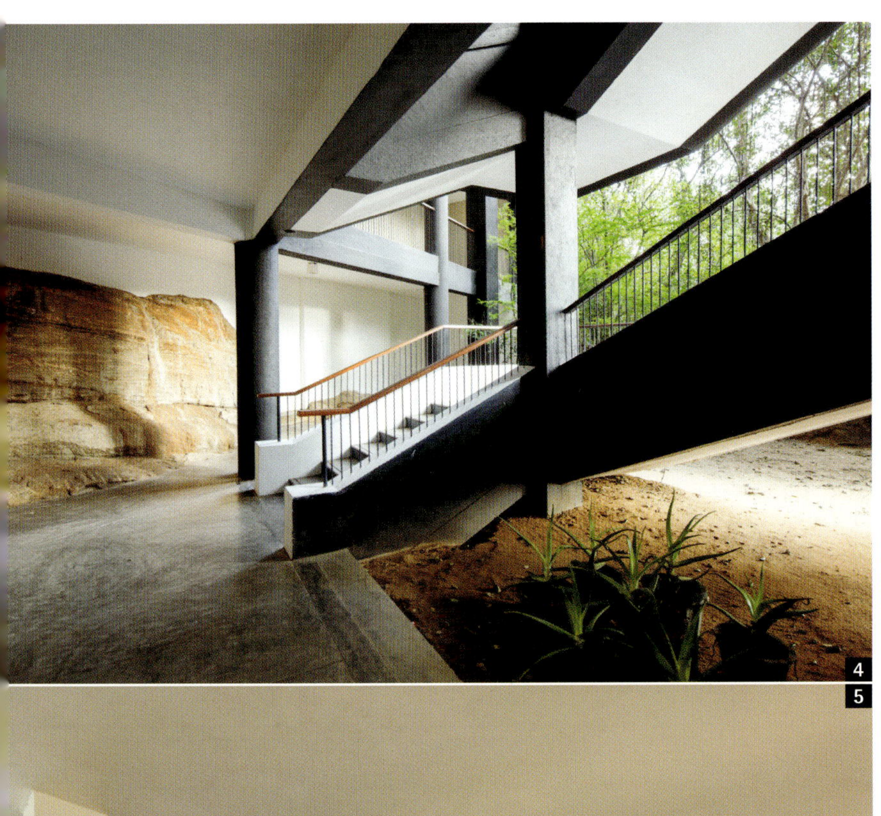

The hotel was built on a ridge against the north-facing cliff and, as predicted, it enjoys views across the reservoir toward Kasyapa's citadel. It takes the form of a long articulated slab that is facetted to follow the shape of the cliff and measures almost a kilometre in length from the eastern tip of the Sigiriya Wing to the western tip of the Dambulla Wing.

After travelling along jungle tracks, visitors are swept up a steep ramp to the hotel entrance that is fashioned like the mouth of a cave. A corridor snakes through the rock and leads them to an open lounge where they get their first view of the reservoir and distant Sigiriya. Below them, perched on the edge of the cliff, they discover the first of the hotel's three magical swimming pools.

As if on a ship, the entrance is in fact on the same level as the uppermost of the five levels of rooms. Above it, on the top deck, are the restaurant and main lounges. Below, a single side corridor that skirts the edge of the cliff serves each level of rooms. Originally each room was conceived as a bed-sitting room with a generous balcony and each had a bathroom that looked out across the tank. Ena de Silva, whose Aluvihare workshops contributed many artefacts to the hotel, once exclaimed: "Where else in the world can you sit on the loo and look out at such a view?"

The roofs are flat, and for the most part covered in vegetation, and the open facades carry a second skin of concrete purlins and timber slats that support a dense screen of foliage and a huge tribe of monkeys. The building

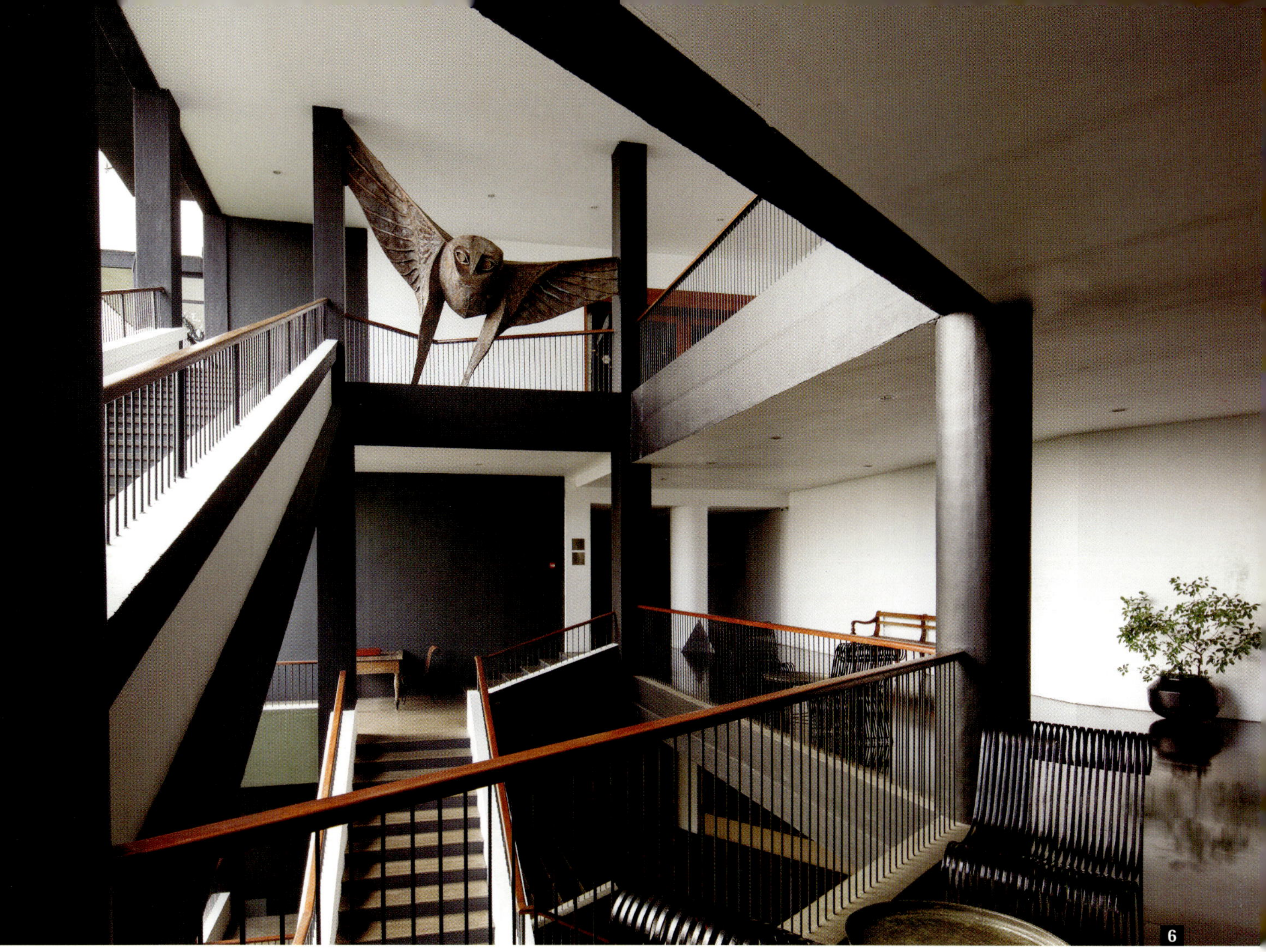

6 The main stair with owl sculpture by Laki Senanayake.

disappears into the surrounding jungle. Its architecture is stark and understated, supporting the notion that this is not a building to look at, but a building to look out of — like a monumental hide or a giant belvedere. It is as if some huge ocean liner, with decks above and cabins below, has come aground on a faraway mountainside.

The detailing is robust; it matches the outcrops of rock that burst through the walls and adds to the illusion that this is, in fact, a reincarnation of Kasyapa's lost citadel.

As it neared completion, the hotel encountered fierce opposition — from the Buddhist clergy, from environmentalists and from politicians. Yet it was one of the most environmentally friendly hotels to have been built on the island and was no more expensive than contemporary hotel developments in Colombo.

Today, the Kandalama Hotel is still very well maintained though, sadly, some of its rooms have been crudely knocked together to create suites and a rather unfortunate conference centre has sprouted from the roof of the Dambulla Wing like a giant silver cabbage. After more than two decades, it continues to surprise and enthrall its guests and stands as a testimonial to its 75-year-old architect and his team of youthful assistants.

# The Strathspey Estate Bungalow

Upcott, Maskeliya

1959–1960

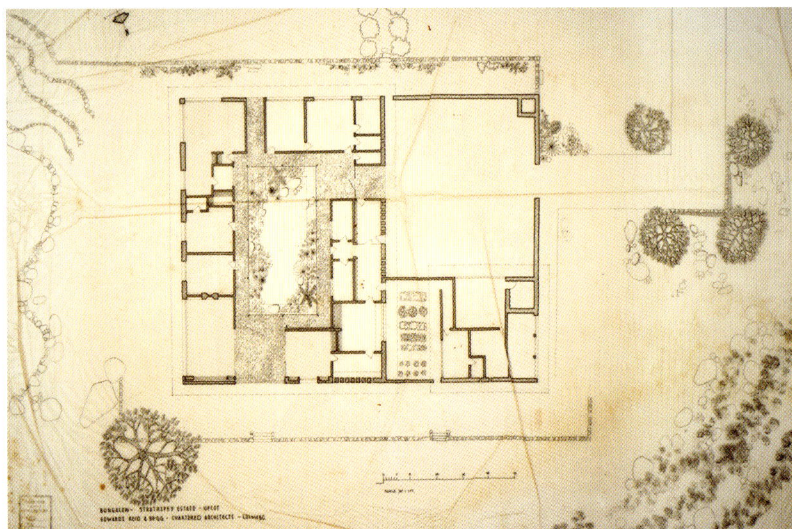

Strathspey is situated at some 1,600 metres above sea level on the eastern slopes of Adam's Peak and is one of the last tea estates to be cleared. Its estate bungalow was designed by Bawa and Plesner at the end of the 1950s. Here the challenge was not to develop a new prototype, but to design one of the last examples of a building associated with a fast-disappearing way of life.

Bawa took his inspiration from the villas of Andrea Palladio that he had visited in 1946 and conceived of the bungalow as a noble homestead set within a working estate on the edge of the wilderness. Traditional estate bungalows were cellular in plan and looked out across manicured lawns to distant views. The Strathspey bungalow, in contrast, was designed around courtyards and was inward looking, its plan conceived as a set of boxes within boxes.

The house is entered through a large outer entrance court containing the garage and staff quarters. Its core bungalow is designed as a sequence of rooms set around an inner courtyard. The sitting room occupies the south-western corner and enjoys views out across the estate. An empty space between it and the dining room is bounded by sliding doors and can function either as an open veranda or as a link.

The bungalow was built by a local estate contractor with walls of white painted rubble and floors of local timber and polished black stone. It is still used as a manager's bungalow and is still in its original condition, though vegetable plots have replaced its lawns and it is now surrounded by dense woodland.

**Above** Plan showing inner and outer courtyards, 1960. Bawa Archive.
**1** The inner courtyard.
**2** The water tower and entrance to the outer court, 1962.
**3** Ulrik Plesner on the veranda (this could be enclosed by a sliding glass screen), 1962.

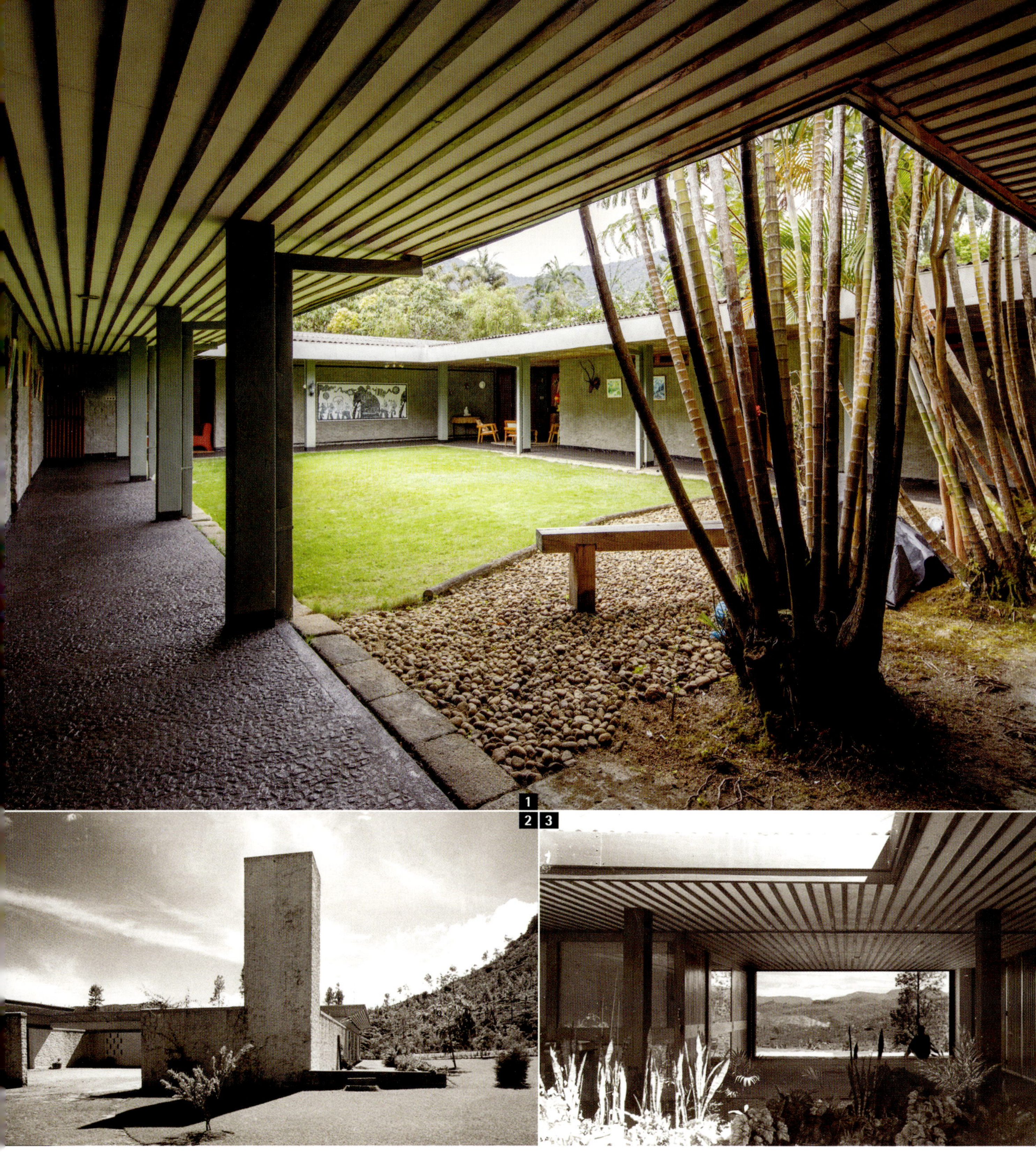
1
2 3

# The Nazareth Chapel of the Good Shepherd Convent

Rasintha Wimalasena Mawatha, Bandarawela
(northeast of the Bandarawela Hotel)

**26**

1965

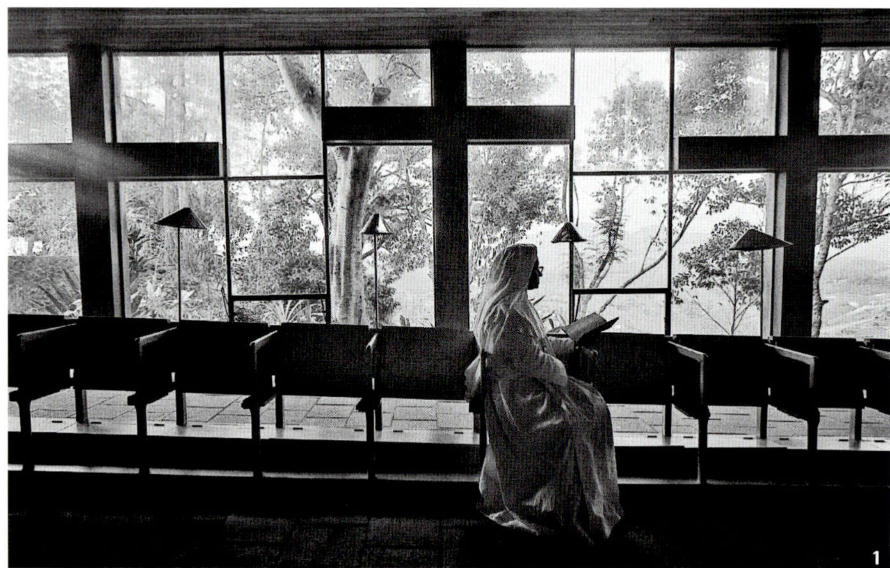

The Order of the Sisters of the Good Shepherd came to Ceylon in 1867 and established a number of convents and schools in and around Colombo. Many of the original nuns came from Ireland.

In the 1940s, the Order acquired an old estate bungalow on the outskirts of Bandarawela to serve as a rest and retirement home for older nuns and as a training centre for novices. In 1961 the head of the Order in Ceylon was an Irish nun called Eileen Mills who was also known as Mother Good Counsel, and it was she who commissioned Geoffrey Bawa to design a chapel to the east of the bungalow. She had been introduced to him by his friend Barbara Sansoni who, at the time, was helping the Order to set up weaving centres. Geoffrey worked on the project with Ulrik Plesner and Laki Senanayake, though Mother Good Counsel and Barbara Sansoni were also part of the team. The design evolved during 1961 and the building was completed in 1962.

From the outset it was clear that the chapel would have to be built on a shoestring. The team opted to use locally available materials: black *kalu gal* stone for the walls, local timber for the ceilings and clay tiles for the roof. They also had to create all the furnishings, light fittings and artworks themselves. In the final analysis they were responsible for every single element of the finished building which could thus be described, truly, as a 'total work of art'.

The chapel occupies a ridge that falls gently towards the east. The south wall faces the street

1 A nun at prayer, 1962.
2 The garden side of the Nazareth Chapel.
3 The street side of the Chapel, 1985.
4 Terracotta mural by Barbara Sansoni depicting the 23rd Psalm.
5 Terracotta 'Station of the Cross' by Barbara Sansoni.
6 Container for Holy Water.

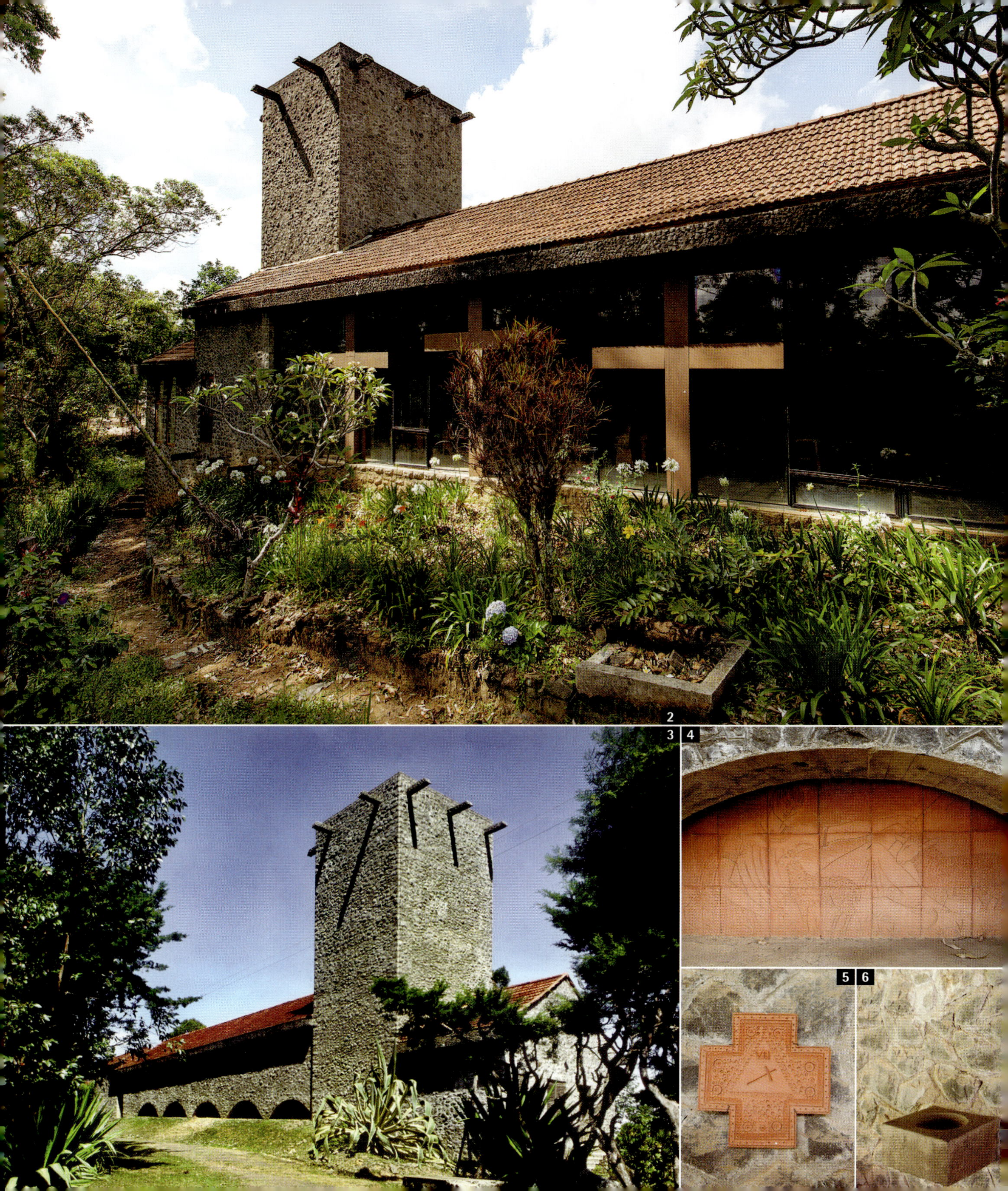

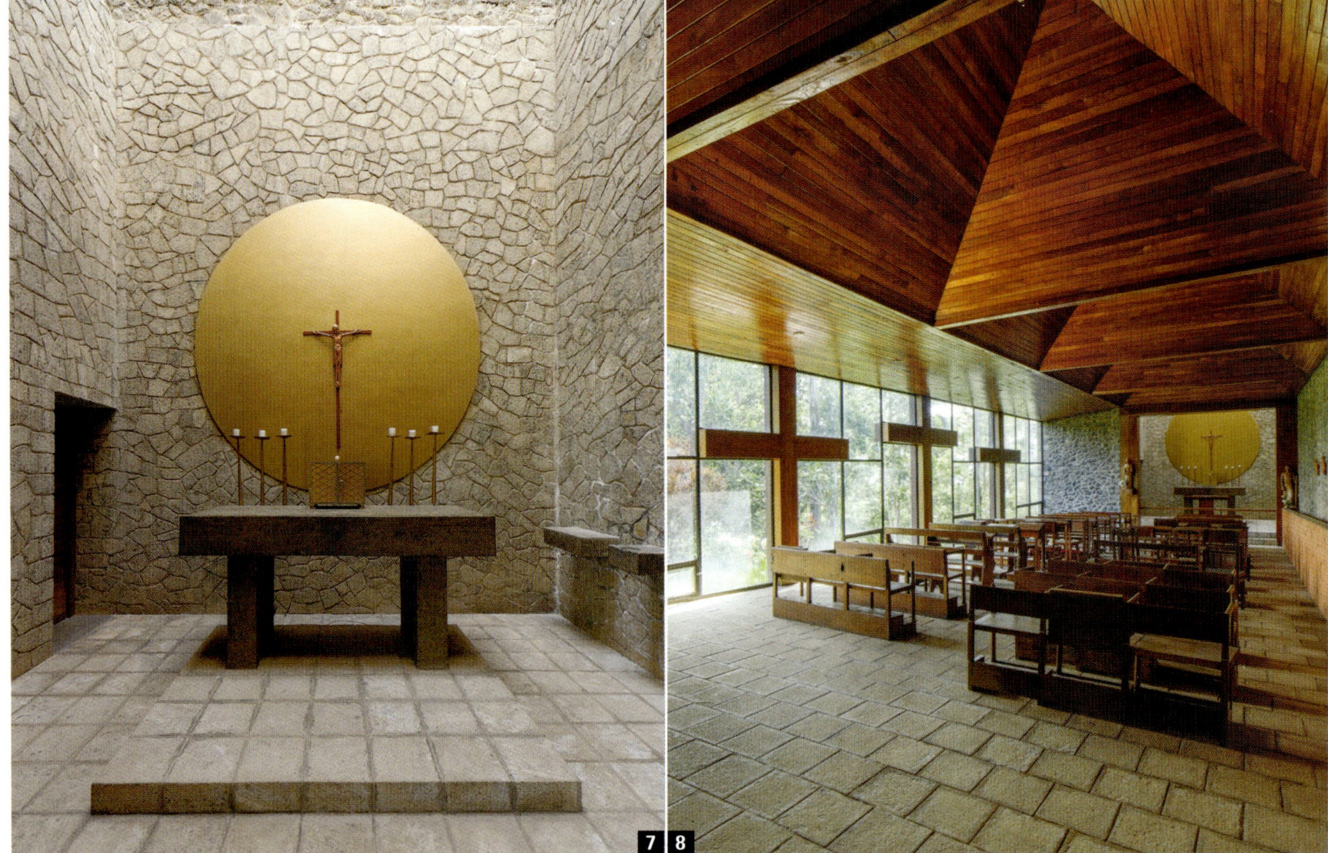

and consists of a long blank rubble wall that terminates in a square tower and is punctuated by five recessed arches at low level. The recesses conceal ventilation slits and are decorated with terracotta tile reliefs illustrating the Psalm of the Good Shepherd designed by Barbara Sansoni.

A small door opens from the street into a long entrance gallery that connects with the garden and the convent and contains two doors into the chapel. The chapel floor slopes gently down towards the altar which sits below the tower and is lit from a hidden roof window. The south wall is solid and is punctuated by small terracotta reliefs depicting the Stations of the Cross, also by Barbara Sansoni. In contrast, the north wall is fully glazed, its four panels separated by massive frames that form three giant crucifixes, and offers views into the garden and the Uva Highlands. The ceiling of the nave is divided into five vaults lined with tuna wood. A door at the side of the altar leads to the vestry and beyond to a small apartment for a visiting priest.

Ulrik Plesner designed the lighting and the furniture. The original pews allowed the nuns to sit facing each other as if in a choir or to turn towards the altar and kneel. They could also prostrate themselves on the stone floor in the aisle between the pews. The pews were later removed when the Second Vatican Council discouraged such practices. Laki Senanayake designed the priest's vestments and the altar table.

Mother Good Counsel and her architects became the best of friends. In 1965 she wrote to them: "Today ... I had a little private laugh in remembering the pre-building days when we each in turn went out to see if the rising sun would be unbearable ... during Lauda. This morning it lit the spirit of the Virgin, turning her into living flames, and us poor mortals standing under her into creatures of light."

The chapel is one of Sri Lanka's most impressive modern worship spaces. The overall effect is one of focused calm and sanctity achieved through the careful manipulation of space, the juxtaposition

**7** The altar.
**8** The nave with the north wall.
**9** The folding confessional screen.
**Opposite** Elevation, section and plan, 1962. Bawa Archive.

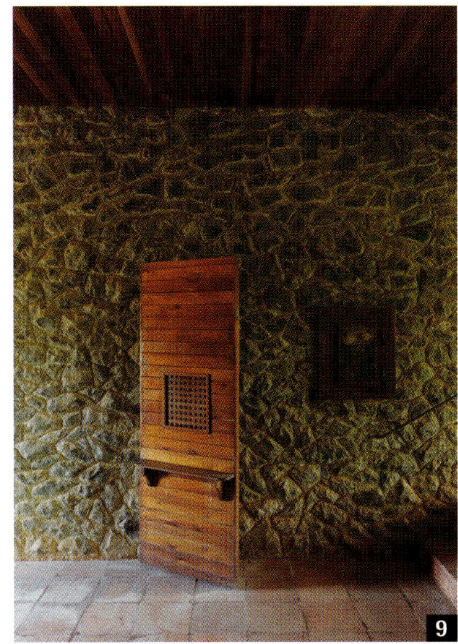

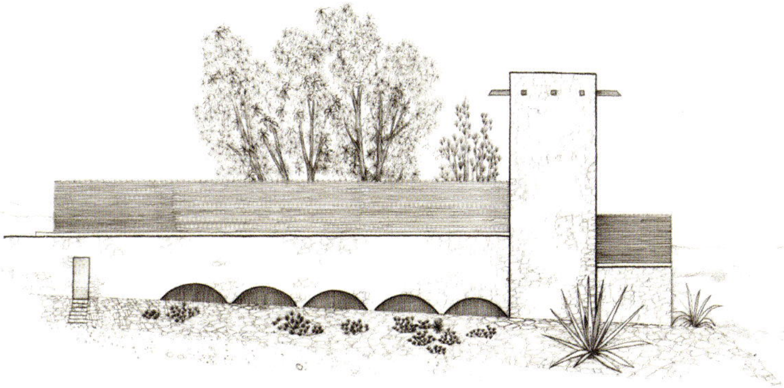

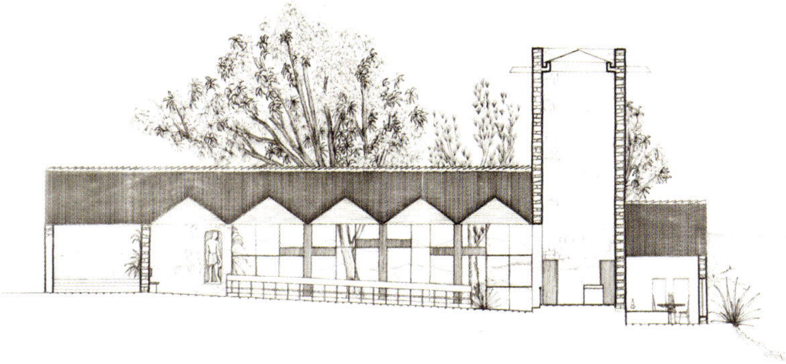

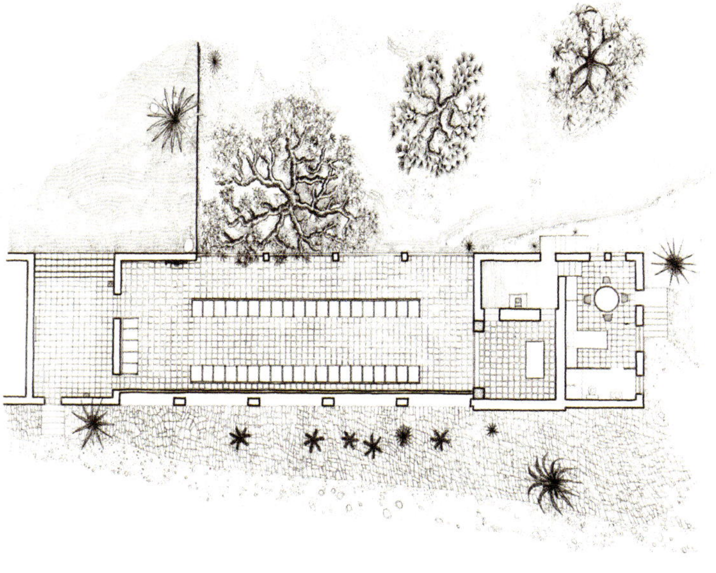

of robust materials and the careful control of light and shade. There is much that is both innovative and unique: the asymmetry of the nave that results from the opposing side walls, one closed to 'keep the Devil out', the other open to invite a view of 'Paradise on Earth'; the use of a trio of massive wooden crucifixes to divide the glazing and provide a vivid reminder of the Calvary; the hidden ventilation arches in the south wall; and the top-lit altar. Also, the simple palette of materials suggests a building that seems to grow out of the ground, one that has been 'unearthed' rather than constructed.

The Nazareth Chapel is a work of great originality which admits to no clear precedents having little in common with the florid Catholic churches of 19th-century Sri Lanka. It may owe a debt to Scandinavian Modernism or to the British Arts and Crafts movement or to the theatricality of the image houses of Polonnaruwa, or it may be that Mother Good Counsel insinuated her memories of the small rural chapels of her native Ireland into the overall design.

# The Jacobson House



Seenimodera, Tangalla
1997

The Jacobson House has come to be known, rather misleadingly, as 'The Last House'. The Jacobsons, who hailed from Hong Kong, met Bawa in mid 1997 and commissioned him to design a house on land that they had bought on a beach near Tangalla. He visited the site and produced a sketch design, but suffered a stroke before he could develop it further. Bawa's associate, Channa Daswatte, with Neelanga Weerasekera completed the project and Bawa had no involvement with its detailed design.

The house sits on a low bluff that slopes gently towards the beach and falls away quickly on the land side. A two-storey pavilion contains an entrance porch from which a short flight of stairs rises to a long veranda which runs along the west side of a generous pool court and connects with a large open loggia at one end of the main building. The main building occupies two floors and fills the south side of the courtyard. A service wing completes its east side. A second pavilion with a smaller courtyard lies to the west of the long veranda.

With its ochre-painted walls and green shutters, the house is more colourful than might be expected of a Bawa design and the first-floor bathroom is also uncharacteristic. This all serves as a reminder that while the general arrangement remains true to his first sketches, Bawa was not involved with the decoration or furnishing. Now functioning as a small hotel, it is advertised online as a 'Breezy Bawa Beachpad' — which says it all really.

1 View across the pool court.
2 Pergola link to the annex.
3 View from the veranda through
sitting and dining rooms.

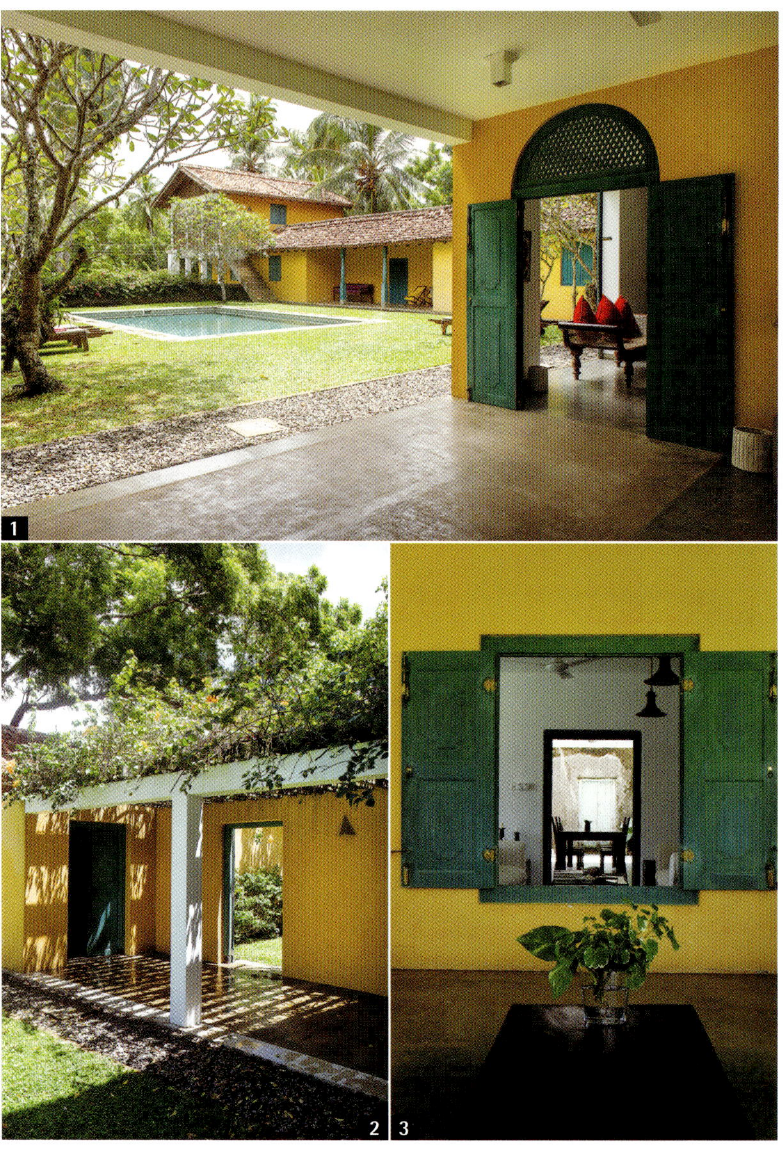

# Claughton Bungalow

Dikwella

1985-1986

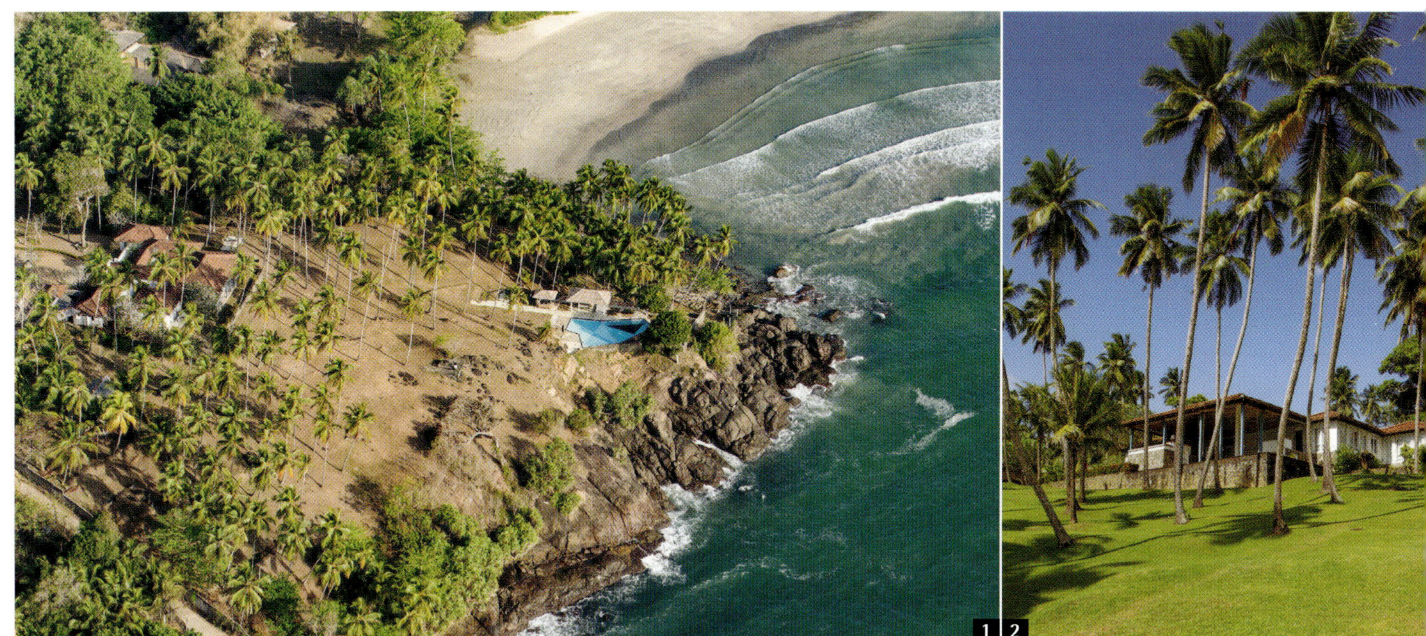

Claughton Bungalow was built for a British estate agent called Fitzherbert. It sits on the crown of a hill which falls steeply away towards the edge of Kudawella Bay. In its original form it contained only three bedrooms, each one within its own courtyard enclosure and each enjoying its own unique view of the sea.

Bawa choreographed the entrance approach so that the house blocked any view of the sea. A Dutch gable with twin arches marks the entrance itself. One arch connects to the kitchens and service areas, the other opens to a narrow corridor that provides a first glimpse of the sea and leads to the main communal space. This takes the form of a split-level loggia under a large hipped roof, with the dining room at the upper level and the open lounge at the lower level. The dramatic level change matches the slope of the site which runs down through a swaying coconut grove to a small polygonal swimming pool perched on the edge of a rocky headland.

The house operated for several years as a small hotel and incongruous rooms were added to one side, though thankfully these are not immediately visible. More recently it has been successfully converted back to a holiday villa.

**1** Aerial view: the villa on left and the pool centre right.
**2** The villa seen from the coconut grove below.

# The Ruhuna University Campus

Matara

1980–1986

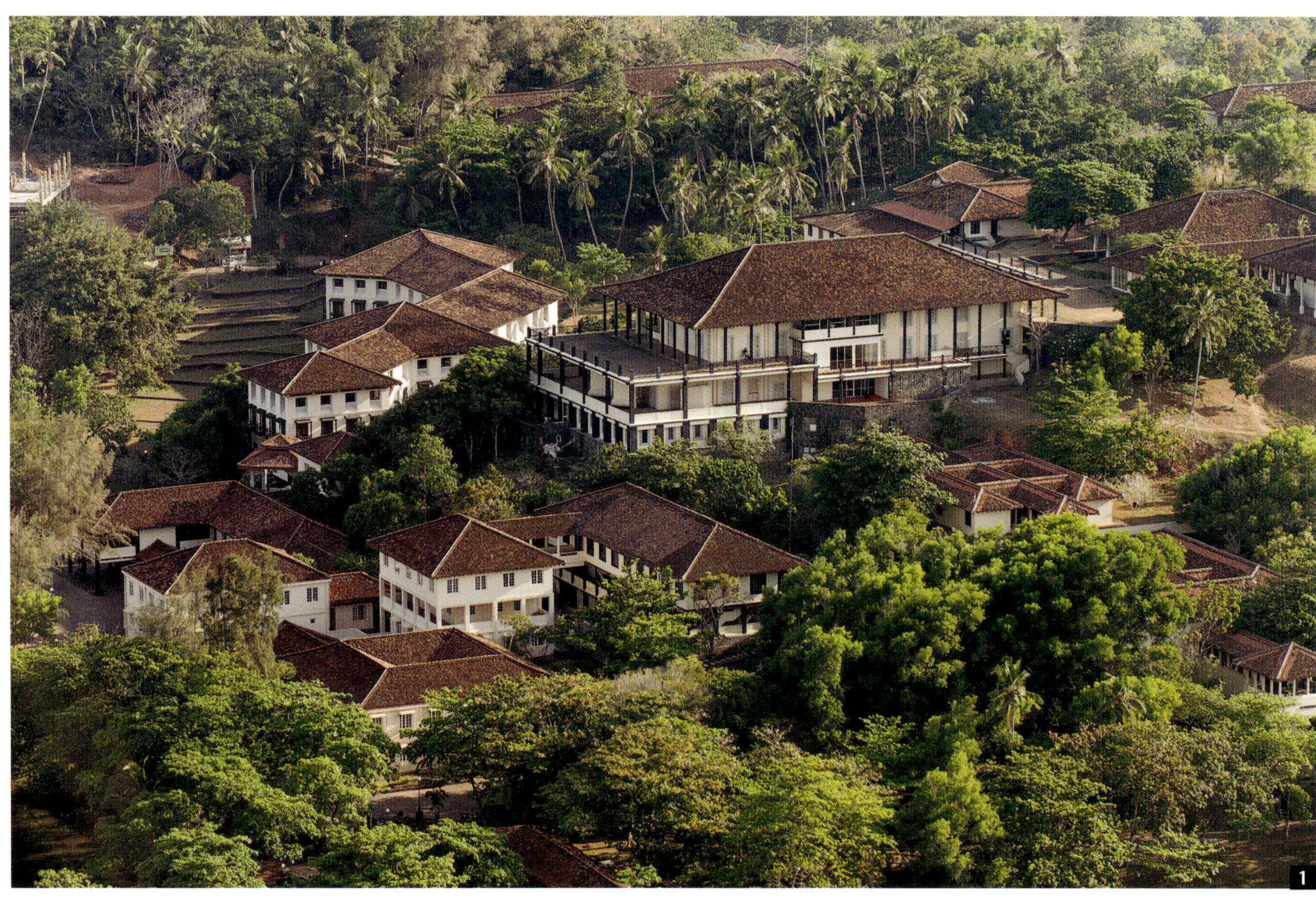

1 Aerial view from the south.

Soon after starting work on the Sri Lanka Parliament, Bawa was commissioned to design the main campus of the new University of Ruhuna near Matara. Suddenly he had to deal simultaneously with the two biggest projects of his career. His main assistant on the University was Nihal Bodhinayake whom he had met in Sydney and who worked on it, almost single-handedly, for seven years.

The brief called for more than 50 buildings with a total area of some 40,000 square metres; the designated site straddled three steep hills

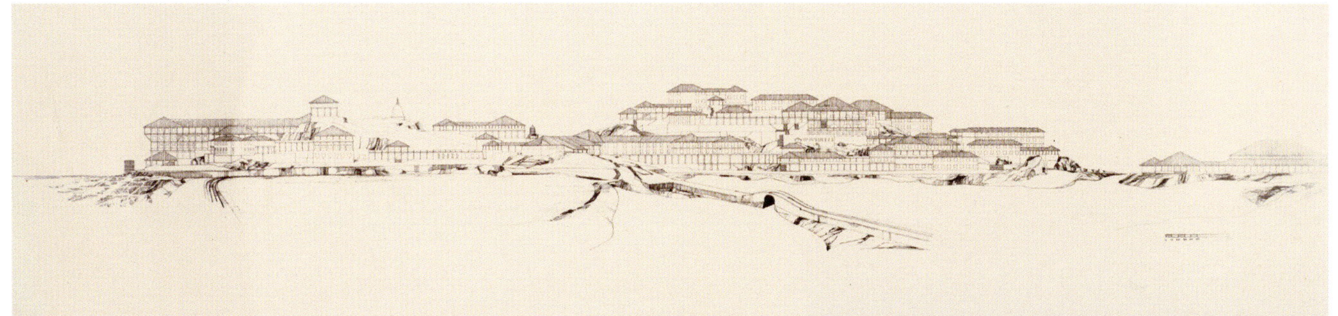

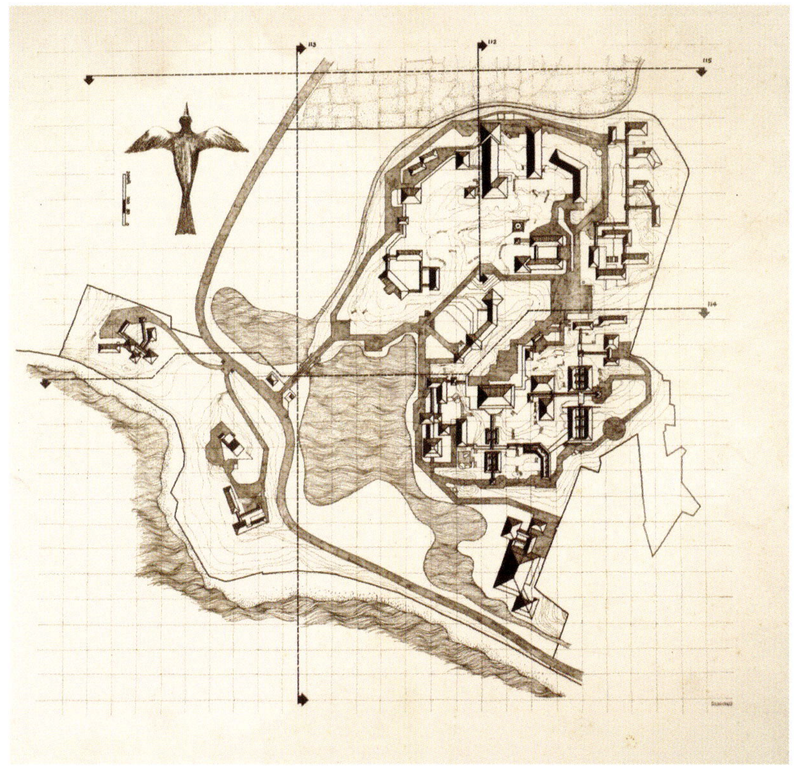

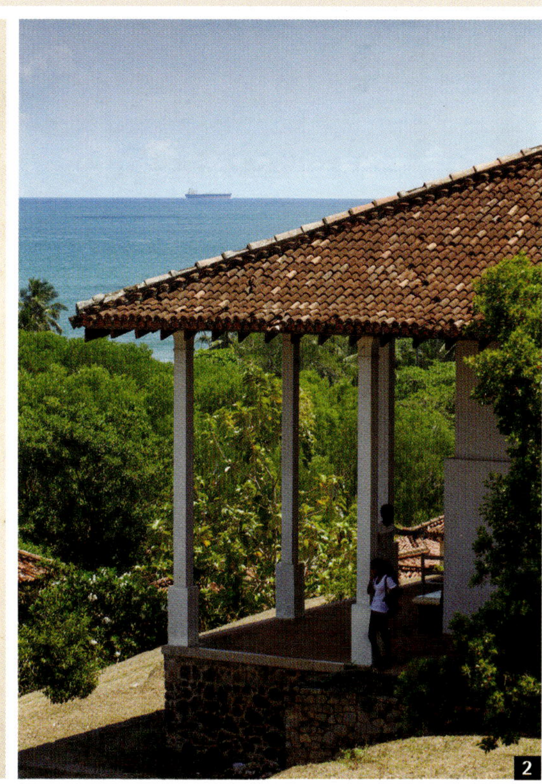

covering an area of 30 hectares. The western-most hill overlooked the ocean and was separated from its siblings by the main road from Matara to Tangalla.

Bawa's strategy was to locate the Science Faculty on the northern hill and the Arts Faculty on the southern hill and to place the shared facilities between them. He then created a lake as a buffer between the campus and the main road and allocated the western hill to staff housing.

Bawa used grids to develop the design: a structural grid of 3 metres (10 feet), a planning

**Top** Panorama from west, 1985. Bawa Archive.
**Above left** Site plan, 1985. Bawa Archive.
**2** View out towards the Indian Ocean.

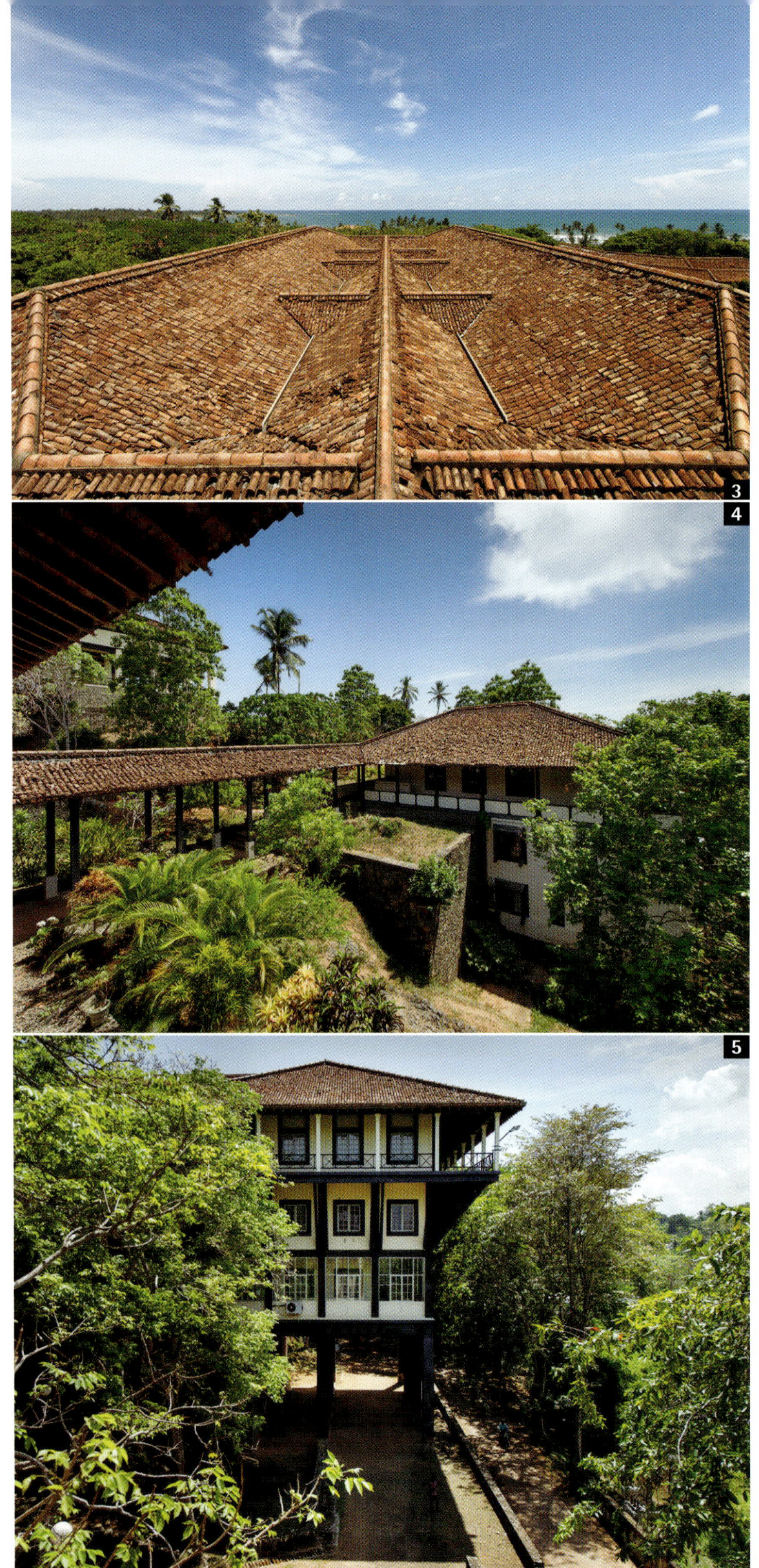

3 Roofs with valley
ventilators.
4 Covered link.
5 The Physics wing.
6 Library and the
central amphitheatre.
7 Library interior.

grid of 30 metres (100 feet) and a vertical grid
of 1.5 metres (5 feet). Uncharacteristically, he
also worked with a large scaled model in order to
locate the various constituent buildings in relation
to each other. His aim was to get the buildings to
'run with the contours' in order to create linked
sequences around the two principle hills, but this
necessitated placing some buildings at angles of
30° or 45° to the main grid.

The design employed a limited palette of forms
and details that were ordered by the grid. However,
the constantly changing dialogue between the
buildings and the site dispelled any sense of
monotony. Having set up a rigid system, Bawa
was happy to break it when the terrain dictated.
As a result the campus developed as a complex
checkerboard of buildings and intervening spaces
which were imbued by an ever-varying sense
of place, adding legibility to the overall plan.

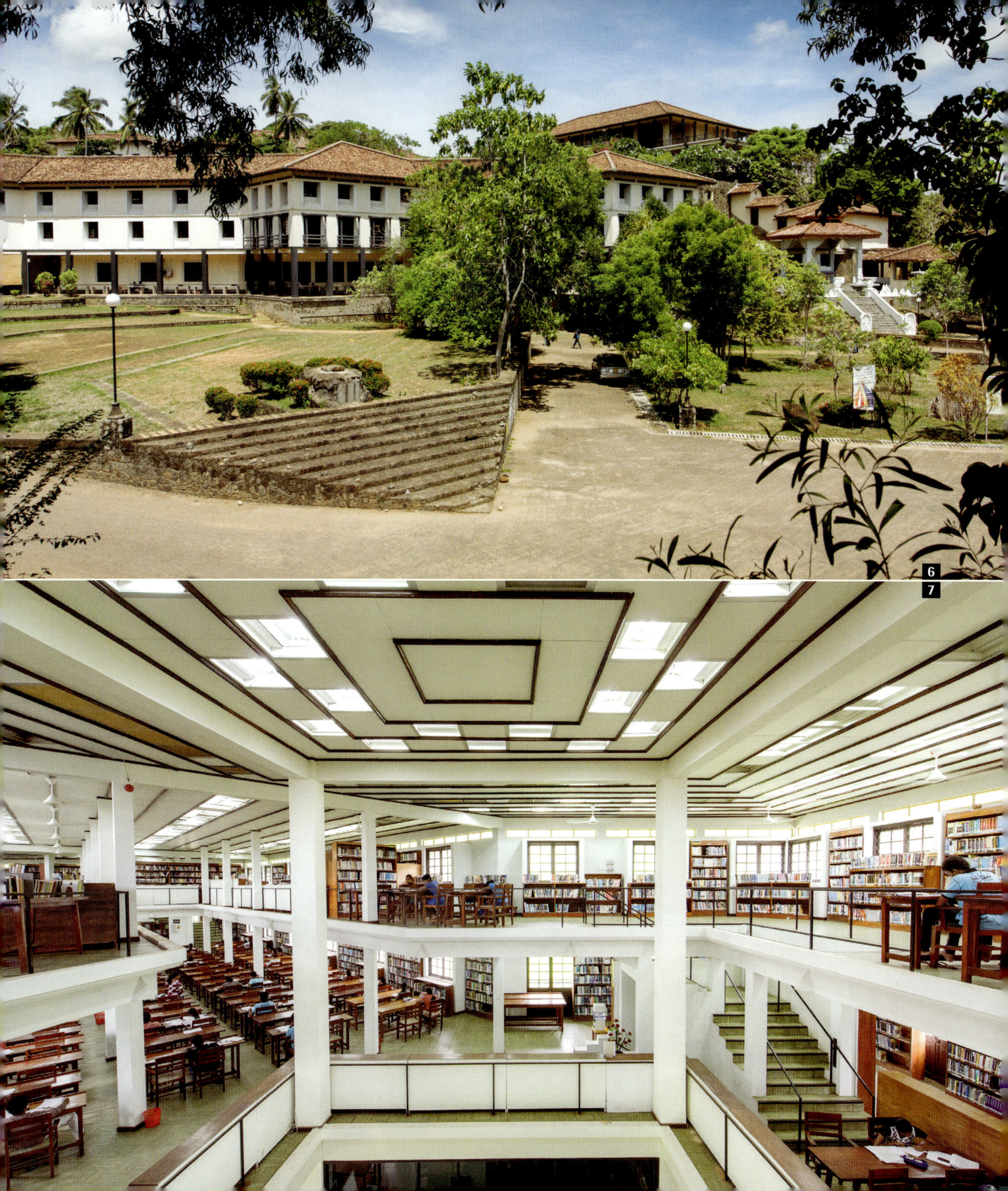
6
7

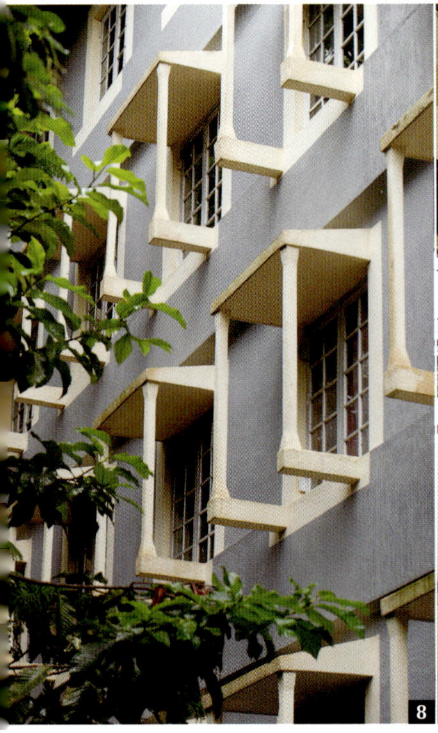

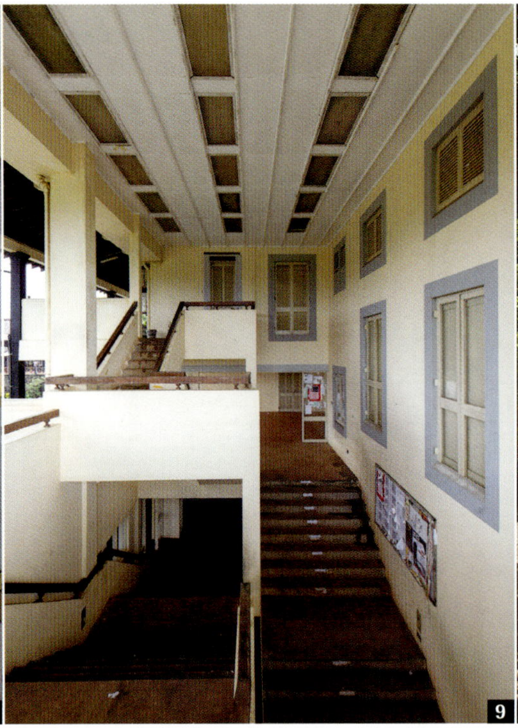

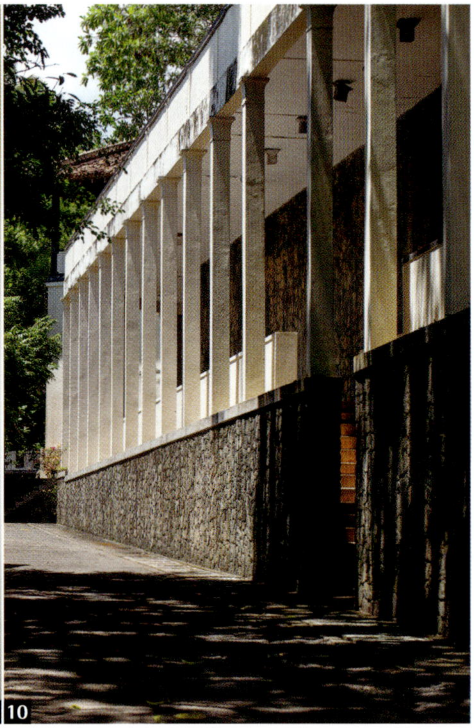

Inevitably, on such a hilly site, there are many changes of level and this gave rise to a series of wonderful staircases.

The campus includes a sports stadium with grandstand and a substantial gymnasium. The library occupies a long building which steps down the valley between the two hills and twice changes its axis through 45°. Here, apparently simple elements are deployed to create a library interior of astonishing sophistication containing a succession of double-height reading rooms framed by book stacks.

The campus faces the full blast of the monsoon winds and has suffered from neglect and lack of maintenance, but its robust quality has helped it to survive its three decades. Bawa's trademark roofs of half-round tile on corrugated cement sheeting have suffered from their exposure to the southern ocean and from the depredations of the hordes of monkeys that seem to outnumber the students. Inevitably, new buildings have been added, some incongruously, but others, more recently, with admirable sensitivity.

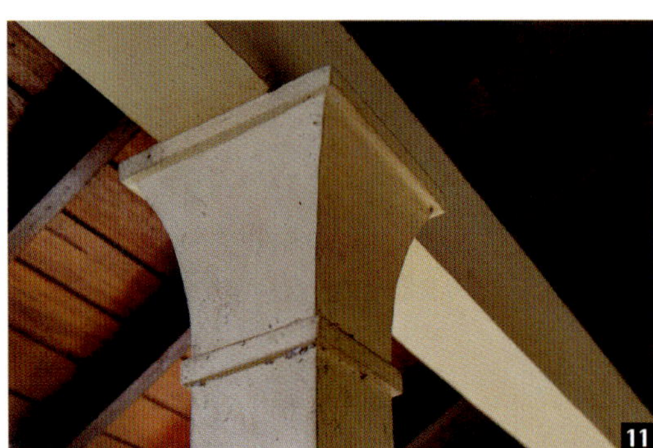

8 Sun-breakers.
9 The main staircase in the administrative wing.
10 A covered way.
11 Typical column head.

# Office Building

Matara

1969

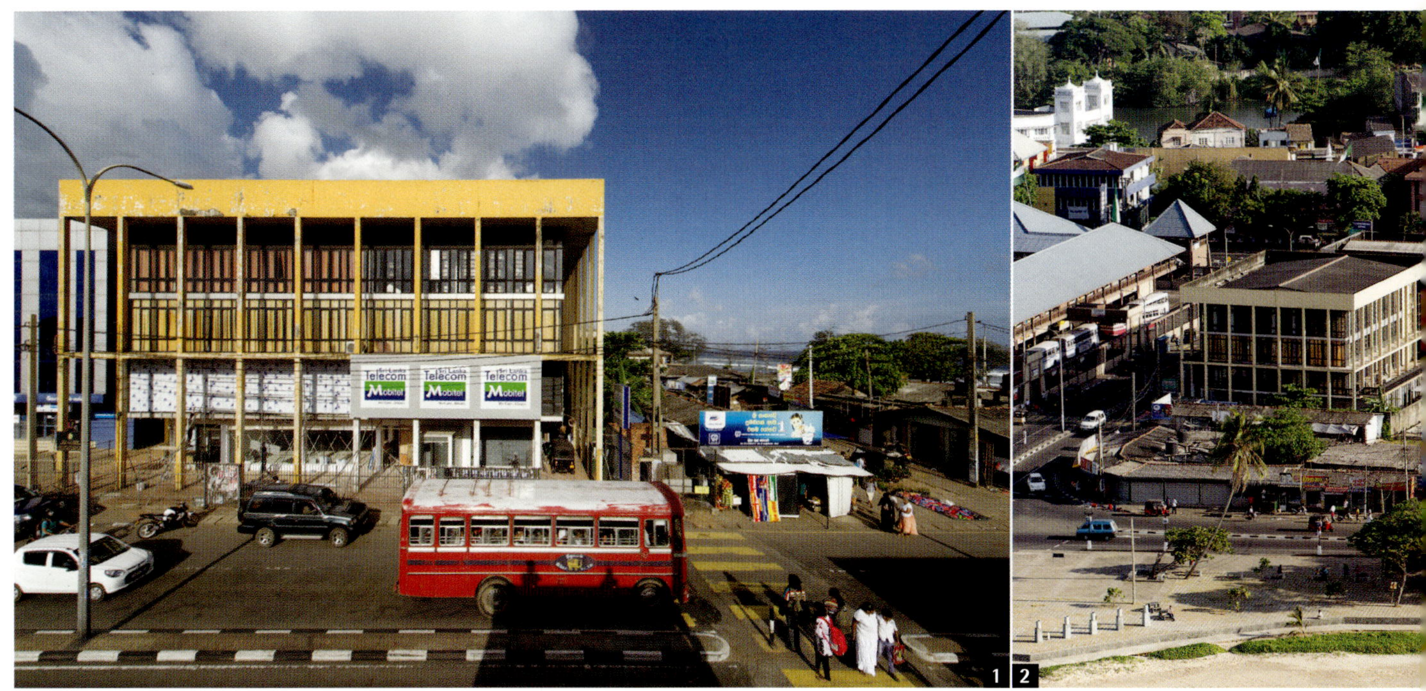

This small office building is located on the seafront at Matara to the immediate east of the bus station. Built for a local businessman, the project architect was Nihal Amerasinghe.

It was designed on four floors in the form of a simple and elegant cube in an uncompromisingly modernist style. A flat roof cantilevers out on all sides to provide shade and rain-screening and is supported on edge columns. The resultant loggia which runs around the building's perimeter is divided horizontally by a balcony at second-floor level.

Although it faces the full blast of the southwest monsoon and has been poorly maintained, this remarkable building carries its 45 years with grace.

**1** View from the bus station.
**2** Aerial view showing the bus station and main mosque.

# The Jayawardene House

Mirissa
1997

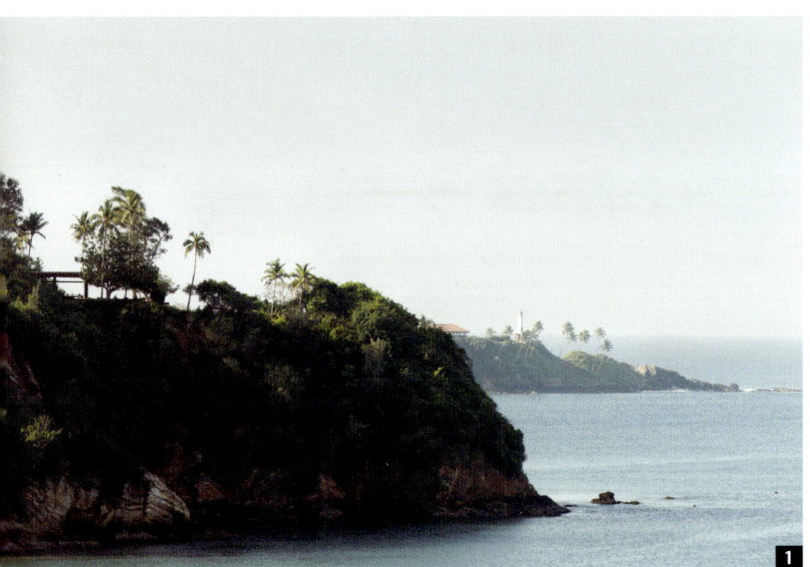

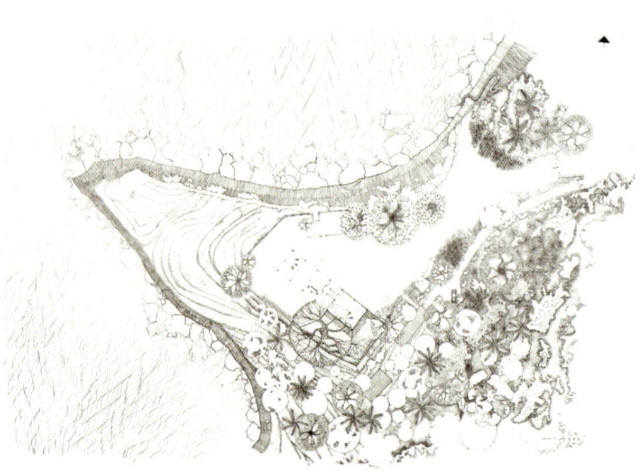

The Jayawardene House — the last house that Geoffrey Bawa built — was designed in 1996 and Bawa continued to make site visits until its completion in late 1997. Commissioned by Pradeep Jayawardene, the grandson of President J R Jayawardene, it was built to replace an earlier house that had been destroyed by Janatha Vimukthi Peramuna (JVP) insurgents at the end of 1980. It is perched on the tip of the Red Cliffs that overlook Welligama Bay.

In its original form, the house consisted simply of a large open-sided veranda defined by a platoon of seven trios of square columns supporting a gently sloping steel canopy. The floor of the two easternmost bays was raised to form an upper plinth under which a couple of basement bedrooms were inserted. These were reached by a central staircase set within a glass enclosure and opened at a lower level to a small patio.

It was as if Bawa had worked for 40 years to distil the tropical house to its bare essentials — an umbrella roof floating in a copse of casuarinas and coconut palms.

Soon after it was completed, the writer, Michael Ondaatje, who was related by marriage to Jayawardene and was a friend of Bawa, penned a poem in its honour:

**Above** Site plan, 1997.
Bawa Archive.
**1** The house on the Red Cliffs above Weligama Bay.
**2** The main pavilion.
**3** Geoffrey Bawa on site with Pradeep Jayawardene and Channa Daswatte. 1997.

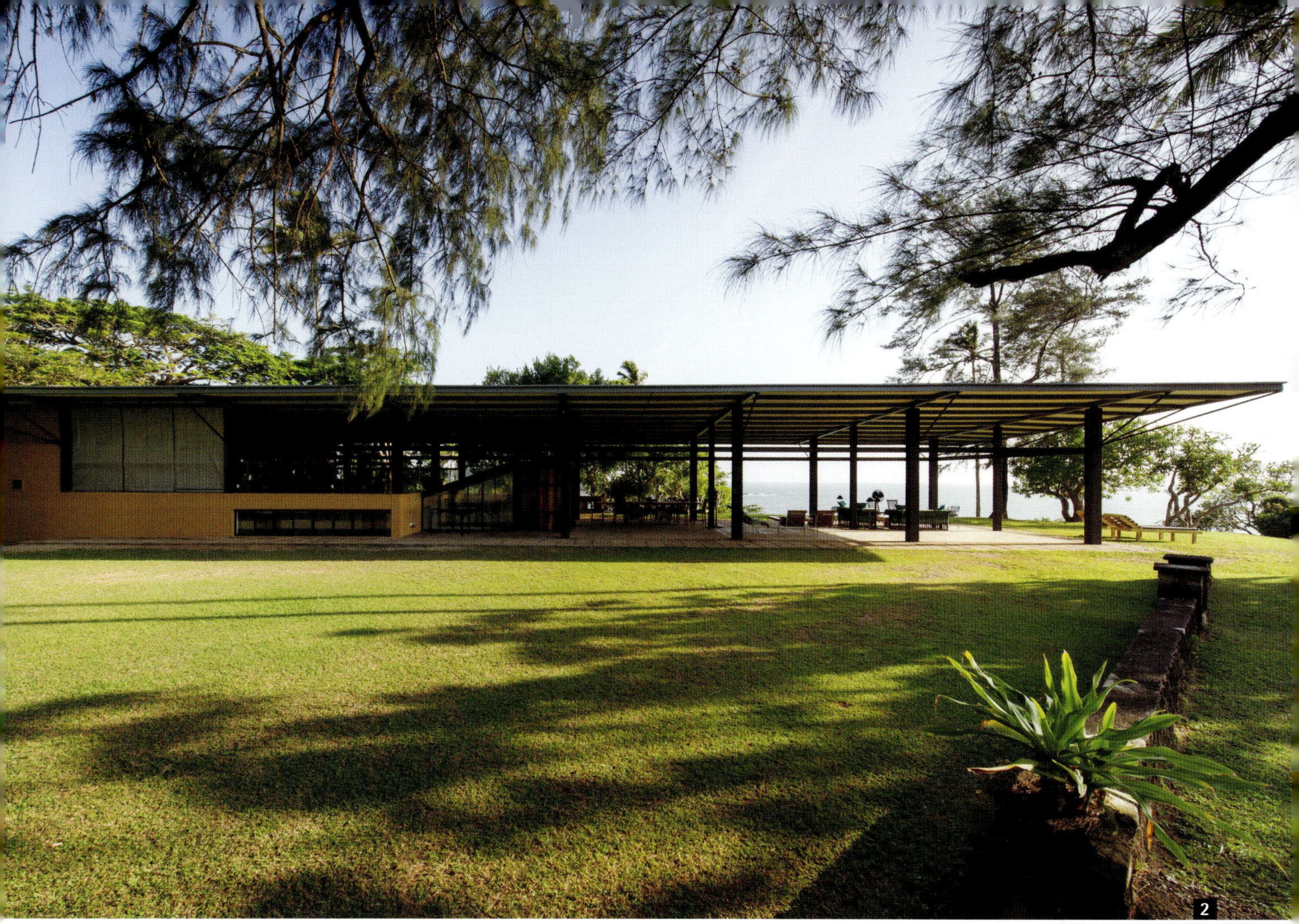

"There is no mirror in Mirissa
the sea is in the leaves
the waves are in the palms
old language in the arms of the casuarina pine
*parampara, parampara*
from generation to generation."
The house was later added to a chain of boutique hotels whose impresario owner proceeded to remodel the bedrooms and enclose the upper plinth, reminding us that those who trade in beauty often destroy what they pretend to cherish. Hopefully, it can one day be restored to its former elegant simplicity.

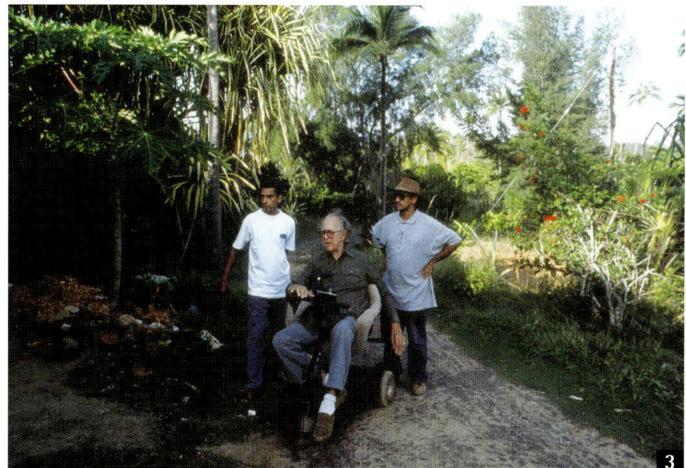

# The ASH de Silva House

Woodward Mawatha, Galle

1959

ASH de Silva was a young doctor who was establishing a practice in Galle and wanted a house with a surgery. Having acquired a steeply sloping site in one of its north-eastern suburbs, he picked Geoffrey Bawa's name out of a telephone book.

Bawa designed the main house as a stepped rectangle around a central courtyard and placed it at the top of the site. He then added an annex for the doctor's sister to the north side of the main entrance, thus forming a small court with a reflecting pool. An arm containing the kitchen and staff quarters was thrust out towards the south. The surgery was housed in a separate pavilion beside the road and was connected back to the house by a long enclosed staircase.

The resultant pinwheel plan was reminiscent of the early houses of Mies van der Rohe, its arms flailing out to entrap semi-enclosed garden spaces. The central courtyard, an innovation that anticipated the Ena de Silva House, was on two levels, with a fountain at the upper level that played gently into a pool at the lower level. Bawa wanted blue glass tiles for the pool but these were unavailable and Laki Senanayake used broken Milk of Magnesia bottles from the doctor's pharmacy.

The house achieved the sort of synthesis that Bawa was striving for: clarity of plan, its formality tempered by asymmetries that derived from the site. It survives in near perfect condition, but its owner and his dog brook no visitors.

**1** The main entrance, 1961.
**2** View from the garden court through the sitting room towards the inner pool court, 1961.

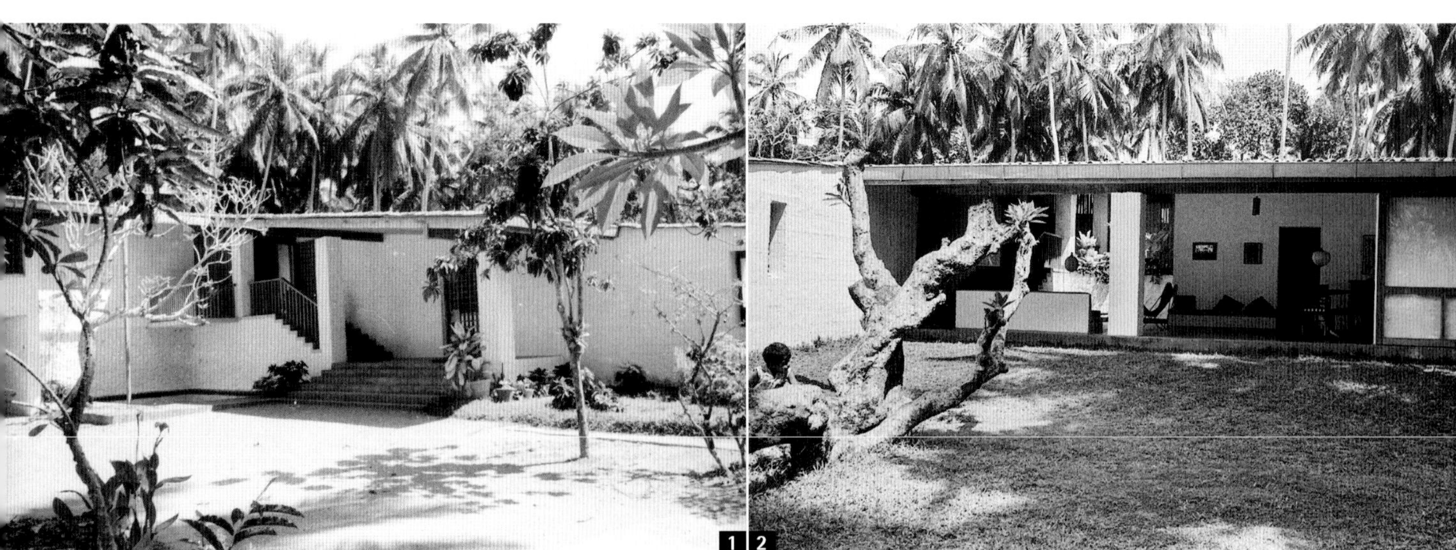

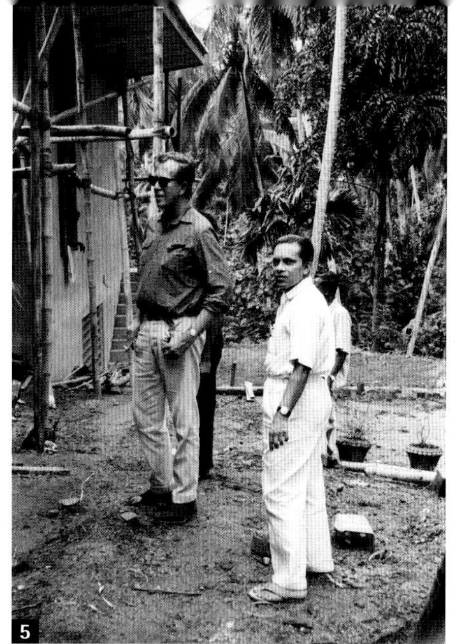

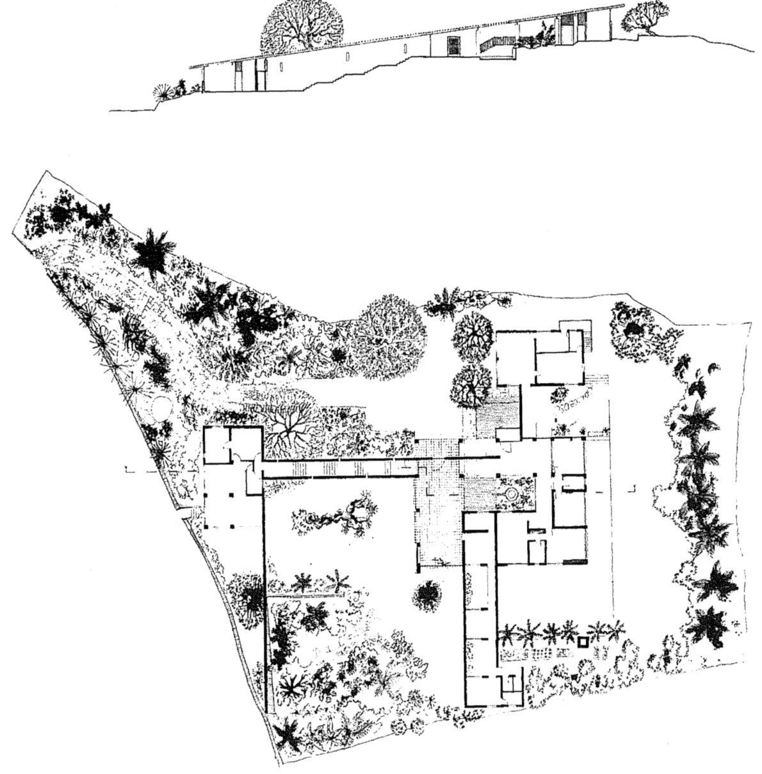

Left Section and plan showing
the main house on the right
and the doctor's surgery on
the left, 1961. Bawa Archive.
3 The sitting room.
4 The upper court and
second entrance.
5 Geoffrey Bawa on site with
Dr ASH de Silva, 1961.

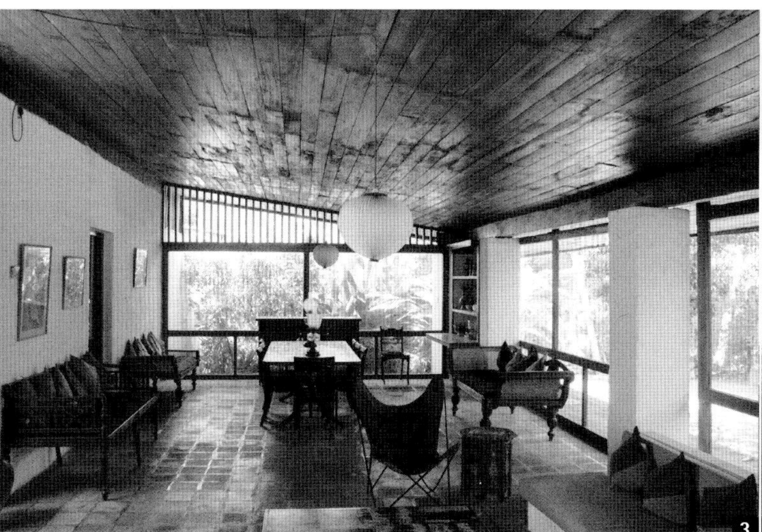

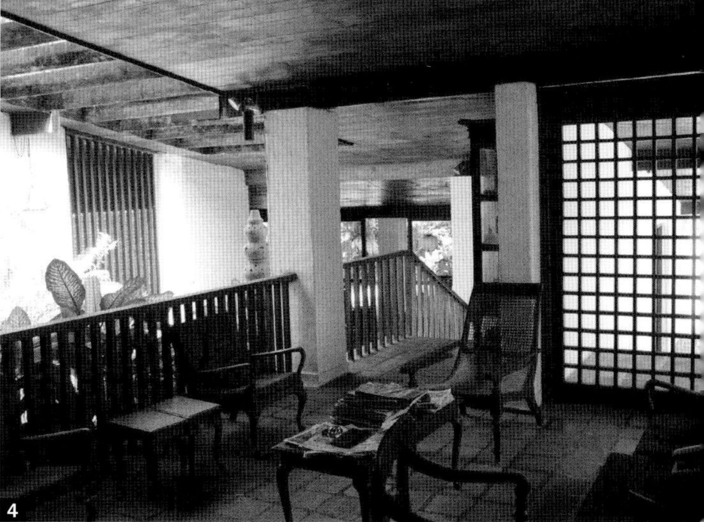

# The Lighthouse Hotel

## Galle

### 1995–1997

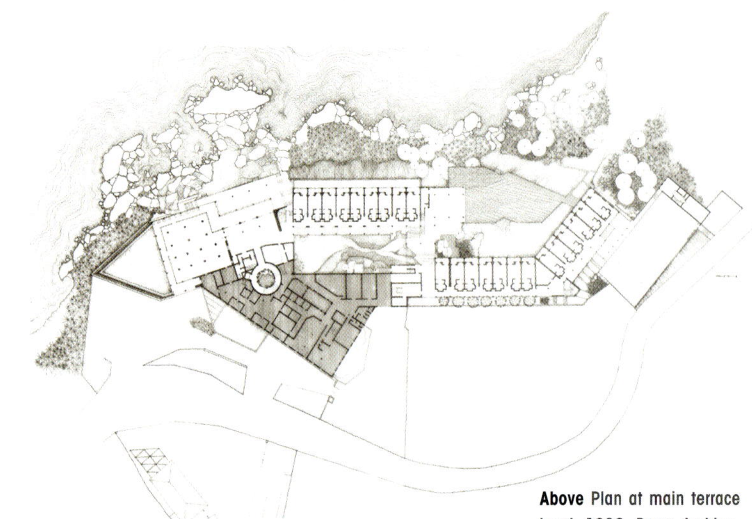

The Lighthouse Hotel was commissioned by Jetwing, a travel company that was founded by Herbert Cooray, a former building contractor and friend of Bawa. It occupies a rocky promontory between the southern ocean and the main road to Colombo and enjoys stunning sea views towards the setting sun. Its principal level is raised up above the road on a stone plinth which shelters the entrance under a massive *porte-cochère*.

The main staircase spirals upwards within a circular drum and is lit from a single oculus in its domed ceiling. Its balustrade is composed from a swirling succession of Sinhalese and Portuguese warriors sculpted in metal by Laki Senanayake in a re-enactment of the 17th-century Battle of Radeniya.

The main restaurant and covered terrace are situated on the first floor and look out across the rocks towards the crashing waves. The second floor produces the surprise of a tiled reflecting pool in an enclosed courtyard that connects to an upper dining room and a bar. The ceiling of the bar is lined with batik panels depicting coats of arms from the colonial period that were crafted by long-time Bawa collaborator Ena de Silva.

The rooms are arranged on three levels in two ranges which slide past each other to create an enclosed court and an open court with a sizeable swimming pool.

Bawa's design exploits the rugged terrain and confronts the relentless crashing of the waves while creating contrasting areas of tranquillity. Complementing this is the muted architecture which offers mixed memories of Moorish palaces, ocean liners and colonial villas.

The hotel has been beautifully maintained and has been extended northwards with an additional wing and a spa designed sympathetically by Bawa associate Channa Daswatte.

**Above** Plan at main terrace level, 1998. Bawa Archive.
**1** The main staircase by Laki Senanayake – a re-enactment of the Battle of Radeniya.
**2** Sketch for the staircase by Laki Senanayake, 1995. Bawa Archive.
**3** Aerial view of the hotel showing the dome over the staircase – the north wing to the left is new.
**4** The dining terrace.
**5** The north end of the pool wing with the stair/ramp.

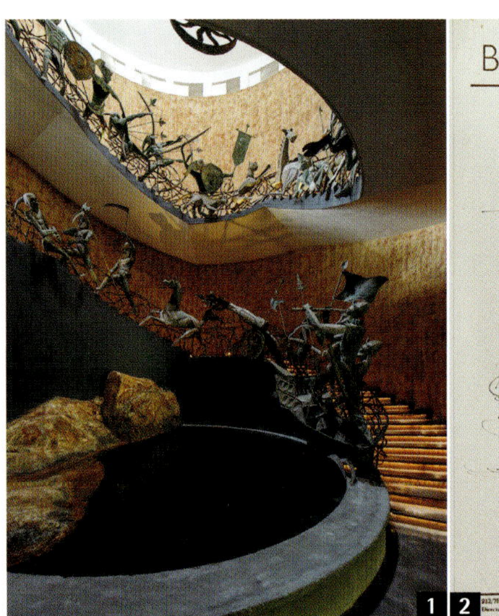

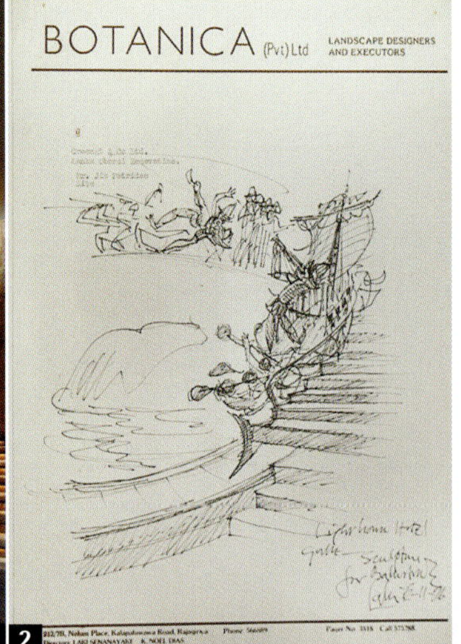

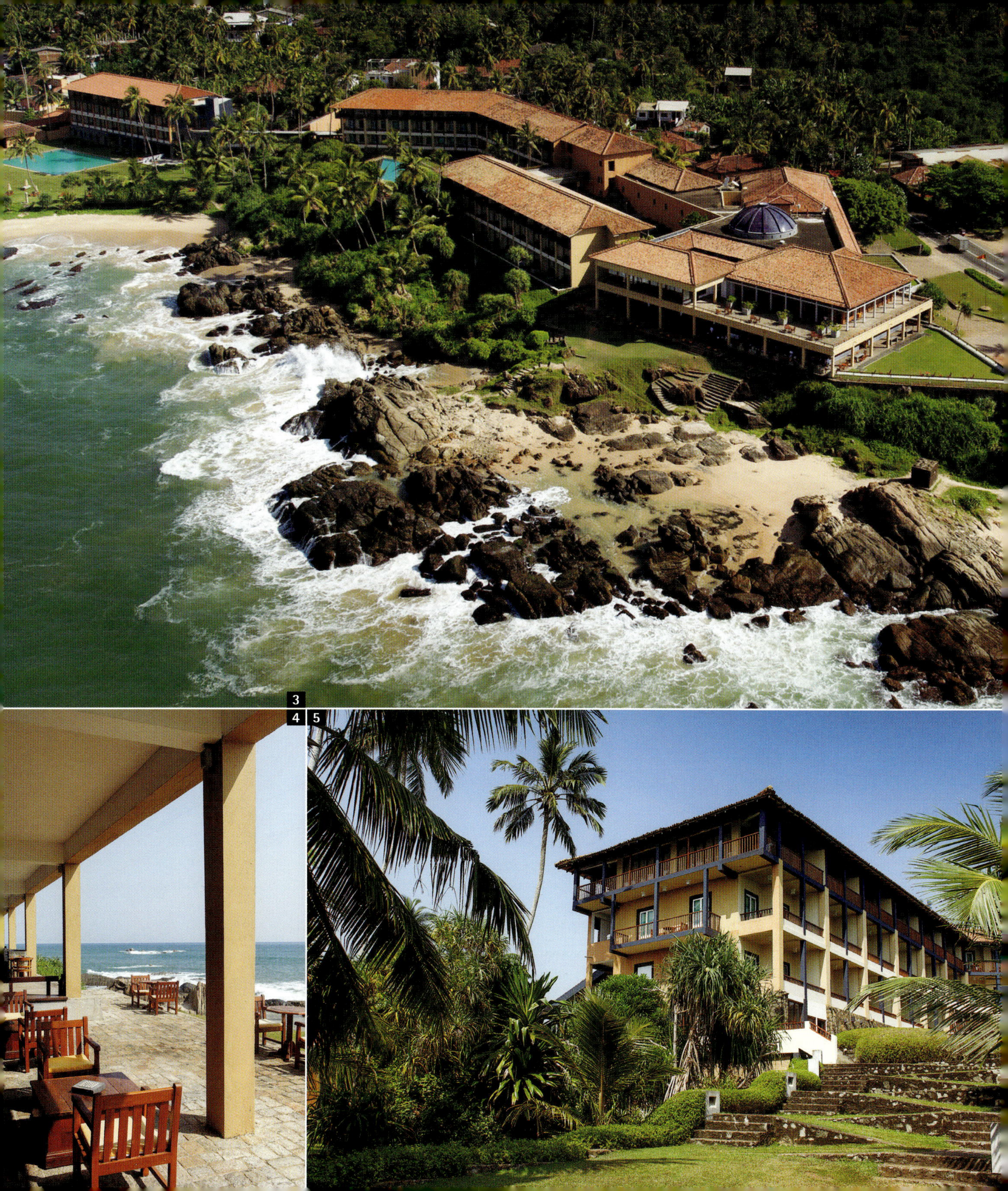
3
4 5

# The Triton Hotel

(aka Heritance Hotel )
Ahungalla
1979

Aitken Spence commissioned Bawa to design the Triton Hotel at Ahungalla in 1979 at a time when he was already busy with the Parliament and the Ruhunu University, and it offered him some light relief. The site was located in a heavily populated area, but enjoyed a wide beach frontage that was connected back to the main Galle Road by a narrow corridor of coconut land.

Bawa began from a straightforward *parti*: a central building with two wings of rooms facing the sea. But he then broke up the wings, sliding them forwards and backwards and turning them through 90°, to create a succession of open-sided courts to face the sea and a corresponding series of enclosed garden courts, at different levels, to enliven the access corridors. A large pool was placed on the axis of the reception hall between the main lounges and the restaurant.

The approach from the main road brought visitors along a winding avenue to the entrance court where a phalanx of swaying coconut palms stood in a large reflecting pool and framed a view which took in the polished floor of the reception hall, the surface of the swimming pool and a distant glimpse of the ocean: a *coup de théatre*! As Bawa put it: "Everything is at the same level: if the world were flat you'd be able to see Africa!"

During the early 1990s Bawa added a new wing and second swimming pool and in 1994 he designed a second hotel, the Orion, for a neighbouring site — but this was not built. The hotel was damaged in the 2004 tsunami and a

number of the coconut palms were lost. Though it has been subjected to the inevitable periodic refurbishments, it retains much of its original quality. However, in an act of corporate myopia, the evocative name 'Triton' was replaced by the non-existent and meaningless word 'Heritance'.

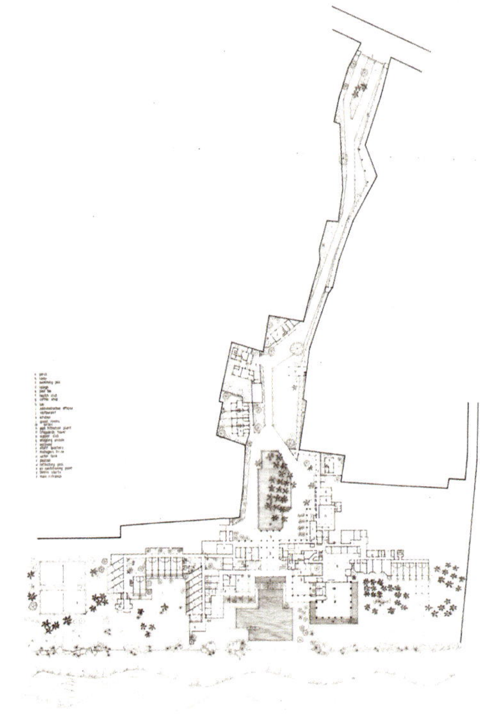

**Above** Site plan showing the approach from the main road, 1980. Bawa Archive.
**1** View through the coconut grove, 1983.
**2** The main pool with the entrance loggia.
**3** The main staircase with a mural by Laki Senanayake.
**4** The cobra stair in the south wing.
**5** An inner courtyard.

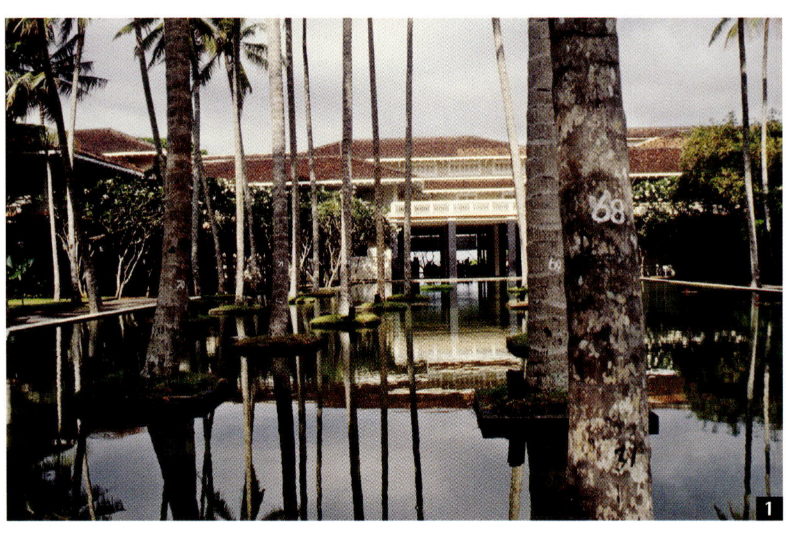

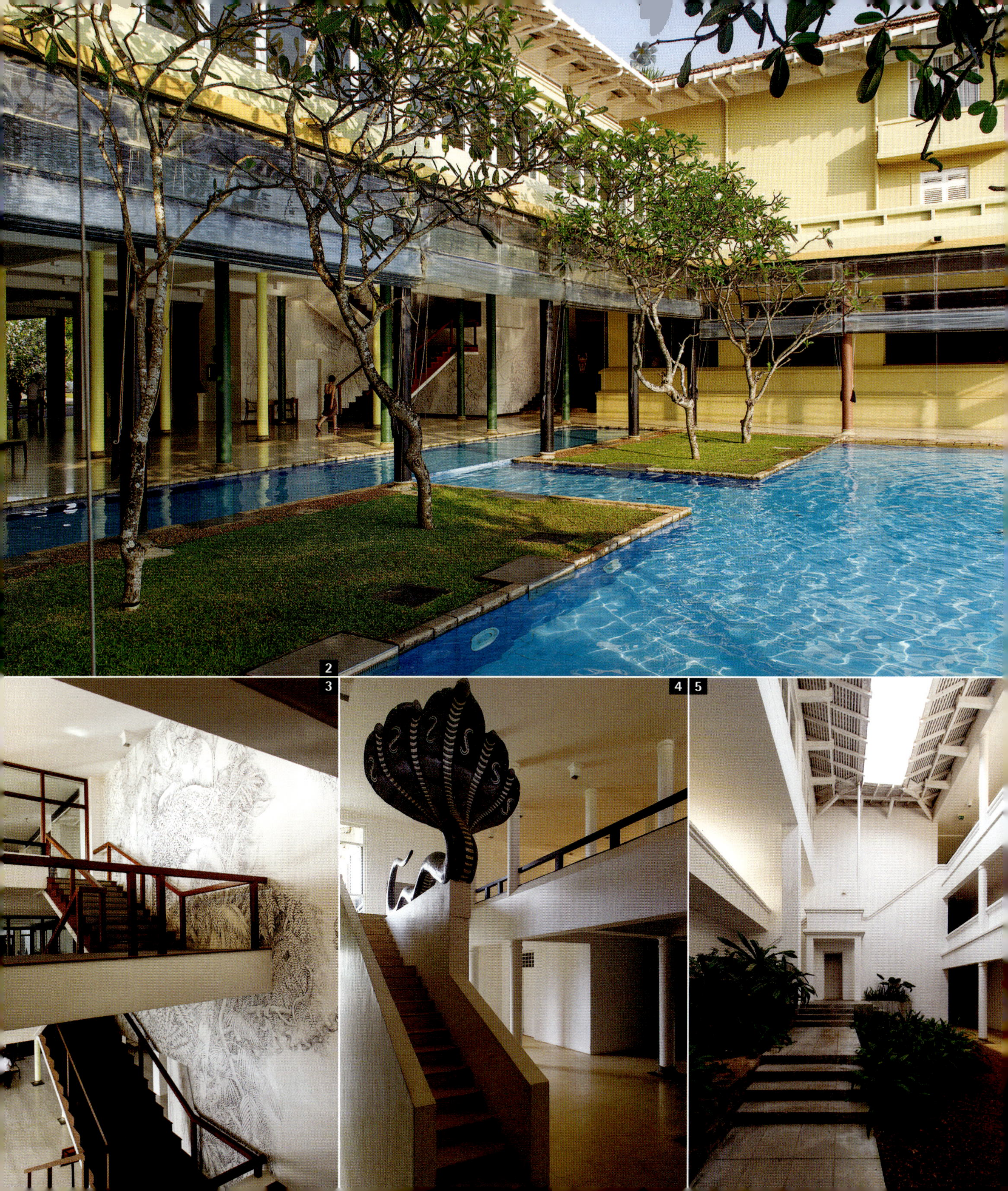

# Club Villa and Mohoti Walauwe

Galle Road, Bentota

1976—

When an old villa lying between the railway and the Galle Road in Bentota came on the market, Geoffrey Bawa tried in vain to persuade his friends to buy it. The Italian sculptor Lidia Duchini preferred instead to buy a pair of nearby houses on either side of the main road, while his friend SMA Hameed, the manager of the Serendib Hotel, opted to buy the empty land to its immediate south.

In despair, Bawa was forced to buy it himself and, having rechristened it 'Mohoti Walauwe', transformed it into a small boutique hotel, creating a new walled pool court and adding a courtyard with additional rooms to the north. The result was a charming labyrinth of courts, verandas and tiny corridors, domestic in scale and ordered with impeccable taste.

In the meantime, Hameed, with his Swiss wife Dani, persuaded Bawa to design a small house for them on the neighbouring plot with a row of rooms that could be let to tour guides. It became known as 'Club Villa'.

It soon became clear to Bawa that he was not cut out for hotel management. For a time Mohoti Walauwe was run by the Hameeds as a joint enterprise with Club Villa. Eventually, however,

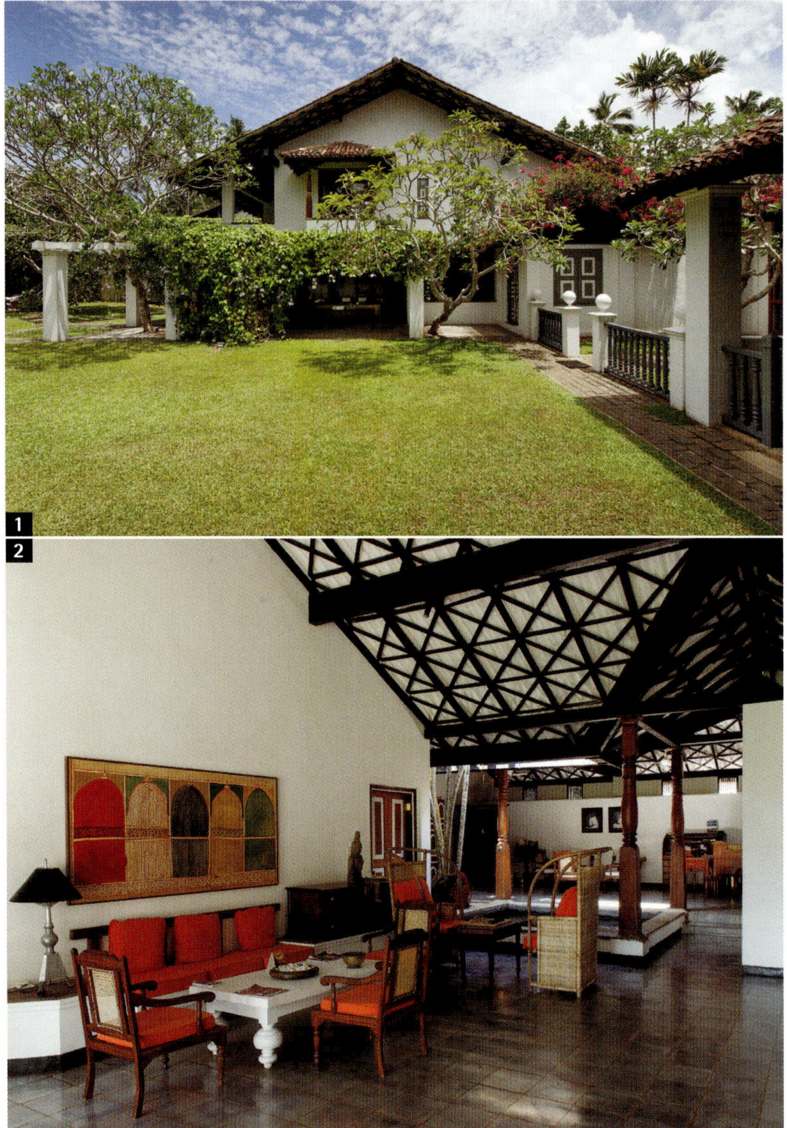

**1** The garden front of Club Villa.
**2** The Club Villa sitting room with a view towards the entrance.
**3** The west front of the original villa.
**4** The pool court of the Mohoti Walauwe.

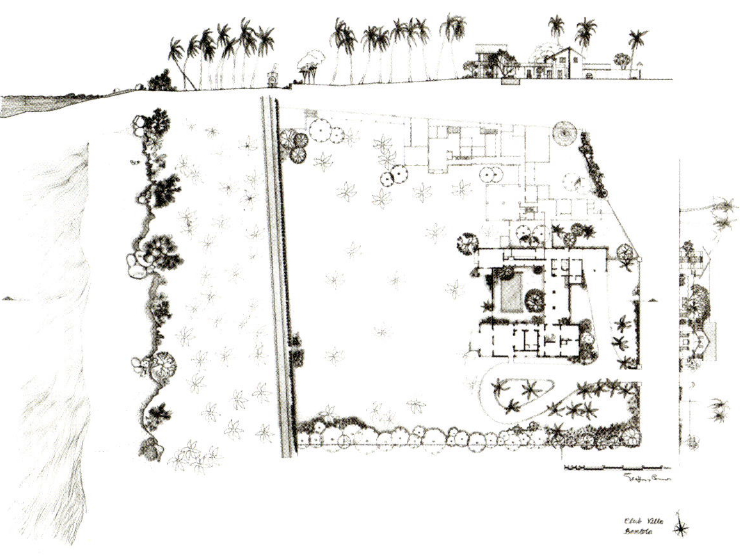



**Above** The original plan of
the Mohoti Walauwe with its
northern additions, 1985.
Bawa Archive.

the Walauwe was sold and run independently.
The Hameeds, meanwhile, extended Club Villa
by employing Anjalendran to add an extra floor
and a dining room and Channa Daswatte to
build an additional villa on the southern
boundary, all under Bawa's watching eye. The
result was less formal than its neighbour, but
was equally impressive.

For a long time the two hotels existed side
by side and offered between them some of the
most pleasant accommodation on Sri Lanka's West
Coast. Then, in 2007, a new proprietor, having
renamed Mohoti Walauwe 'The Villa', proceeded
to destroy its intimacy, removing Bawa's subtle
details and adding a paved car court, a monstrous
reception building and a new dining pavilion.

The Hameeds have now sold the Club Villa, but
its new owner has resolved to preserve it — and it
still retains its original charm.

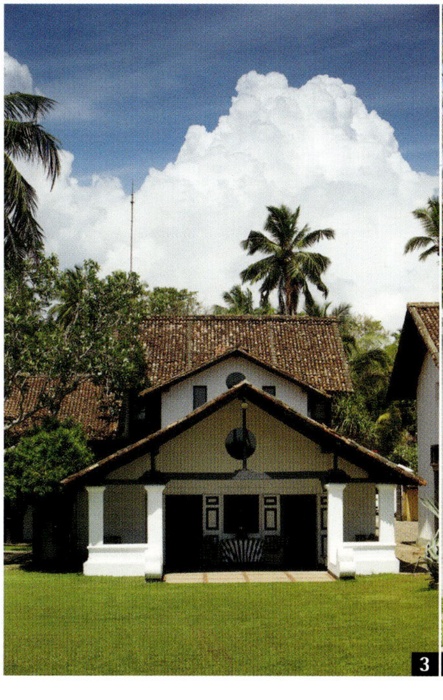

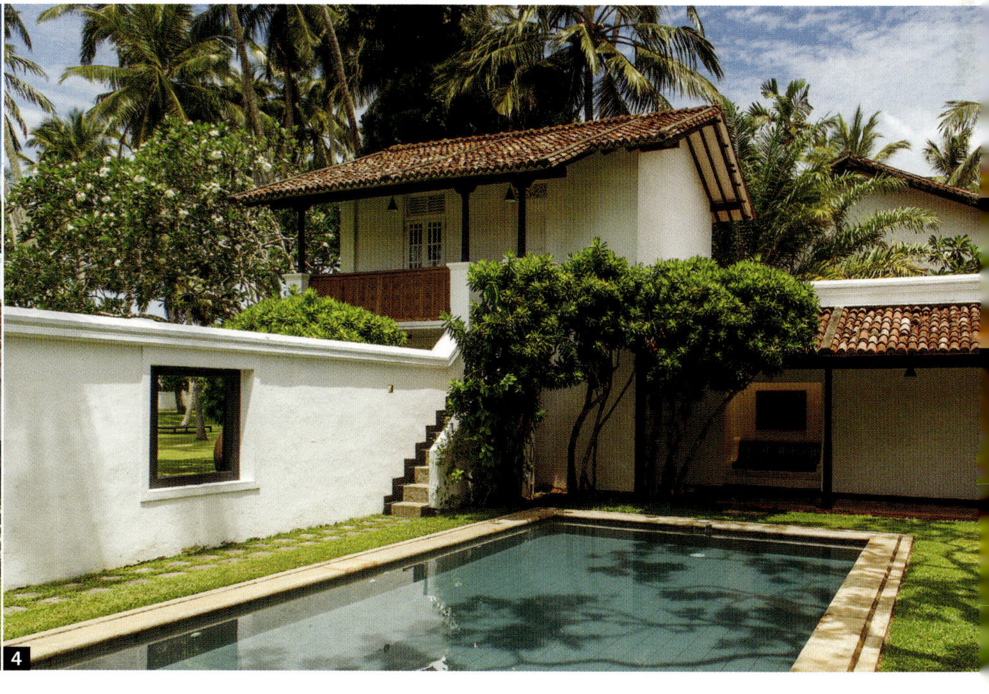

# Villa No 87

Galle Road, Bentota
1978

Having ignored Bawa's entreaties to buy Mohoti Walauwe, the sculptor Lidia Duchini opted instead to buy two old houses on either side of the Galle Road, and used one of them as a showroom for her sculpture. Later, she persuaded Bawa to remodel both houses. The house on the east side of the road stood on the edge of a large secluded garden which looked out across an expanse of jungle swamp. Bawa turned that house around so that its main veranda faced the garden and, having demolished the house on the west side of the road, rebuilt it within the garden at right angles to its neighbour. He then added a third pavilion along the southern boundary that served as a reception building with staff accommodation. In the final composition the three buildings turn their backs on the busy road and develop a careful but casual relationship with each other, with the trees and with the view across the swamp.

After Lidia's death the houses were neglected for several years until they were bought by the Colombo flower merchant Rohan Jayakody. He restored them with great care and, with Bawa's help, created a magical lap pool along the northern boundary. He also proceeded to develop the swamp as a picturesque water garden with follies of his own devising.

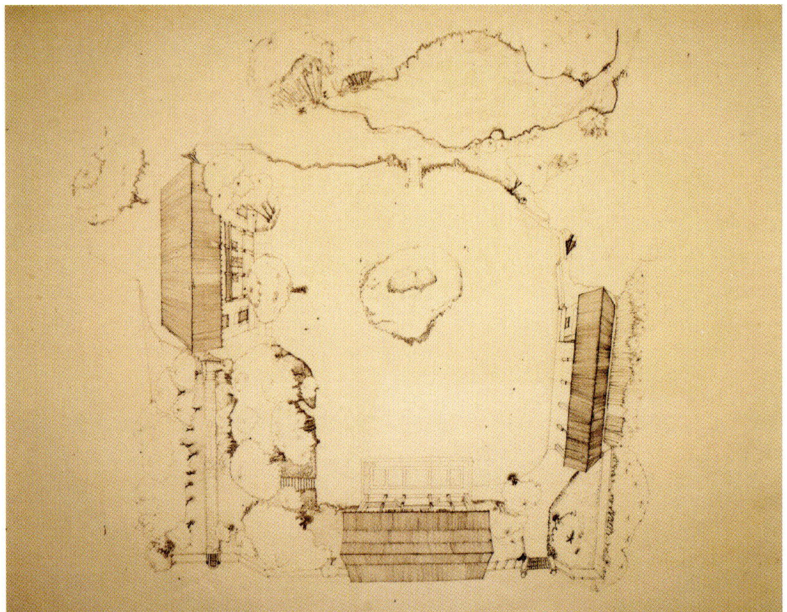

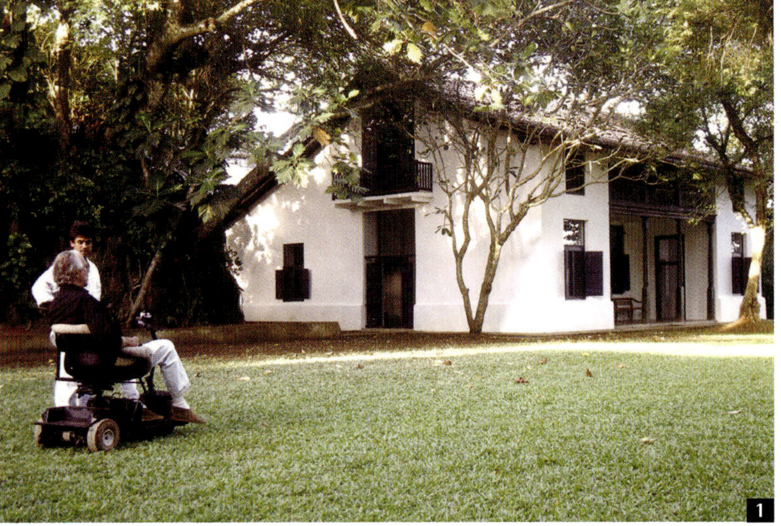

**Right** Bird's eye perspective showing the three pavilions, 1985. Bawa Archive.
**1** Geoffrey Bawa with Channa Daswwatte.
**2** The central hall and staircase in the East Villa.
**3** The East Villa with the West Villa beyond.
**4** The East Villa's upper storey.

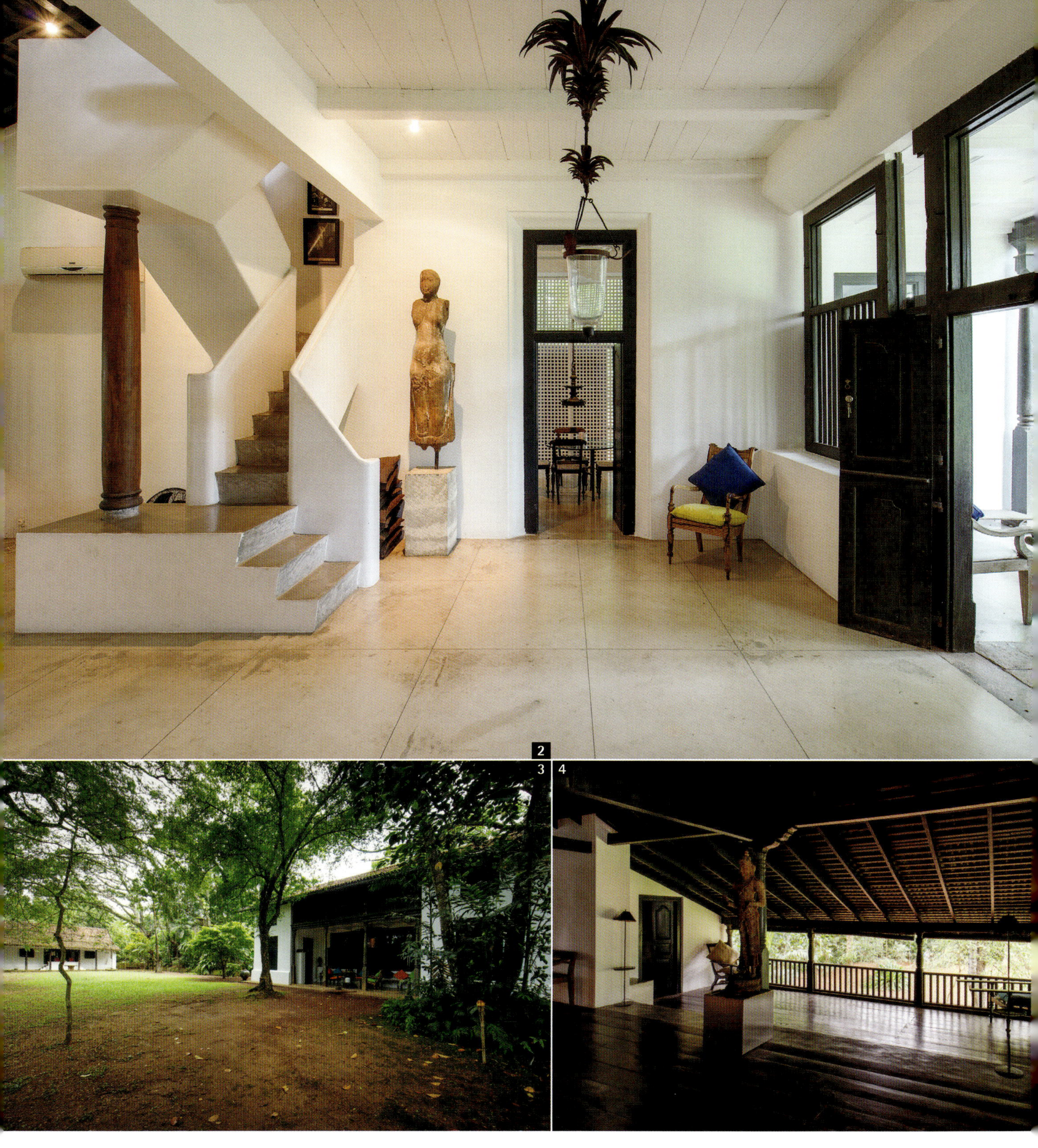

# The Bentota Tourist Village

Bentota

1967–1969

In 1967 Bawa was recruited by his friend Cecil de Soysa, the Chairman of the newly created Hotels Corporation, to help develop a self-contained tourist resort on land between the railway line and the beach at Bentota. Cheap air travel still belonged to the future and Sri Lankan tourism was in its infancy. It was assumed that most foreign visitors would arrive by boat in Colombo and would travel the 50 miles down the coast to Bentota by train.

Bawa's masterplan identified locations for five major hotels, including two that he would eventually design: the Serendib and the ill-fated Bentota Beach. He also drew up detailed plans for a tourist village. This included a new railway station with a footbridge linking it to the beach, a small public square with a police station and a bank, an artificial lake and a meandering shopping arcade. The beachside land opposite the railway station was designated as a public recreation space and was provided with shelters in the form of traditional *ambalamas*.

Astonishingly, much of the village has survived the intervening 50 years, in spite of the efforts of hoteliers to confine their guests and their wallets within their hotels. The station still welcomes visitors who prefer a more sedate mode of travel; the shopping arcade is still home to hopeful jewellers and knick-knack sellers; and the public beach remains, though its shelters have disappeared. Sadly, the popular hopper bar at the north end of the shopping arcade has been replaced by a hideous piece of public sculpture.

A planned village where foreign tourists could meet with locals, buy local products and eat local food in a traffic-free environment now seems to be hopelessly utopian. Some of these things do happen in places like Negombo and Hikkaduwa, but they happen in a much more confrontational and less harmonious way.

1 The bank and post office.
2 The station platform.
3 View of the station from Bawa's railway bridge.

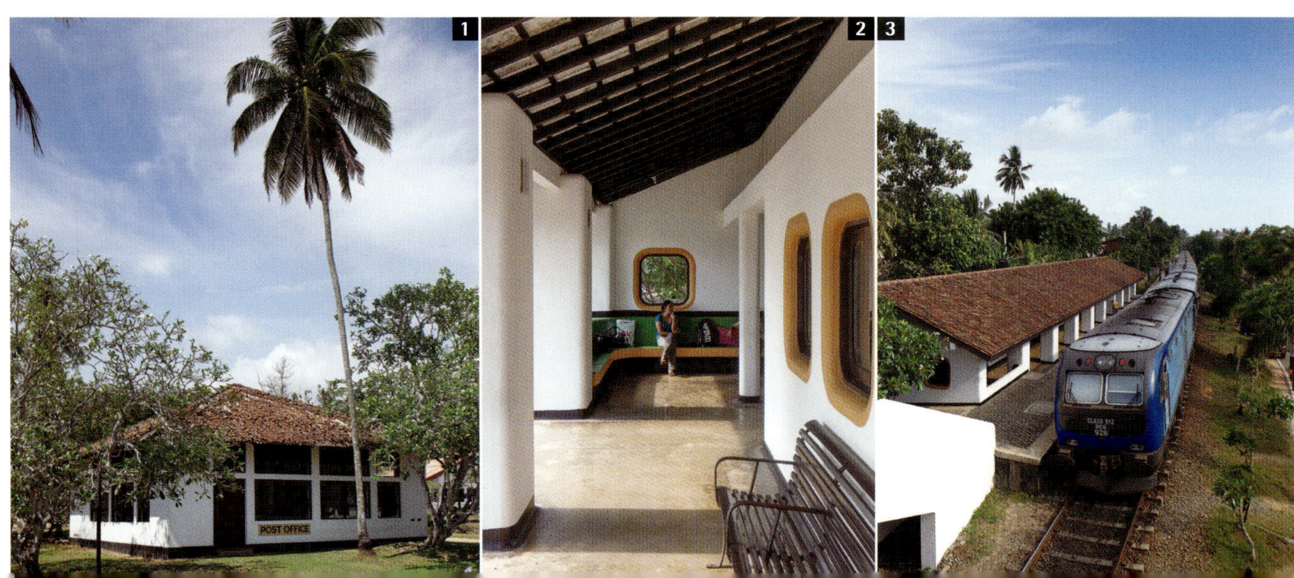

# The Serendib Hotel

(aka Avani Hotel)
Bentota
1969



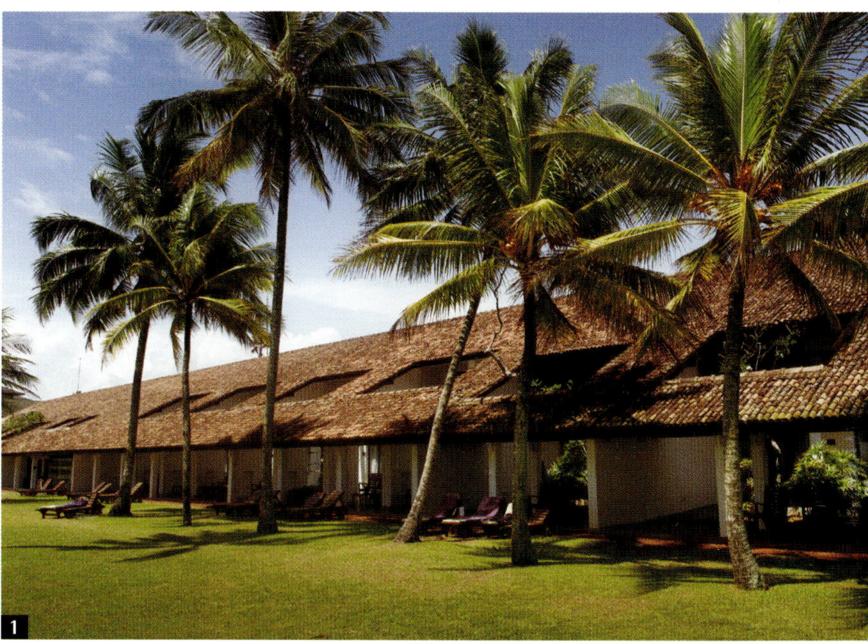

1 The original Serendib wing dating from 1970.

The Serendib was one of two hotels that Bawa built beside the beach at Bentota. While the Bentota Beach was conceived as an up-market hotel, the Serendib was intended to cater to budget travellers and was inspired by traditional government rest houses: two levels of rooms stretched out along the back of the beach on either side of a central restaurant with corridor access along the land-side.

The service accommodation was arranged along the side of the road to create a courtyard garden and shield the landside of the hotel from the railway. A perpendicular entrance route ran from a large *porte-cochère* across the courtyard, past a peacock enclosure and a bar, and through the dining room to the coconut grove at the edge of the beach. Visitors arrived to the crashing sound of distant waves and the screech of peacocks and were met by staff in brightly coloured sarongs and saris — designed by Bawa's assistants. The simple rooms were cross-ventilated and included a sculptural bathroom unit and a protected outside sitting area. The public areas were adorned with artworks by Ismeth Raheem and the furniture was designed by Pheroze Choksy.

The Serendib proved to be very popular and five years later a new three-storey wing was added to a design by Raheem and Choksy along with a swimming pool and a beautiful café pavilion, beginning a gradual process of gentrification. The new wing was configured to solve the noise problems that resulted from cross-ventilation — the access corridors were set back from the rooms and linked across by staircases.

More recently, the Serendib has lost its beautiful name and has been upgraded, but in gaining extra stars much of its original charm has been sacrificed. The rooms, now bigger, are in tropical anywhere-land while the beautiful poolside café has been bowdlerised. On the plus side the original restaurant has been moved to make way for a welcome open-sided lounge area, though the new restaurant which runs along the northern edge of the garden is hot and airless. Bizarrely, Raheem's artworks have survived almost 50 years, though, like Michelangelo's paintings on the ceilings of the Sistine Chapel, they have been regularly restored by waiters with felt-tipped pens.

# Lunuganga

Three kilometres inland from Bentota
1948

Geoffrey Bawa bought an abandoned rubber estate in 1948 with a view to transforming it into a landscaped garden that would evoke memories of the English and Italian gardens that he admired. He named it 'Lunuganga' or 'Salt River'.

The estate covered an area of about eight hectares and straddled two hills on a promontory that projected out into the Deduwa Lagoon, about three kilometres inland from Bentota. A dilapidated bungalow sat on the summit of the northern hill with limited views of the lake and was surrounded by a forest of tired old rubber trees.

Over the next 50 years, the garden project would take much of Bawa's free time and money. It evolved as a serendipitous journey without a fixed plan, though its progress was recorded in a series of beautiful drawings, executed at ten-yearly intervals.

"The garden evolved over a long time. The contours showed what the first moves must be. As the land was cleared a wide and splendid view of the lake emerged. Once the initial clearing was done, the main views established themselves ...".

Bawa replaced the drive with an arrival court, hidden in the trees below the southeast corner of the bungalow and turned the original *porte-cochère* at its north-western corner into what would become the main sitting area. The car court was linked by a series of terraces and broad staircases that led to an entrance loggia formed beneath a guest bedroom and then finally to the bungalow's south terrace.

He then cut a swathe through the trees to open up a vista across the southern hill towards the other side of the lake and a distant *dagaba* (stupa). The

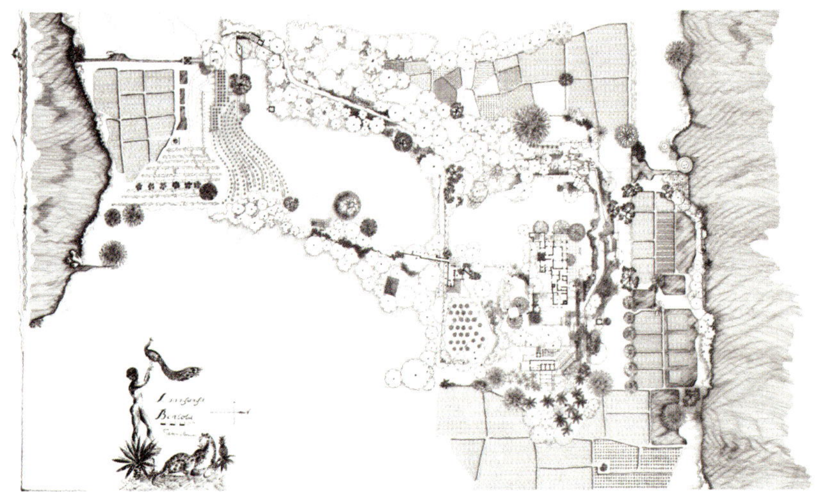

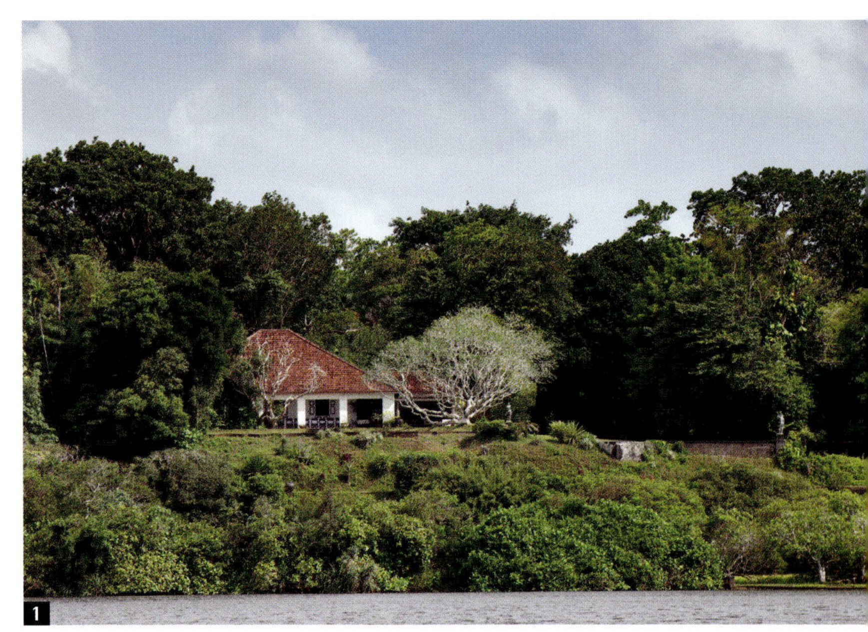

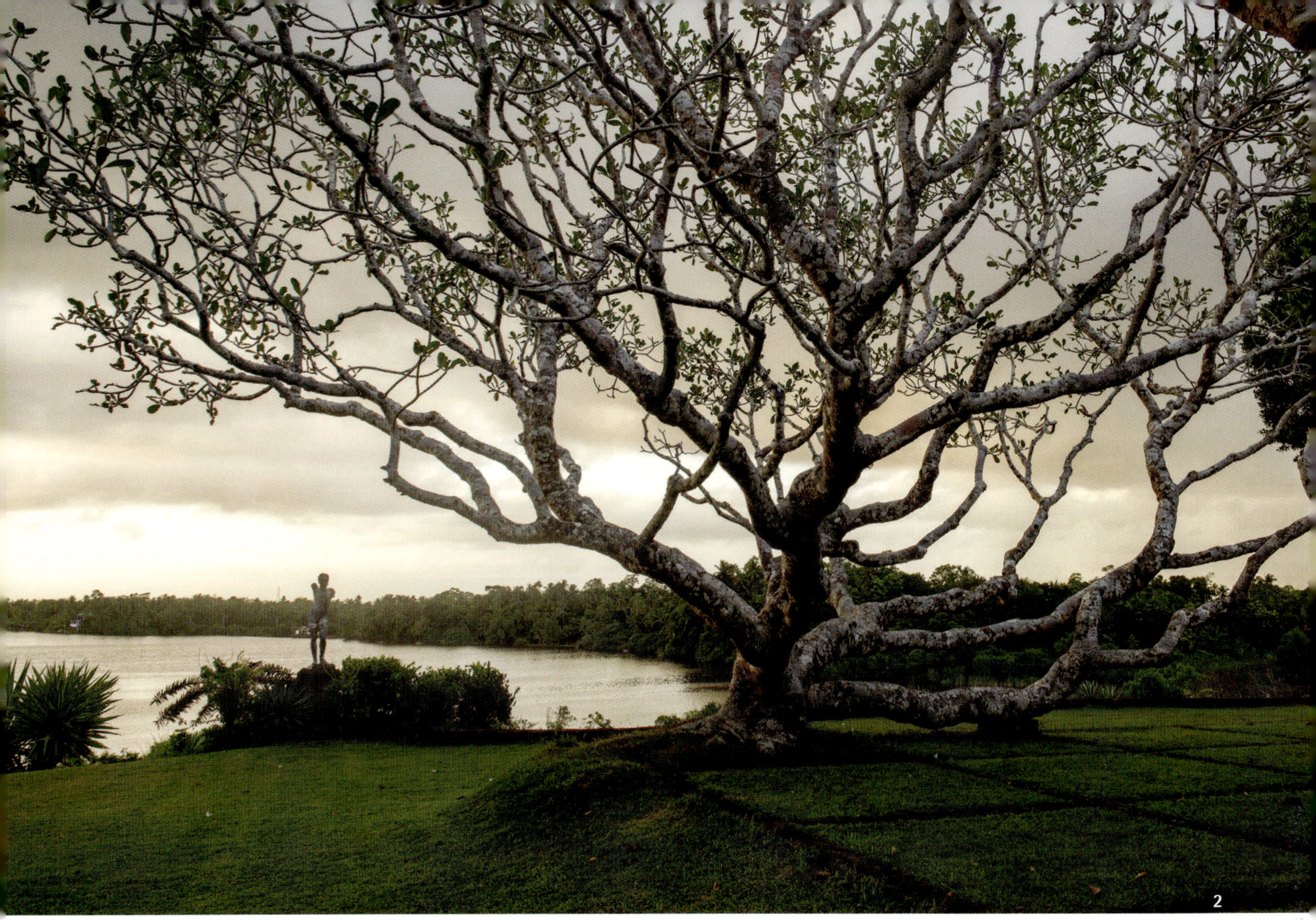

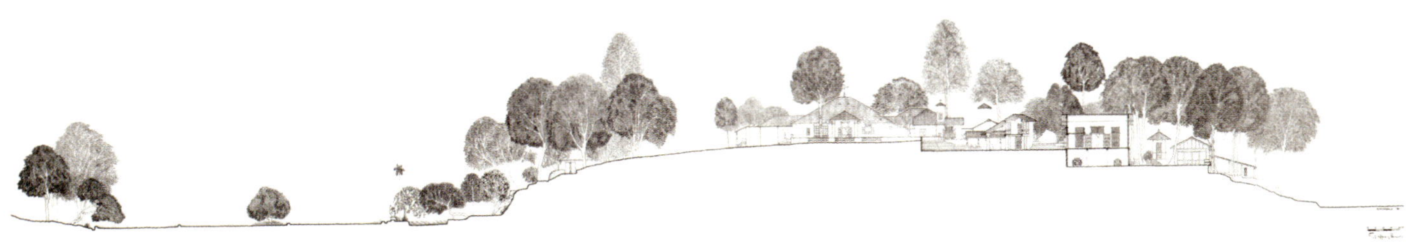



**Opposite** Plan of the Garden, 1985. Bawa Archive.
**1** The first view of the House and the North Terrace as glimpsed from across the lake.

**2** The *araliya* (*Plumeria* sp) on the North Terrace.
**Below** Section through the hill looking north, 1989. Bawa Archive.

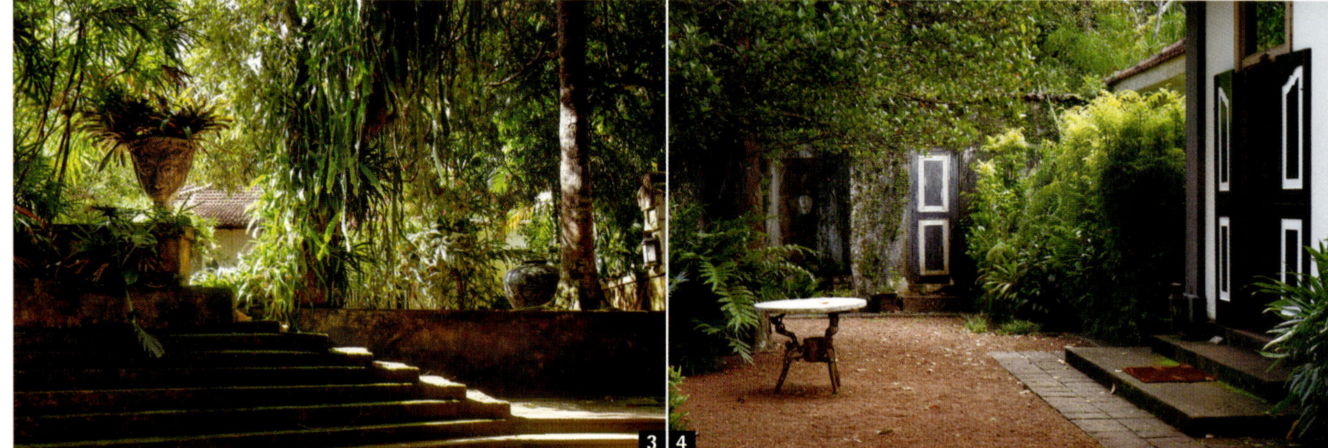

two hills were separated by a road that served the neighbouring property. He buried this in a ha-ha, but connected the hills by a covered bridge.

"The long view to the south ended with the distant temple, but in the middle distance was a ridge with a splendid *moonamal* tree. When I placed a large Chinese jar under it, the hand of man was established in this middle distance. Now the eye stops there, travels to the glimmer of the lake beyond and to the stupa on the crown of the far hill ...".

The bungalow itself contained two bedrooms with a conventional sitting room and dining room as well as kitchens and staff accommodation. Bawa wrapped the bedrooms in a series of verandas and small courtyards. His own room, occupying the southwest corner, developed as a suite of rooms that included a study and a bathroom as well as two pool courts. The sitting room and dining room were barely ever used and acted simply as a route towards the main veranda on the north-western corner.

The land to the north of the bungalow was levelled to make a lawn while, beyond it, the hillside was cut away to create an artificial cliff, criss-crossed by narrow pathways and staircases, with a flat area of water meadows at its foot. This connected to a paddy field that lay below the west end of the main hill and terminated in the mysterious 'Plain of Jars'.

To the east, beyond the kitchens and servants' quarters, Bawa created a series of stepped terraces framed by various buildings. The principal terrace was dominated by a noble pavilion, known as the Sandela, which served as a library and studio. Below it lay the Gothic Court which gave access to a series of farm buildings that were later converted into a gallery and studio.

In the early 1990s Bawa added a bungalow to the southwest corner of the garden beyond the summit of the Cinnamon Hill, but plans to develop the southern terraces came to nothing.

Bawa conceived of Lunuganga as a moving spectacle, a series of scenographic images that change with the season, the time of day, the mood. Its separate but connected spaces can be moved through at leisure — and an infinite number of different promenades combining different areas are conceivable. On arrival, however, there is a carefully choreographed route: The visitor is offered a first distant glimpse of the north front of the house from the causeway over the Dedduwa Lake, but the approach route swings

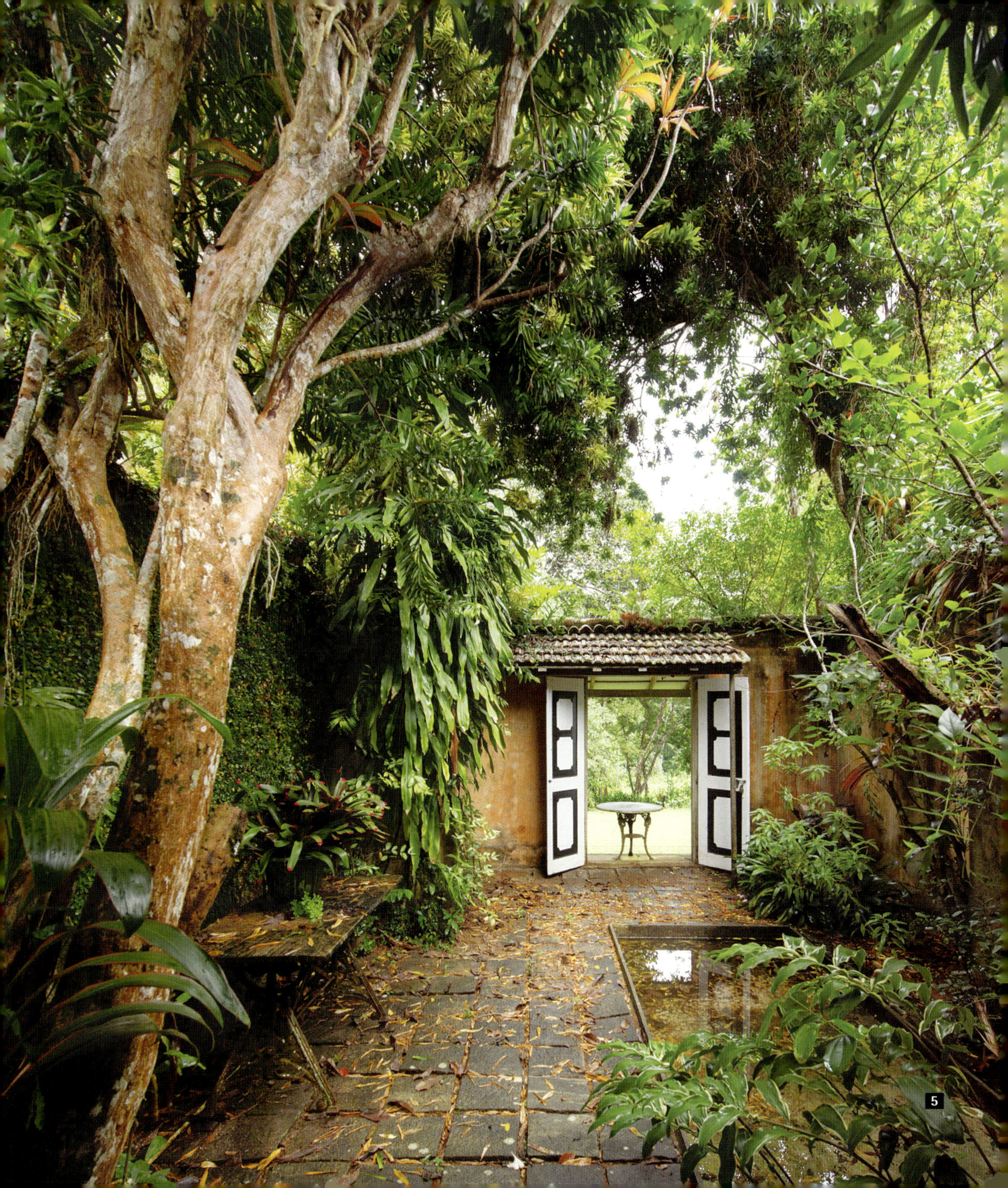

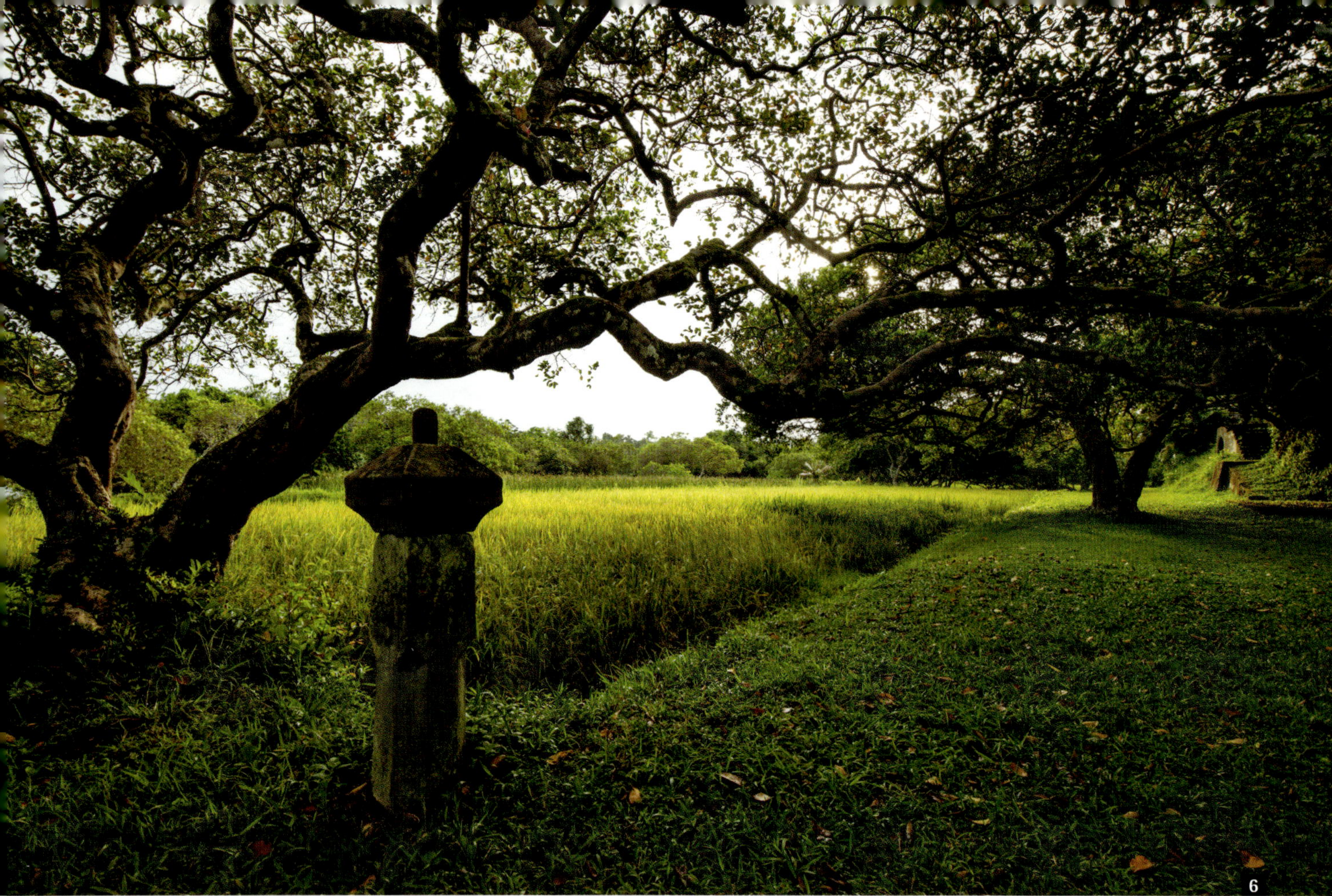



around in a circle to arrive from the south east at the main gate which lies, hidden in the trees, at the foot of the northern hill. From there the disoriented visitor climbs up through the trees to arrive on the southern terrace at the epicentre of the garden where, as if in a game of Blindman's Bluff, the blindfold is removed and all is revealed.

Over the years the original rubber trees were replaced by a rich variety of mainly indigenous trees and plants and the garden was been liberally embellished with pavilions, walls and statues. The result is a civilized wilderness. It is not a garden of manicured parterres, of flowers and fountains, but a succession of hidden surprises and sudden vistas, a composition of green on green, an ever-changing play of light and shade, a landscape of memories and ideas.

Unlike his brother Bevis's introspective garden at Brief, some 15 kilometres away to the north, Bawa planned Lunuganga around a series of outward vistas, drawing distant features into the composition to create a civilised garden within the larger garden of Sri Lanka.

By 1990 the garden was in its prime and Christopher Bon joined forces with Dominic Sansoni to produce a book of haunting black and white photographs that was published in Singapore. Geoffrey supplied the minimal texts[1]:

"Looking back on the making of the garden, seeing it as it is now, it seems to me almost inevitable that it should be there ...".

The garden now seems so natural that it is hard to imagine how much effort went into its creation. Nor is it apparent how much effort is

6 The rice paddy and the Broad Walk.

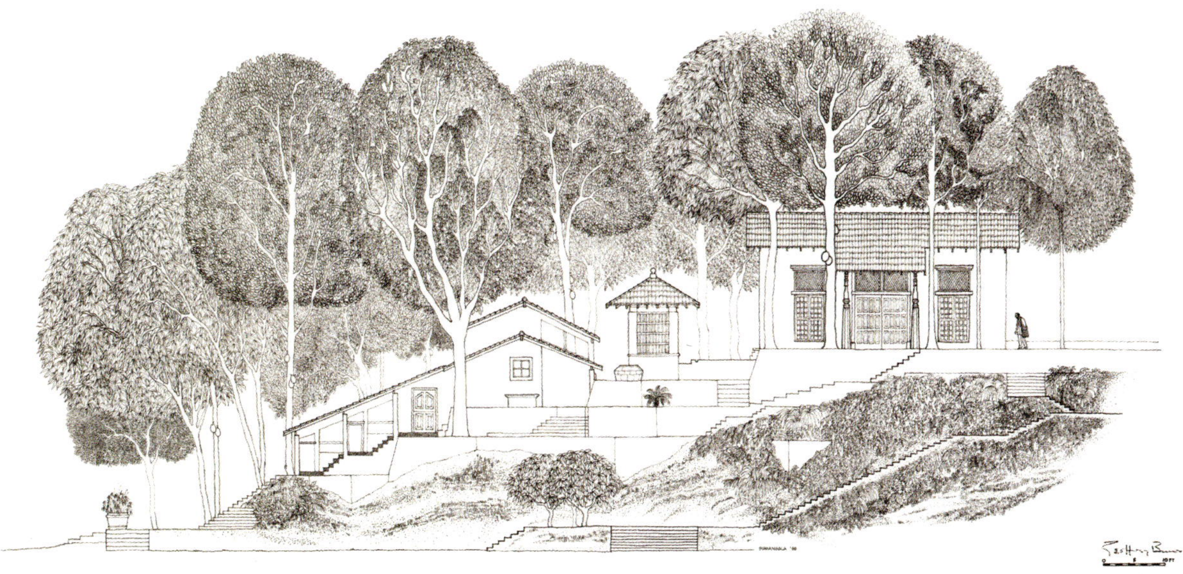



needed to maintain its air of careful casualness:
ignore it for a week and the paths will clog up
with leaves, for a month and the lawns will run
wild, for a year and the terraces will crumble and
the jungle will return. It's a work of art, not of
nature, the contrivance of a single mind and a
hundred pairs of hands working with nature to
produce something that is 'supernatural'.

Today Lunuganga is owned by the Geoffrey
Bawa Trust and managed by Michael Daniel and
Asha de Silva, both landscape architects. It is open
to the public and operates as a boutique hotel.

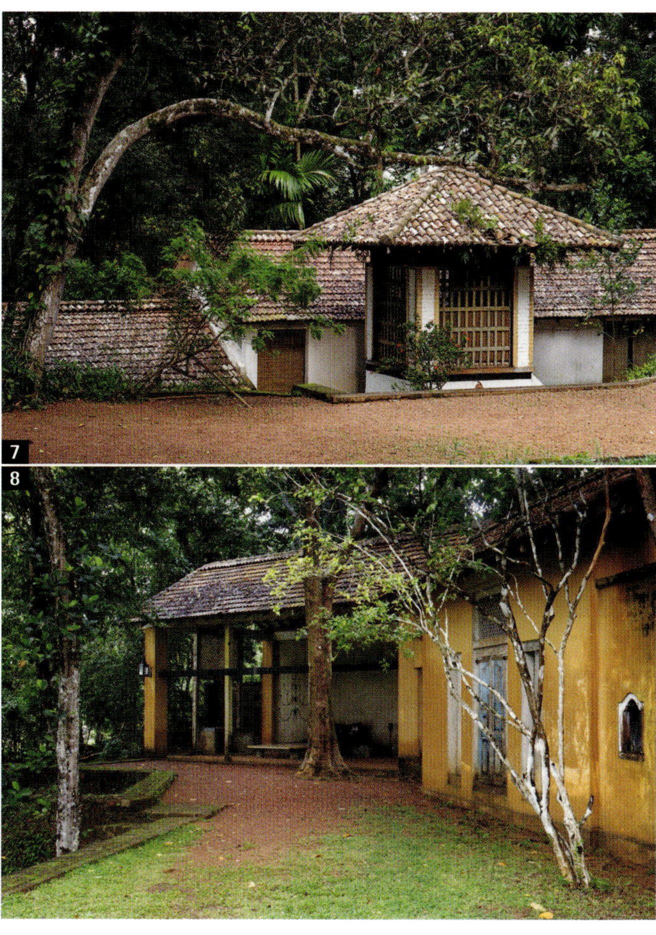

[1] Bawa, Geoffrey, Christoph Bon and Dominic Sansoni. *Lunuganga*.
Singapore: Times, 1990

# The Ena de Silva House

## Lunuganga, Bentota

First built in 1960 in Colombo; recreated near Bentota in 2015–16

Bawa's design for the Ena de Silva house marked a shift away from Tropical Modernism to what might be termed 'Contemporary Vernacular'. The client was an aspiring artist/craftsman, married to a retired Inspector General of Police and she and her husband had acquired a corner plot on Alfred Place with an area of 750 square metres — considered at that time to be small. She wanted a modern house that would incorporate traditional features, with an office for her husband and an atelier for her and her son.

Bawa worked closely with Ena de Silva and together they created an introspective house that turned its back on the busy street and focused on a large internal courtyard or *meda midula*. Contained within a high surrounding wall, the house was prefaced on its street frontage by a long covered loggia. A diminutive street door opened to a transverse strip of garden and revealed the main entrance, an ancient temple door from Jaffna. This opened to a narrow stone-paved tunnel through the outer single-storey front wing of the house that led to the encircling veranda of the main courtyard. The outer wing contained the garage, the office, a guest suite and the atelier. Across the court, a two-storey pavilion contained the dining space and the open sitting room on its ground floor and three bedrooms on its first floor. On the right a low linking wing contained the kitchens and staff quarters.

The courtyard was the main lung of the house and its surrounding verandas served as its principal living spaces. Initially covered in grass, it was later paved in river pebbles and incorporated four massive grinding stones at its corners. The verandas were supported on turned trunks of

**1** View across the courtyard towards the studio, 1962.
**2** View across the courtyard towards the dining veranda, 1962.

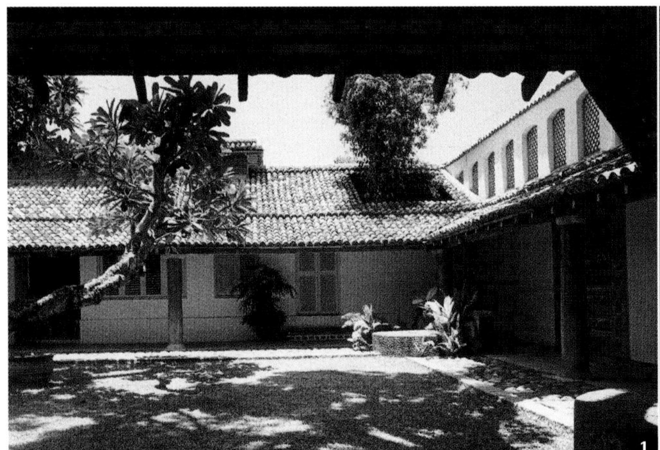
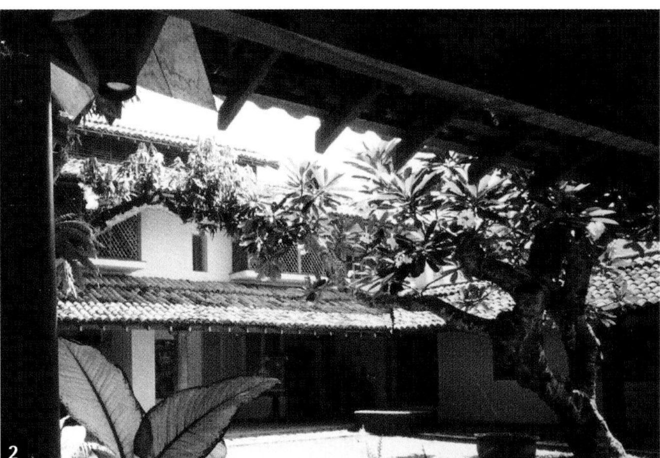

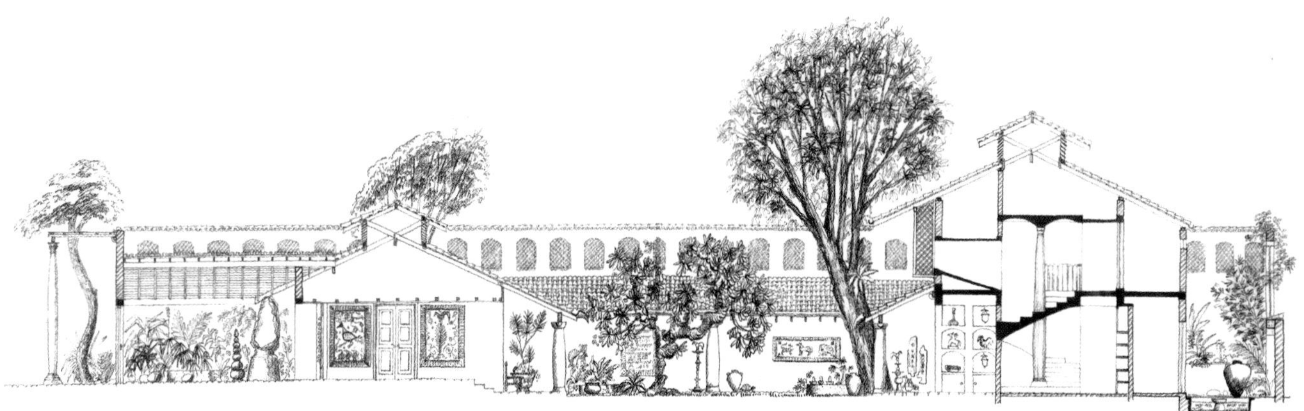

satinwood that incorporated granite headstones and bases. The roofs were of half-round clay tiles. Ena wanted 'windows that could be used for serenading at night' at first-floor level, so Bawa created projecting bay windows that were enclosed by timber lattice. The staircase was a spiral, but unlike the free-standing concrete stair of the Deraniyagala House it was contained within walls, as if in some ancient castle.

Soon after occupying the house, Ena set up a batik workshop with Laki Senanayake. After the death of her husband she retired to her family home at Aluvihare where she ran a craft cooperative and rented her house to the artist Saskia Pringiers. When the Pringiers moved out in 2010 she was forced to sell the house to a private hospital and, in spite of it being one of the most important Asian houses of the 20th century, it was tragically demolished to make way for a car park.

The Geoffrey Bawa Trust managed to acquire many of its key elements and it is currently being rebuilt on the edge of the Lunuganga Estate where it will house an exhibition of Ena de Silva's work.

**Above** Section by Laki Senanayake, 1962. Bawa Archive.
**3** The dining veranda, *circa* 2015.
**4** One of four millstones in the courtyard, *circa* 2015.

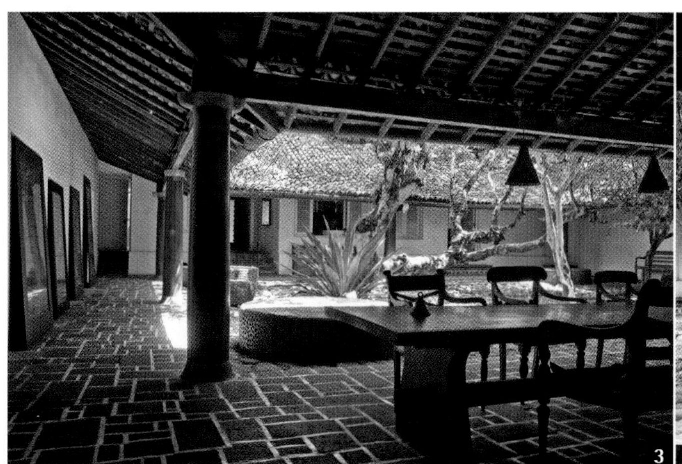

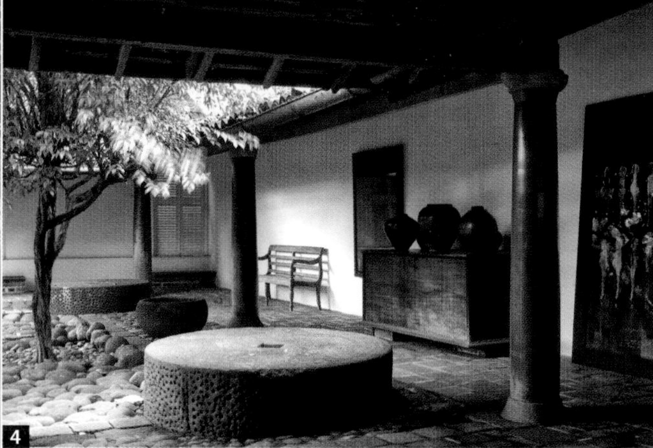

# The Neptune Hotel

(aka Heritance Ayurveda Maha Gedara)
Beruwela

First built 1974; remodeled in 2010

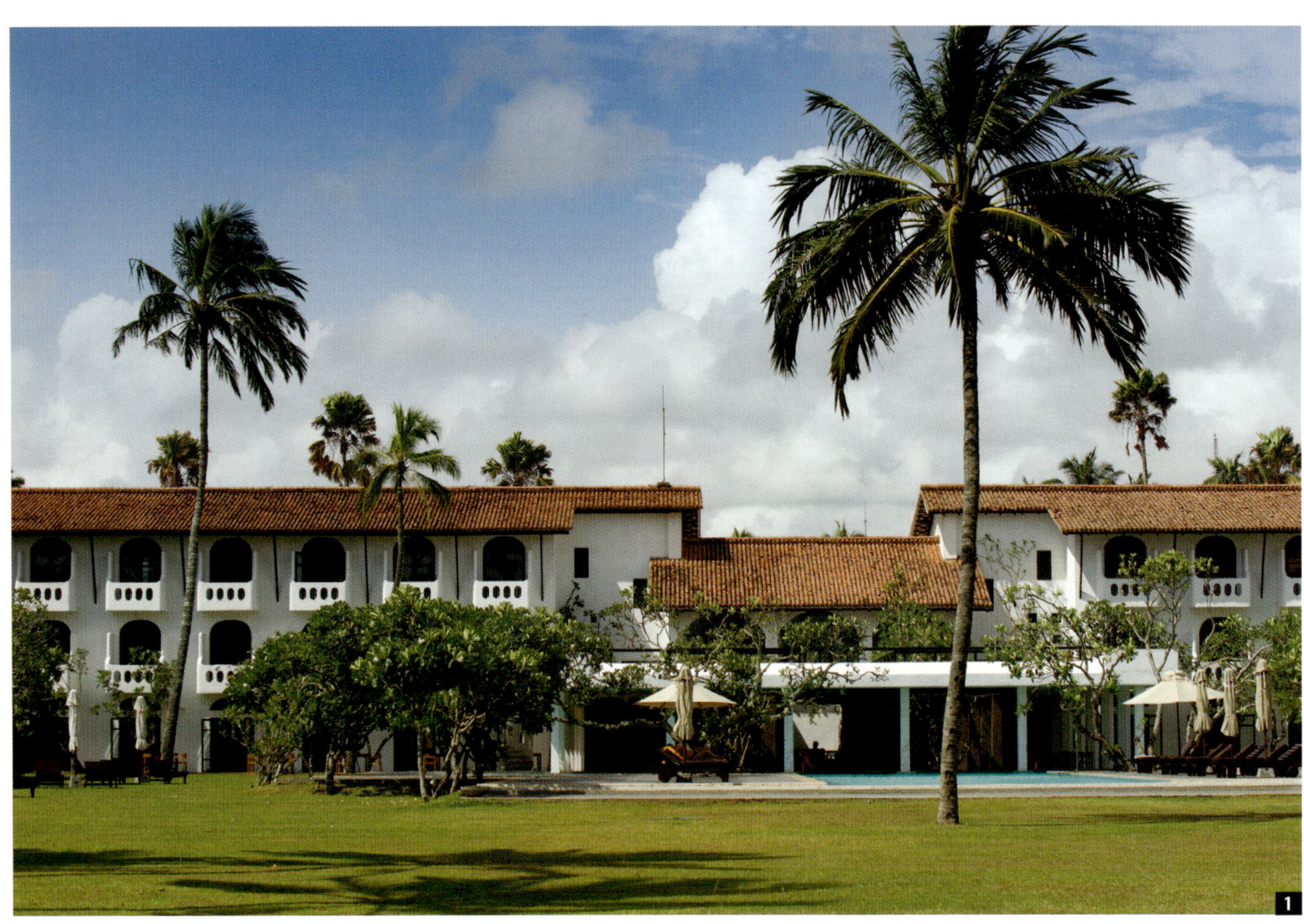

1 View from the edge of the beach to the pool and hotel.

The Neptune Hotel was built on the fringe of the Moorish coastal town of Beruwela. Although it faces an expanse of wide sandy beach, the sea is quite treacherous for much of the year. Bawa therefore deployed three double-storey ranges of rooms to create a large garden court that opened to the back of the beach with a generous swimming pool at its centre. He then turned the entrance approach into a mini jungle around a large wildlife pond, and used the excavated

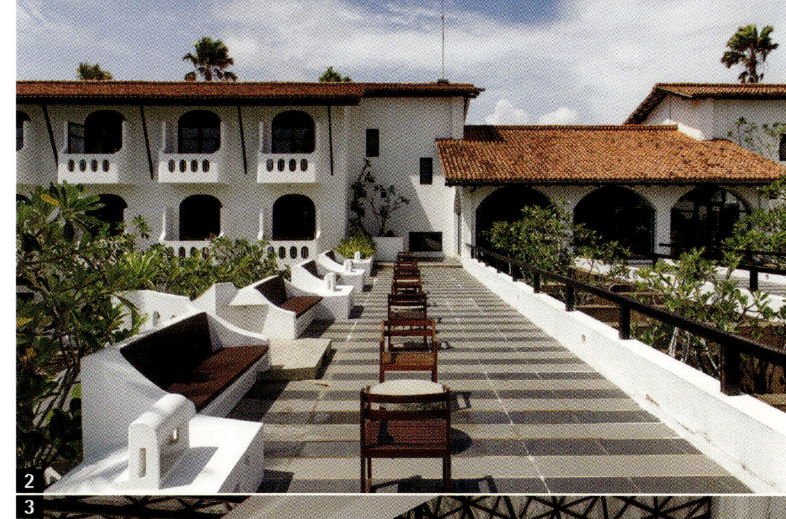

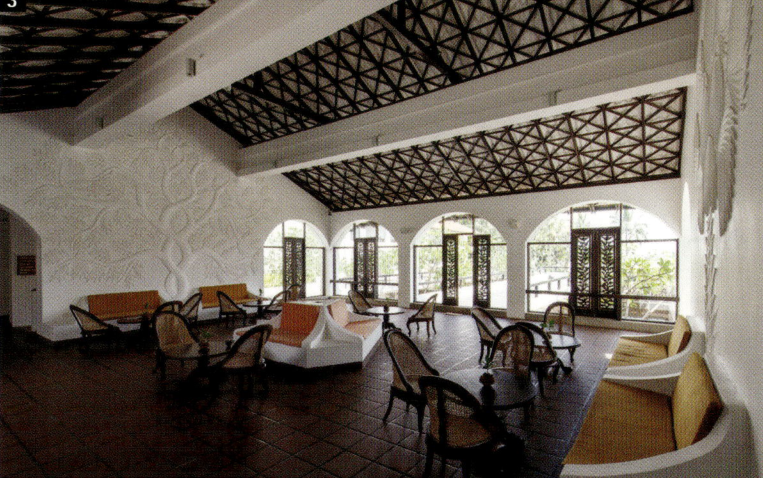

2 The raised terrace above the
dining room and pool.
3 The upper lounge with reliefs
by Laki Senanayake.
4 Façade detail.
5 Staircase linking the pool to
the raised terrace.

material to form a ramp that brought visitors
to an entrance at first-floor level. The reception
space opened on to a generous terrace that gave
views of the sea and covered the main restaurant
and a part of the pool.

Anura Ratnavibushana was the project
architect and the design reveals a sculptural
plasticity which often characterised his work.
Laki Senanayake produced the plaster reliefs that
adorn the walls of the upper reception area. Bawa
was concerned that loose paintings were often
removed by light-fingered guests and persuaded
Laki to create individual murals for every bedroom.
This he did in relay, one colour at a time, with a
team of assistants.

In 2010 the hotel was converted to a spa
and rechristened with the instantly forgettable
mouthful 'Heritance Ayurveda Maha Gedara'.
Vinod Jayasinghe expertly refurbished the core
Bawa hotel, while the spa facilities were added
within a new group of buildings to one side of
the hotel. Sadly, Laki's miraculous murals were
painted over.

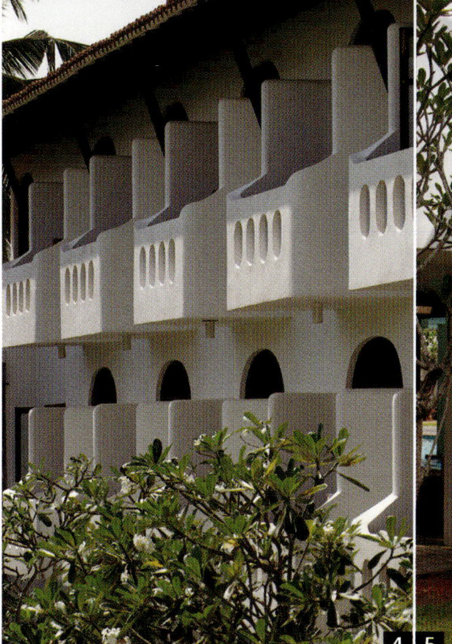

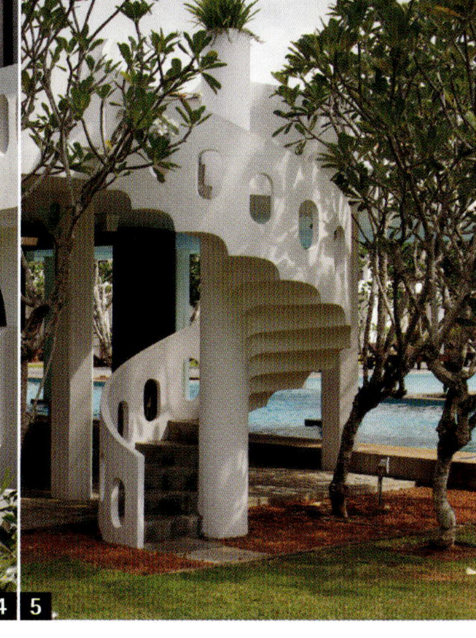

# The Blue Water Hotel

Wadduwa

1996

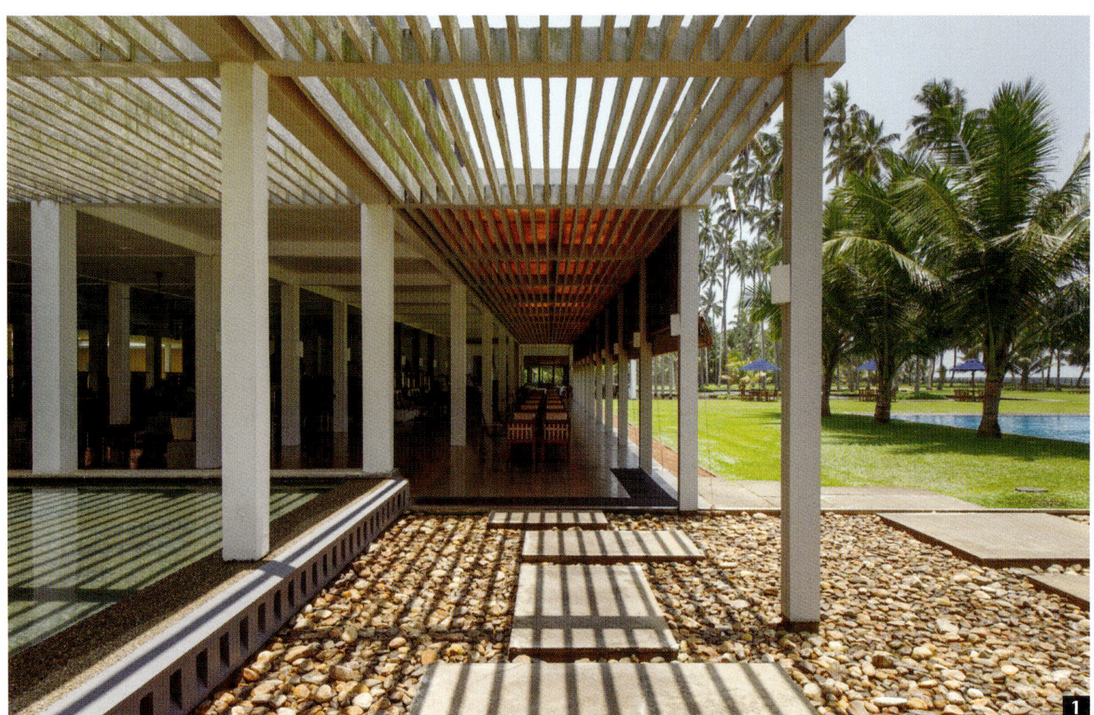

1 The restaurant pergola.

Although Bawa designed a number of hotels for sites in Colombo, including two projects for extending the famous Mount Lavinia Hotel, none of these was actually built. His closest hotel to the capital is the Blue Water, built for Ajit Wijesekera at Wadduwa in 1996.

The hotel occupies a coconut grove that stretches from the railway line to the sea and overlooks an inhospitable beach. It was conceived as a vast suburban *palazzo*. A monumental *porte-cochère* indicates an entry point through a high boundary wall; this opens to a long covered walkway that runs beside a large grass court, passing the reception and ending in a columnated loggia that offers a view through the coconut trees towards the sea. Beyond this, a large swimming pool connects to an outside café.

The sequence of spaces is carefully controlled and the palette of materials is light in tone and muted in colour. The hotel's generous scale and its proximity to the capital have made it popular for ceremonies and celebrations. It has recently been extended towards the south and now incorporates a conference centre and a spa, both designed by Channa Daswatte.

1 The restaurant pergola.
2 View from the edge of the beach.
3 Staircase.
4 The reception desk.

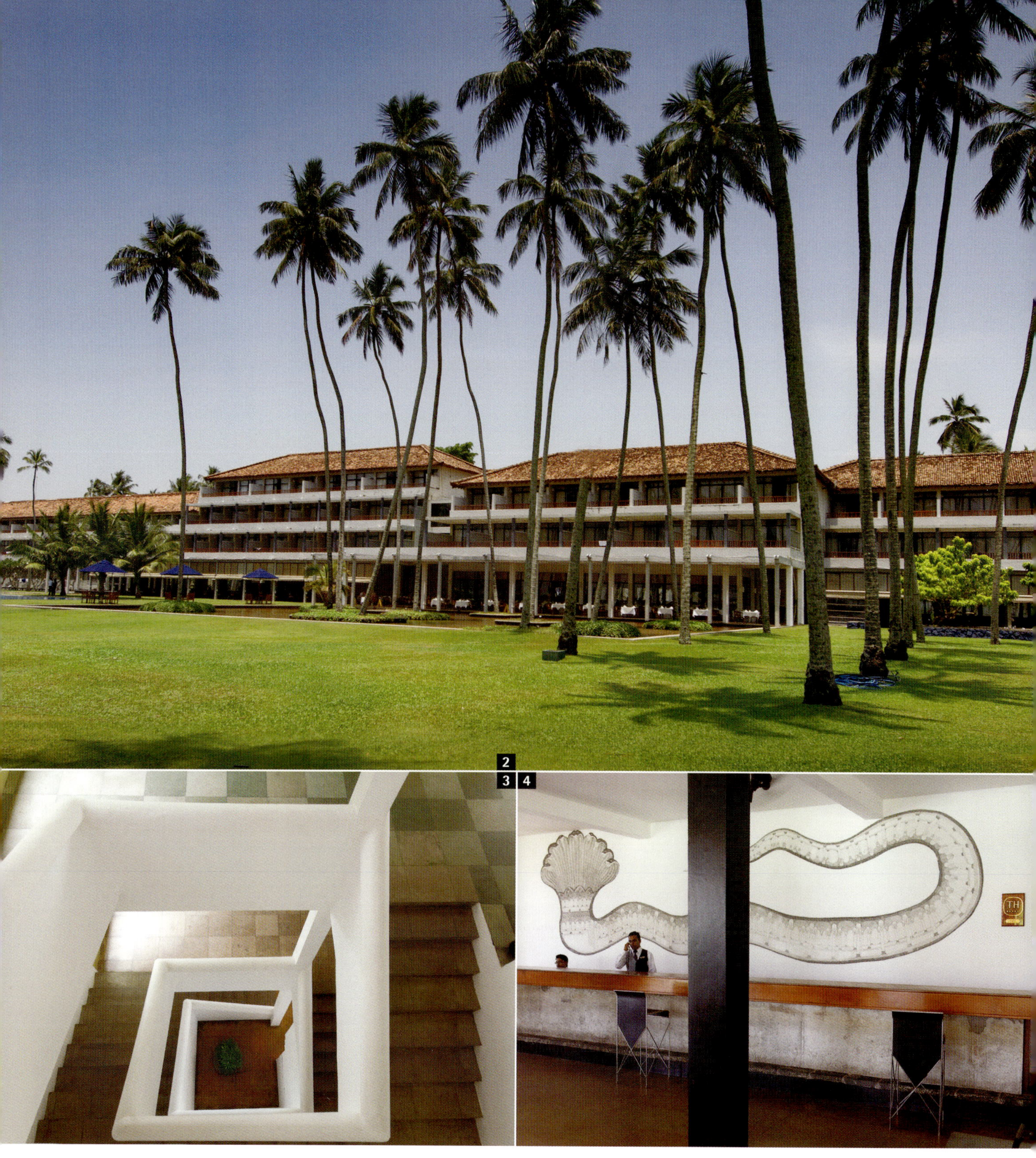

# The Institute for Integral Education

(aka The Subodhi Centre)
Pilyandala
1978—1981

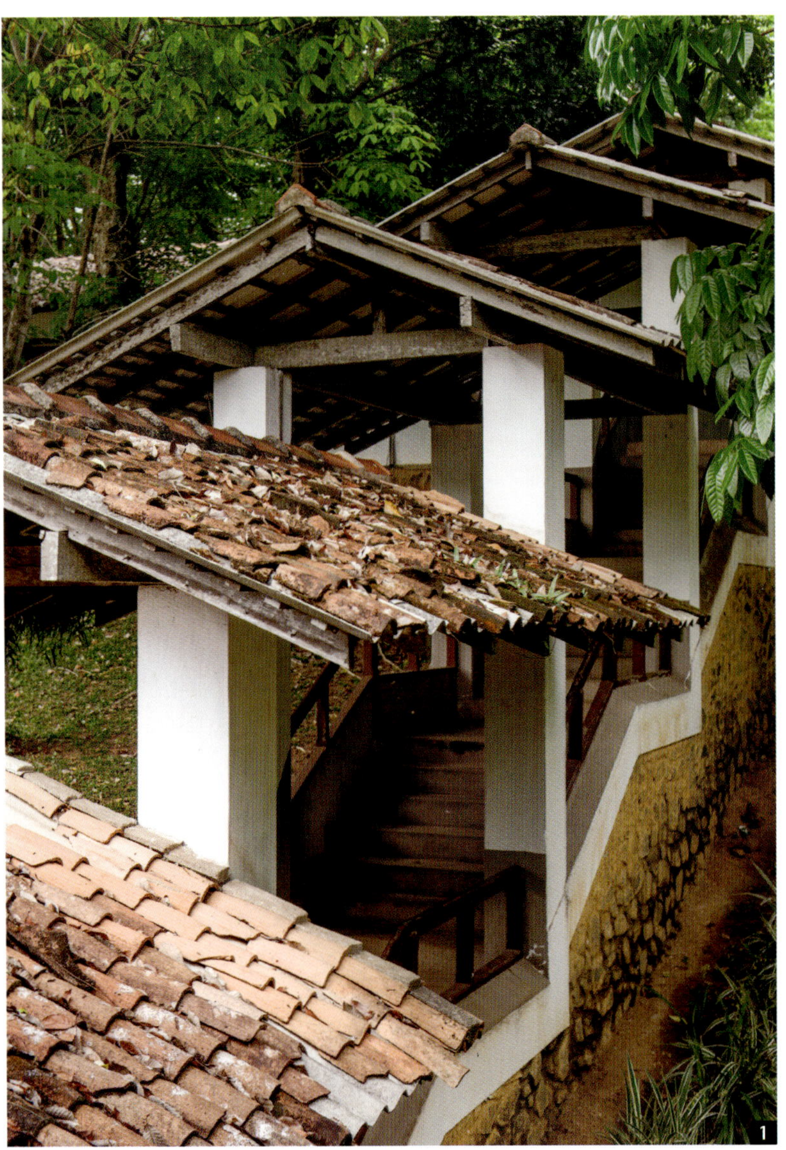

**1** The staircase linking up to the dormitories.

The Institute for Integral Education was created by the Catholic Church as the setting for residential courses intended mainly for school-leavers and young people, and was funded by a German charity called Misereor. It occupies a former rubber plantation on the sloping east bank of the Bolgoda Lake and is close to the Moratuwa University campus. The site is divided by a steep-sided valley that has been cut by an occasional stream.

The general layout, established by Bawa on site using 'sticks and string', was conceived as a sequence of pavilions, loggias and links. The buildings are modest and simply built and demonstrate Bawa's skill at exploiting a terrain.

Visitors arrive at an entrance pavilion at the top southeast corner of the site. To one side is the library, a square building with a stepped roof, reminiscent of a Buddhist preaching hall. Below to the right is the main open-sided auditorium. A covered link plunges into the earth to become a subterranean passage before breaking out to join the central loggia that bridges over the bed of the stream. To the north a wonderful cascading staircase climbs up the side of the valley and connects to residential blocks that are strung out along the contours.

Although fairly run down, the centre is still a place of peace and contemplation.

**2** A typical Bawa roofscape.
**3** The auditorium.
**4** In-built seats in the central bridge building.
**5** The auditorium interior.

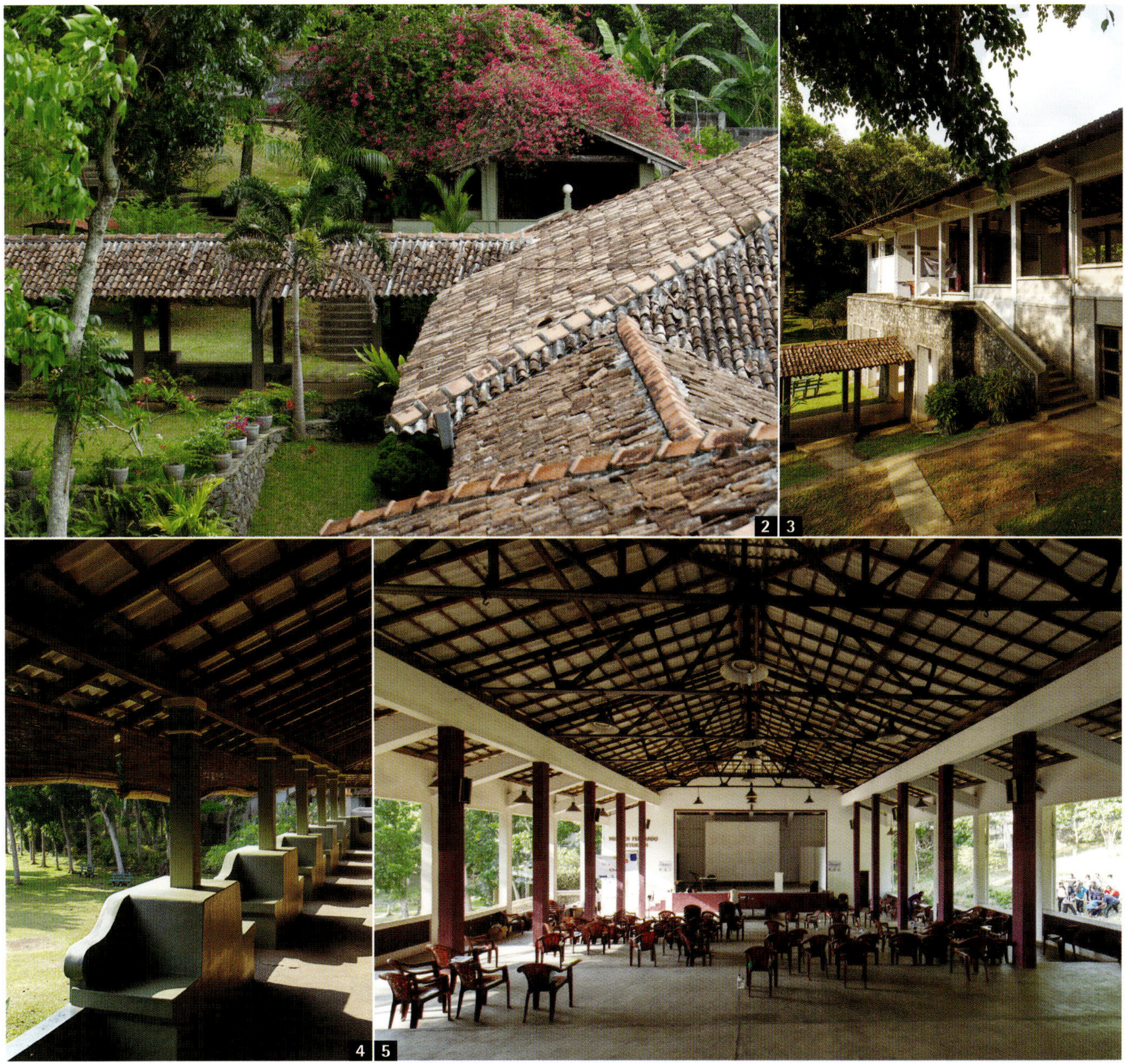

# Bawa at Risk

These are buildings that have suffered from insensitive refurbishment or are in need of drastic repairs and are threatened with extinction.

## a The Keuneman House (1967)
### 27th Lane, Colombo - Colpetty

Pieter Keuneman was Bawa's distant cousin and became housing minister in the SLFP government of 1970. Bawa created for him an inverted house on a tiny plot: the ground floor was given over to a car port and the MP's office; the bedrooms were on the middle floor; and the sitting room and garden terrace were on the top. The ground floor is now used as a hairdressing salon and the house is in poor condition.

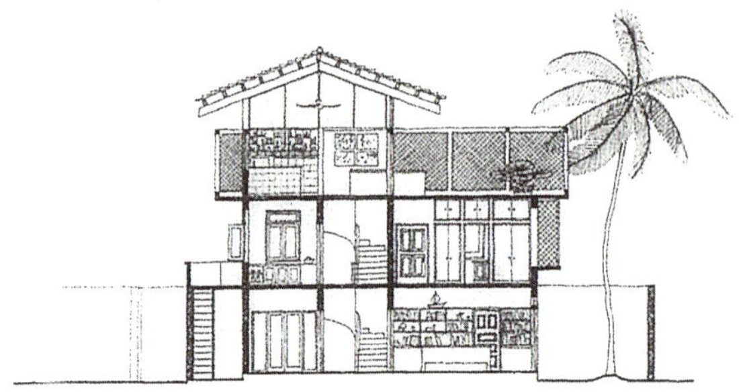

**Above** Section through the house showing the top-floor sitting room and garden terrace, 1985. Bawa Archive.

## b Classroom Block for Bishop's College (1960–63)
### Boyd Place, Colombo - Colpetty

The classroom block occupied three storeys with two upper floors of classrooms and an open loggia at ground floor. The clearly articulated façades were designed as a breathing wall with perforated concrete panels hung from cantilevered beams in the manner of Tropical Modernism. A sculpted bishop by Bawa's friend Lydia Duchini stood at the foot of the staircase. The block has been much altered and is now in poor condition.

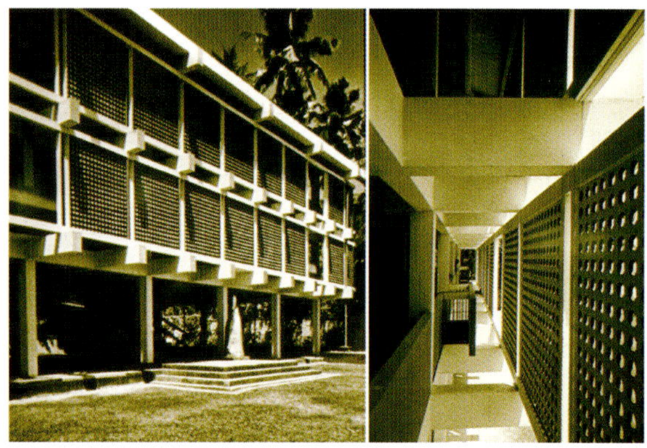

**Above** Photographs from 1962 showing the façade.

## c Two Classroom Blocks for St Thomas' Prep School (1958–60)
### Galle Road, Colombo - Colpetty

This was one of the first projects assigned to Bawa after he joined Edwards Reid & Begg. The western block, parallel to the railway line, is on three floors and was clad in a breathing wall of hollow concrete blocks. The two-storey eastern block was placed at right angles and had deep overhanging eaves and a continuous spandrel panel at first-floor level decorated with concrete reliefs made by artist Anil Jayasuriya. The reliefs have sadly disappeared and both blocks are in poor condition.

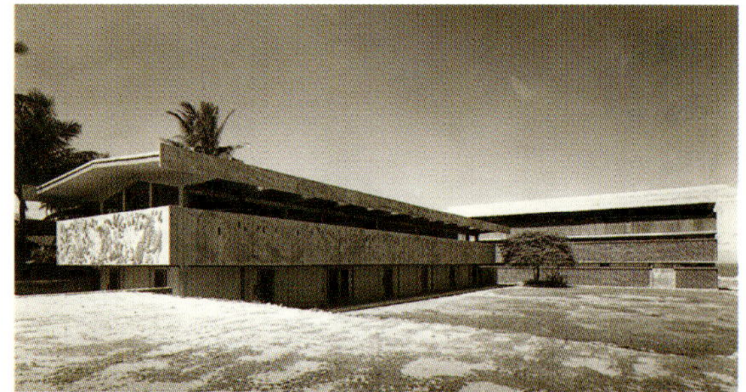

**Above** Photograph from 1962 showing the sculpted relief panels.

### d   Automobile Association Offices (1959-60)
#### Marcan Markar Mawatha, Colombo - Galle Face

This was designed to house the headquarters of the Automobile Association with a member's bar on its ground floor. The front façade carried a dramatic upward-curving concrete canopy which shaded a small terrace. Now in poor condition, it is hemmed in by a new building.

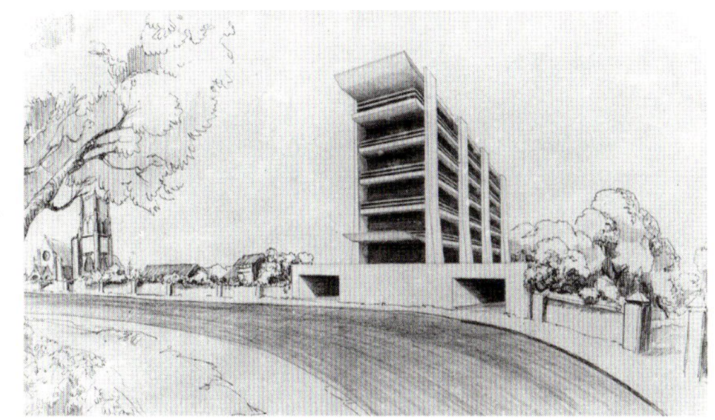

**Above** Perspective drawing from 1960. Bawa Archive.

### e   Druvi de Saram Houses (1987-94)
#### Ward Place, Colombo - Cinnamon Gardens

Miriam de Saram owned a substantial villa in Ward Place. In 1987 Bawa converted the back part of the house, adding new pavilions and courtyards to create a separate dwelling for her son Druvi. Later, Druvi commissioned Bawa to remodel the front part of the house. The front house was occupied by a succession of shops and is now home to an advertising agency, while the rear house has fallen into disrepair.

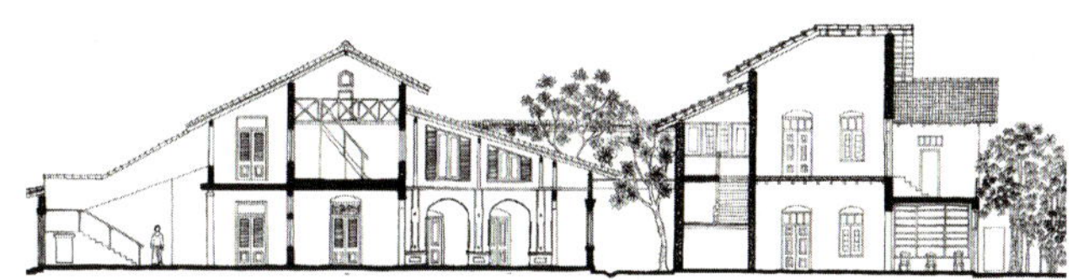

**Above** Section through the front part of the house (Anjalendran, 2015).

### f   Wattala Convent (1965-71)
#### Church Road, Wattala

The convent was conceived as a chain of cells arranged in echelon pattern around a lozenge shaped courtyard. The project architect was Anura Ratnavibushana. Though still occupied by a small core of elderly nuns it is now quite run down.

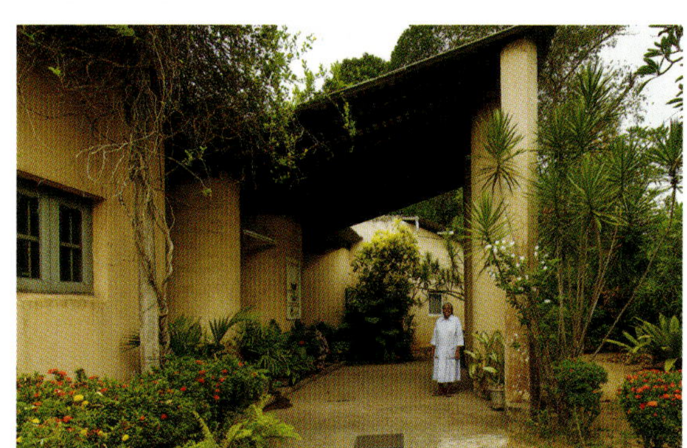

**Above** The entrance to the convent.

## g Yahapath Endera Farm Convent (1965-71)
### Halgasena – south of Hanwella

Bawa was commissioned by the nuns of the Good Shepherd Convent to create a residential farm school for girls. The nuns occupied a converted estate bungalow at the southern end of a dramatic ridge. Assisted by Anura Ratnavibushana, Bawa added a chapel, a dormitory and various agricultural buildings and, in a later phase, a silk farm. The buildings employed simple traditional technologies with locally-produced building materials and were built at minimum cost. The nuns eventually sold the farm to the la Salle Brothers who ran it as a Boys' Town for a few years. It was then sold to a brewery and is now in a very dilapidated state.

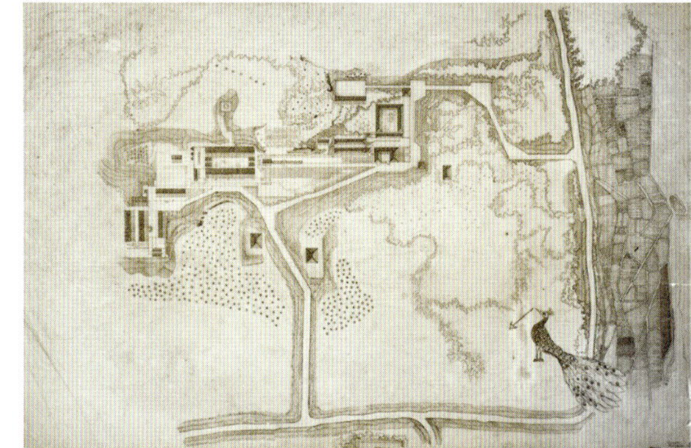

**Above** Site plan, 1969 (Ratnavibushana & Raheem). Bawa Archive.

## h The Ratnapura Tennis Club (1959)
### below the Ratnapura Rest House

The Tennis Club was located on steep ground near the Rest House. The two tennis courts were cut into the hillside below a raked tribune. Tribune, bar and changing rooms were protected by a single sloping roof of corrugated cement supported on jungle timber columns. The buildings survive in dilapidated condition and are used by a martial arts club.

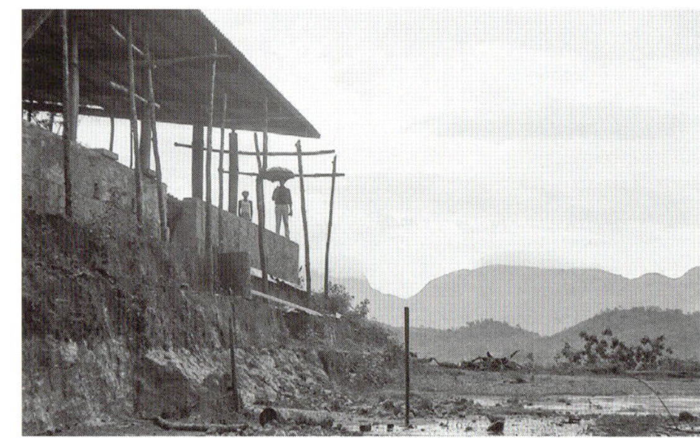

**Above** Geoffrey Bawa on a site visit in 1959.

## i Kalutara Public Library (1970)
### Galle Road, Kalutara (opposite the *dagaba*)

This modest building is tucked away behind the garland boutiques that line the road opposite the Kalutara Temple. It takes the form of a square enclosure under a pyramid roof. The project architect was Turner Wickremasinghe. Though still in use as a library, it is in a poor state of repair.

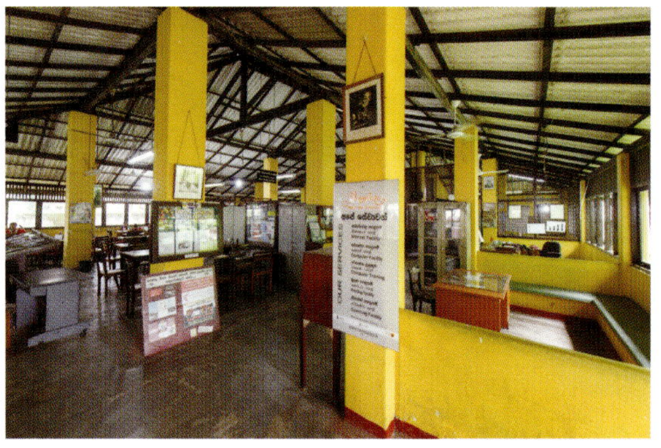

**Above** View of the interior.

# Bawa Transformed

These are buildings that have been altered by the owners to such an extent that they no longer resemble the original. Whilst several are travesties, there are a couple which could be said to have undergone something of a rebirth.

## 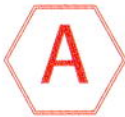 The de Saram Row Houses (1970)
### 5th Lane, Colombo - Colpetty

This design for a row of four houses can be viewed as an experiment with a new urban housing typology. Each house occupied a narrow strip of land and was planned around a series of internal courtyards in the manner of Bawa's own nearby town house. The experiment was not entirely successful — there were problems of noise transmission both from room to room and from house to house, problems that Bawa would later address in his design for the Albert Teo houses in Singapore. Of the four original houses, one has been demolished and two have been ruined by unsightly additions.

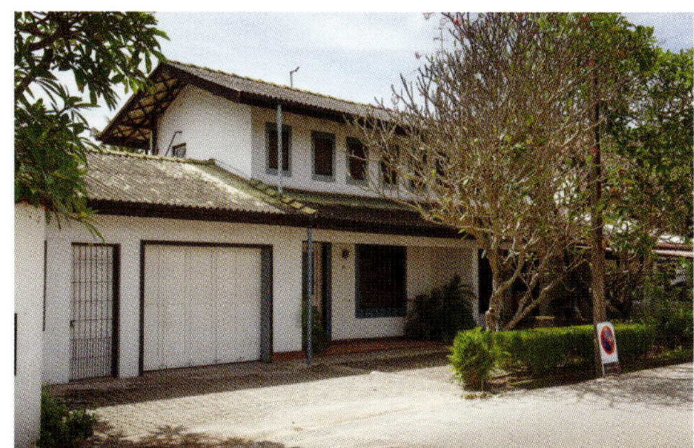

**Above** The sole survivor.

##  The Fernando and Martenstyn Houses
### (1963 and 1978)
### Kannangara Mawatha, Colombo – Cinnamon Gardens

The house that Bawa built for Pin and Pam Fernando in 1963 at the end of a short lane off Kannangara Mawatha was an unremarkable two-storey pavilion set at the centre of a garden. Then, 15 years later, in the corner of the same garden he inserted an astonishing minimalist tower house for their daughter within the branches of a massive Bo Tree. A concrete staircase with thin steel handrails rose as a canted dog-leg connecting a double-height dining space to a first-floor sitting room, a bedroom floor and finally to a tree-top roof terrace.

Now the Bo Tree has gone and the houses have been transformed by a new owner.

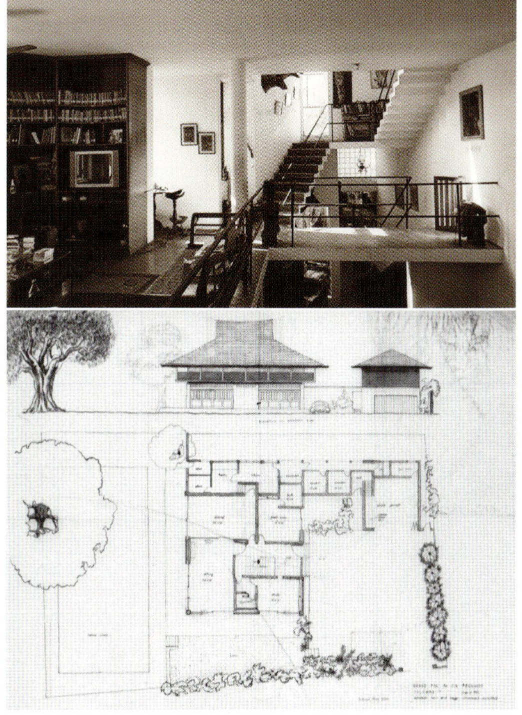

**Top** Photograph of the Martenstyn House staircase, 1998.
**Above** Drawing of the Fernando House, 1963. Bawa Archive.

## C  The National Institute of Management Studies (1975)
### Vidya Mawatha, Colombo – Cinnamon Gardens

This five-storey pavilion adopted the stepped-out section of the Bentota Beach Hotel. This enabled Bawa to insert a surprising internal courtyard at fourth-floor level. The project architect was Vasantha Jacobsen-Chandraratne.

Today the courtyard has been swallowed up in a programme of wholesale internal remodelling and the exterior has been reclad in powder-coated aluminium sheeting.

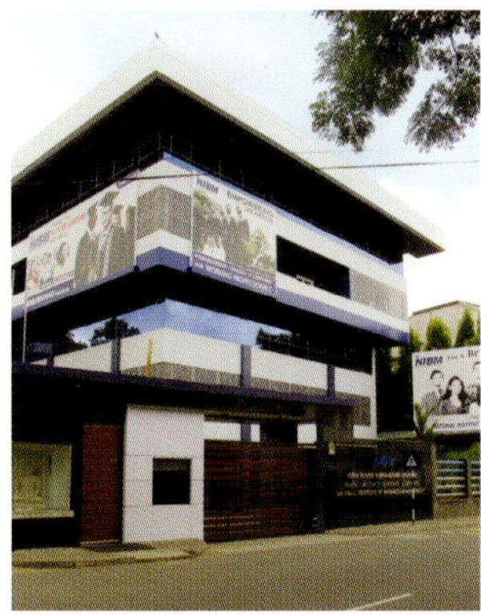

**Above** The new aluminium façades.

## D  The Blue Lagoon Hotel (aka Jetwing Blue) (1965, 2012)
### Talahena, south of Negombo

Bawa's first hotel was built for entrepreneur GEB Milheusen on a spit of land twixt sea and lagoon. The main reception building was placed on the edge of the lagoon and the accommodation was arranged in a series of villas between the lagoon and the sea. Having enjoyed initial success it went into decline after Milheusen's death and operated for a time as a hotel school. In 2012 it was rescued from extinction by architect Vinod Jayasinghe with the travel company Jetwing. Although the new hotel is not a reproduction of its former self, it is faithful to the original idea and many key features, such as the water tower, the *porte-cochère* and the villas, have been retained.

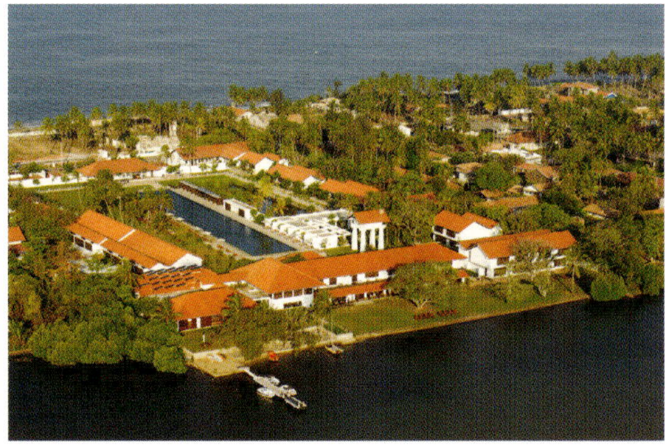

**Above** Aerial view of the newly refurbished hotel.

## E  The Royal Oceanic Hotel (aka Jetwing Beach ) (1986, 2005)
### Negombo

This hotel was designed in 1986 when Bawa was recovering from the two biggest projects of his career. Not one of his best, its most remarkable features were the raised reception area and the associated swimming pool loggia. In 2005 it was acquired by Jetwing who commissioned architect Vinod Jayasinghe to refurbish it. The result is a more stylish version of the original.

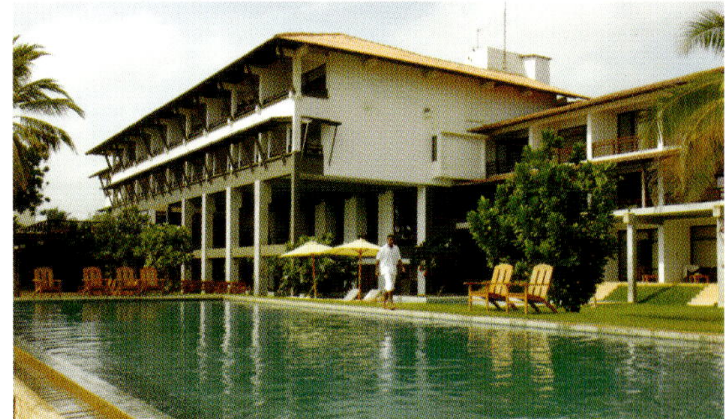

**Above** View of the refurbished reception building, 2010.

## ⬡ F  Bentota Beach Hotel (1967-69)
### Bentota

Bawa raised the hotel on a mound that had once supported a small Dutch Fort, enclosing its base within a massive stone bastion. The main reception areas were located around a pool court and the original 30 rooms were arranged as an 'L' plan on two upper levels with views to the sea and the estuary. It was built in a time of austerity using a palette of local materials. The architects designed all the furniture and fittings and created all of the artworks.

Although it was one of the most beautiful hotels in Asia, it was torn apart by its owners in the mid 1990s: the tiled roofs were replaced with plastic corrugated sheeting, the pool-court was stripped of its vegetation and reduced to a terrazzo trough, the handloom ceilings were ripped out, the beautiful furniture junked. Today, though it bears only a shadowy resemblance to the original design, it is still advertised as a 'Bawa Hotel'.

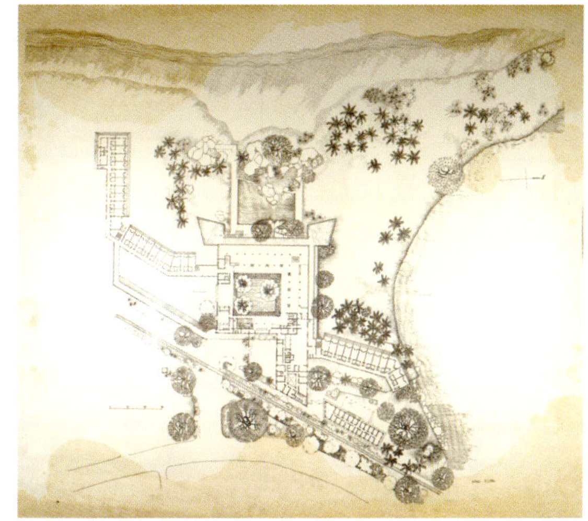

**Above** Plan at upper plinth level, 1975. Bawa Archive.

## ⬡ G  Tourist Police Station (1978)
### Galle Road, Beruwela

This small police station was built to serve the growing number of tourists in the Beruwela area. An external staircase led straight up to the main office at first-floor level. It still survives, though it is now a brightly painted riot of colour — one suspects that Bawa would have approved.

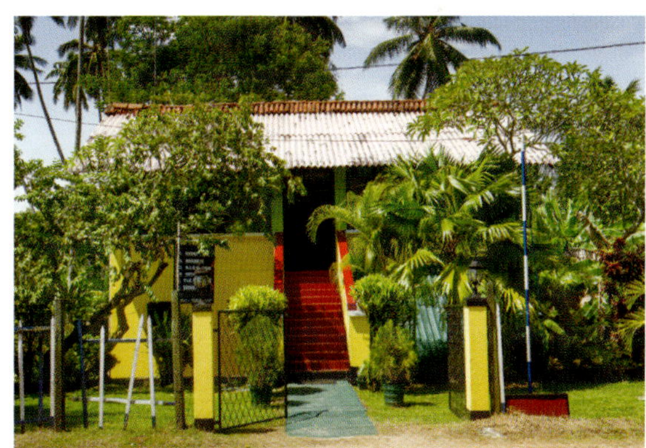

**Above** The brightly coloured Police Station.

# Lost Bawa

These are buildings which have either been demolished or have succumbed to the ravishes of time.

## The British Council Library and Offices (1980)
### Duplication Road, Colombo - Colpetty

Bawa converted a colonial mansion into a new Library and Offices for the British Council in 1980, organising the new additions, which included an auditorium and a residence for the Representative, around a pleasant garden courtyard. British Council Representatives rotate every three years and each one seeks to leave his mark by tinkering with the buildings. Within a few short years Bawa's work was undone and today almost nothing remains of his sensitive intervention.

## Upali Wijewardene House (1959)
### Thurston Road, Colombo - Colpetty

Built for the newspaper proprietor, Upali Wijewardene, this house was an exercise in simple Miesian Modernism, employing a black frame with white-painted brick infill panels. The main living spaces were built at first-floor level around internal courtyards. Later, an extra floor was added with a rooftop swimming pool and a helicopter pad. After Wijewardene's death in an aeroplane crash in 1983, the house began a slow decline and was finally demolished in 2014.

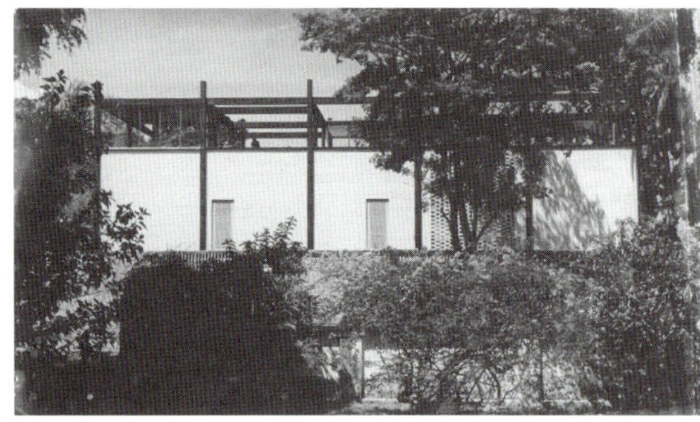

**Above** The garden elevation, 1962.

## Carmen Gunasekera House (1959)
### Dharmapala Mawatha, Colombo - Colpetty

One of Bawa's first projects after he joined Edwards, Reid & Begg, this house was planned as two connected pavilions, which were slid to create implied courtyard spaces. The front pavilion incorporated a Montessori school at basement level.

After serving for several years as a foreign embassy the house was converted to a restaurant in 2014 and most of its distinguishing features were lost.

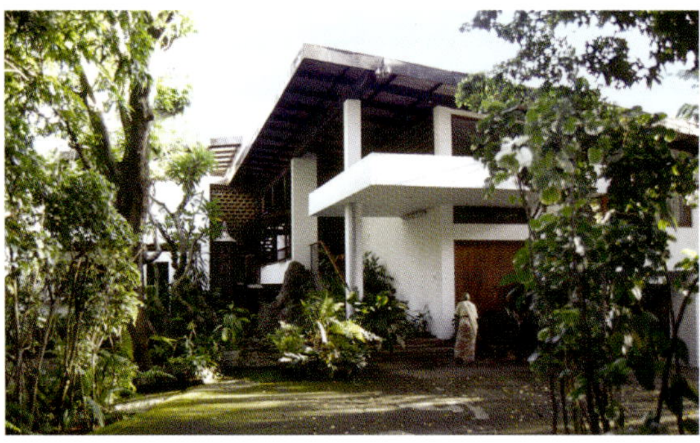

**Above** View from the street, 1998.

# Ekala Industrial Estate (1959)
## Jaela

Bawa designed the Ekala Industrial Estate with Ulrik Plesner on a former coconut estate to the south of Colombo's international airport. The design was in Tropical Modern mode and proposed standard factory units in the form of simple white prisms with long shallow monopitch roofs and pre-cast concrete clerestories. The units proved to be hot and stuffy and the white walls were soon stained with mould, suggesting to the architects that they should look for other ways of building.

The estate was later demolished to make way for an Air Force training facility.

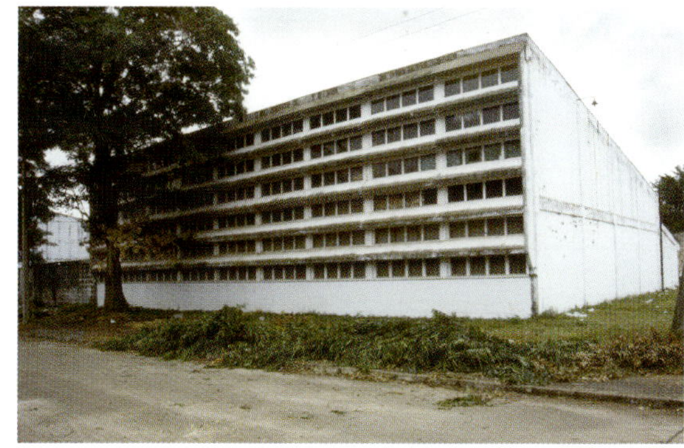
**Above** A factory unit, 1998.

# Shell Circuit Bungalow (1960-61)
## Anuradhapura

This simple bungalow, designed with Ulrik Plesner, consisted of a long shallow plan under a large over-hanging umbrella roof and was an attempt to break away from the 'Tropical Modern' mould. It no longer exists.

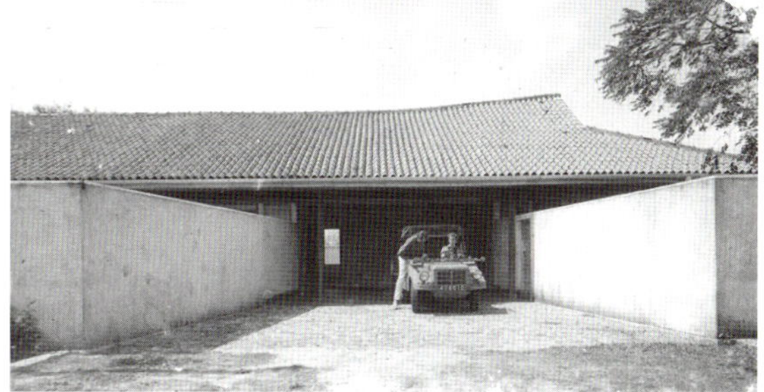
**Above** Geoffrey Bawa and Ulrik Plesner on a site visit, 1961.

# Mahahalpe Silk Farm (1969-73)
## Galaha near Kandy

Bawa built the Silk Farm at Mahahalpe for the nuns of the Good Shepherd Convent with Anura Ratnivibushana as his project architect. It comprised a cluster of small agricultural and residential buildings on a steep hillside. Silk production failed, the farm was sold and the buildings fell into disrepair.

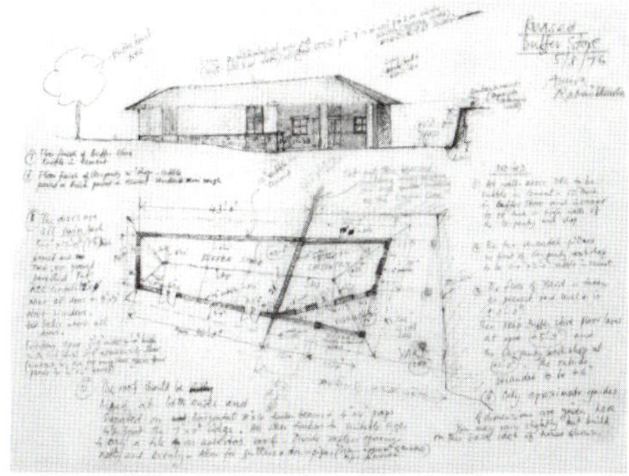
**Above** A design development drawing by Anura Ratnavibushana, 1970. Bawa Archive.

## Pallakelle Industrial Estate (1970-71)
### Digane, near Kandy

The Pallakelle Industrial Estate was built close to what would become the site of the Victoria Reservoir. It was planned as a cluster of square factory units. The pyramidal tiled roofs incorporated raised clerestories to admit light and encourage stack ventilation. Many of the units were later altered and the few that survive are in poor condition.

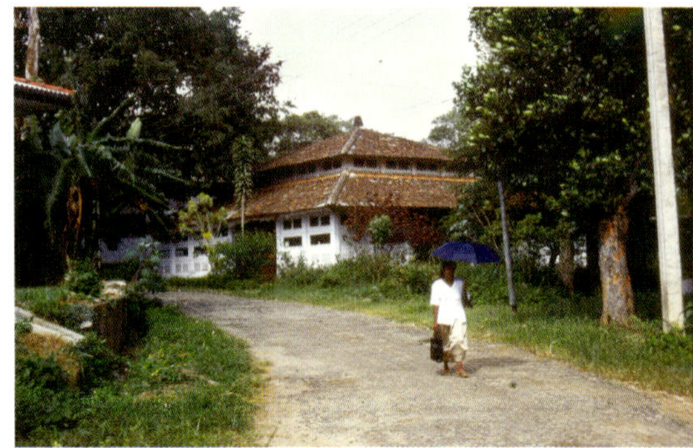

**Above** A standard factory unit, 1998.

## The Sinbad Hotels (1990, 1994)
### Kalutara

The original Sinbad Hotel was designed by French architects on the spit of land that separates the mouth of the Kalu Ganga from the sea. When it was taken over by the Serendib Group in 1990, Bawa carried out a refurbishment with the help of his friend, the retired Swiss furniture designer, Rico Tarawela. Bawa breathed new life into the reception buildings and Tarawela remodeled the bedroom blocks. Some of this work still survives.

Four years later Bawa was commissioned to design a new hotel on a site a little to the south. After the Central Bank bombing of 1995, however, work stopped when building was 75 percent complete. Now, after 20 years, a new hotel is being created out of the ruins of the old.

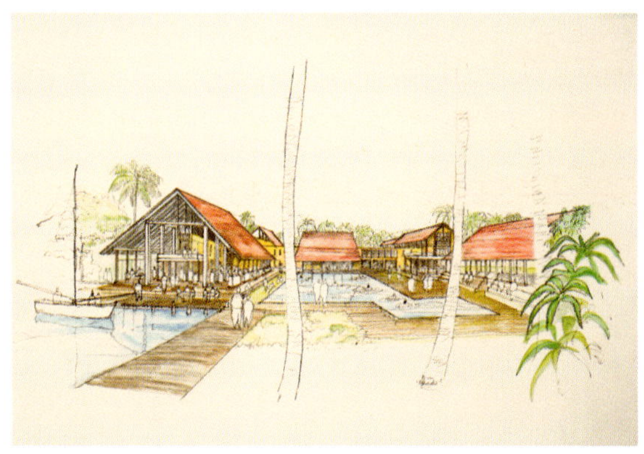

**Above** Perspective sketch of the 1994 project. Bawa Archive.

# Bawa Abroad

After 1970, as someone of mixed parentage, Bawa felt less and less secure in a Sri Lanka that was edging towards Sinhalese hegemony and, like many Sri Lankans in his position, he considered emigrating. He actively solicited work in India and for several years ran a small office in Madras. He also took on projects in Bali and Mauritius.

Later, following the publication of the *White Book* in 1986, he produced designs for a number of projects in India and Southeast Asia, including a house for the Sarabhai family in Ahmedabad, a pyramidal conservatory for the Botanic Gardens in Singapore and a new Hyatt Hotel in Bali, though none of these was built.

A detailed account of the unbuilt projects lies beyond the scope of this book and the projects described below are those that were actually built.

## INDIA

### Boys' Town for the de la Salle Brothers (1965-67)
#### Nagamalai, near Madurai

Bawa had successfully completed a number of projects for the Catholic Church in Sri Lanka and his first commission in India came in 1965 when he was asked to design a Boys' Town for the de la Salle Brothers on the outskirts of Madurai in Tamil Nadu. Bawa worked on the design with Ulrik Plesner though he never visited the site and Ulrik was responsible for its detailed development. The various parts of the plan were organised in checker board fashion on the hillside site in a manner reminiscent of the monasteries of Anuradhapura and the boys' dormitories were arranged in groups of four, swastika fashion, around walled compounds.

After Plesner quit Bawa's office in 1966, the project went into limbo and was eventually completed by Laurie Baker, an expatriate architect based in Trivandrum.

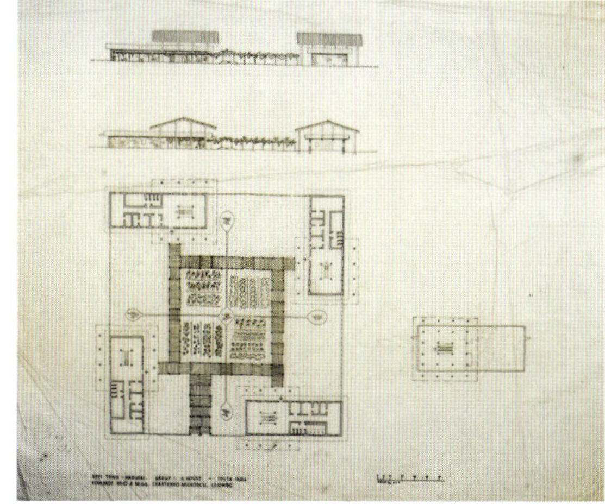

**Above** A typical cluster of dormitories, 1966. Bawa Archive.

### Extensions to the Connemara Hotel (1971)
#### Madras

Bawa established an office in Madras in 1971, largely on the strength of a commission to build an extension to the Connemara Hotel. The new wing was built around a pool court. The hotel has since undergone a number of changes and little remains of Bawa's intervention.

## Staff Club for Madurai Mills (1973)
### Madurai

While working on the Connemara Hotel, Bawa was introduced to Martin Henry who was the new CEO of the vast thread-making company, Madurai Coates. Henry had inherited two staff clubs in Madurai, one for European staff and one for locals, but was determined to amalgamate them and challenged Bawa to come up with a design. Bawa determined to use local materials and technologies and to acknowledge Western and Hindu traditions. He used honey-coloured stone from the Nagamalai Hills for walls, floors and columns and incorporated ancient doors from Chettinad. His design proposed residential accommodation for visitors as well as a library, a restaurant, generous lounges and a discreet bar.

When the company was wound up, the staff club was sold to a Sri Lankan travel company and architect Vinod Jayasinghe was employed to convert it to a hotel. While some original features of the club were retained, its unique atmosphere was lost.

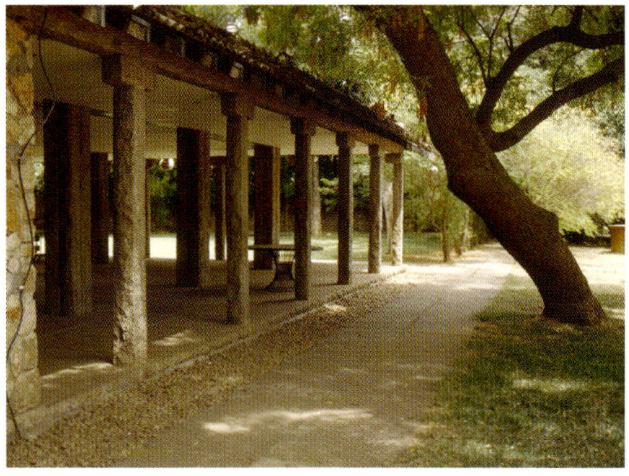

**Above** View of the main club room showing the split stone columns, 2000.

## INDONESIA

## Batujimbar Estate (1973)
### Batujimbar, Sanur, Bali

Bawa had first met Australian artist Donald Friend when Friend was living on Bevis Bawa's estate at Brief in the late 1950s. Friend later moved to Bali where he set up a house and studio on the beach at Sanur and collaborated with Indonesian entrepreneur Wija Waworuntu to create the Tanjung Sari, hailed by some as the world's first boutique hotel. When Waworuntu and Friend bought a strip of land in order to develop an estate of beachside villas, Friend summoned Bawa to be their architect.

Bawa made several visits to Bali during the course of 1973 and drew up a masterplan for 15 villas. Each villa was designed in detail and conceived as a unique checkerboard of pavilions and courtyards inspired by traditional Balinese architecture. Only three were realised: Friend's own villa with its museum and performance space, and house nos 6 and 11. Today only the museum and house 11 survive.

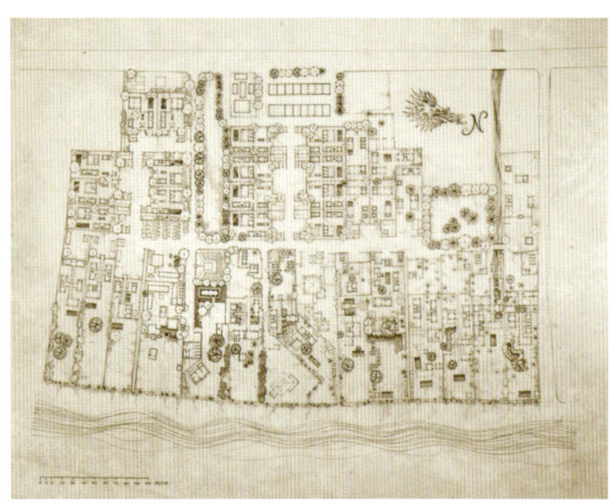

**Above** Site Plan, 1973. Bawa Archive.

## MAURITIUS

### Peter White House (1973-74)
### Pereybere

Peter White had started out as a tea broker in Colombo but later moved to Mauritius as a sugar estate manager. Having bought an abandoned sugar mill with a view to creating a weekend house, he remembered Bawa and invited him to be his architect. Bawa visited the site and developed the design concept with White. Detailed design was undertaken in Colombo by Ismeth Raheem while site supervision was entrusted to Nihal Amerasinghe, a former colleague who happened to be working in Mauritius.

The main house was developed within a pair of vaulted store rooms and incorporated a lap pool. A smaller store room became a guest house.

After White retired and returned to the UK, the house was abandoned and was later converted into a printing factory.

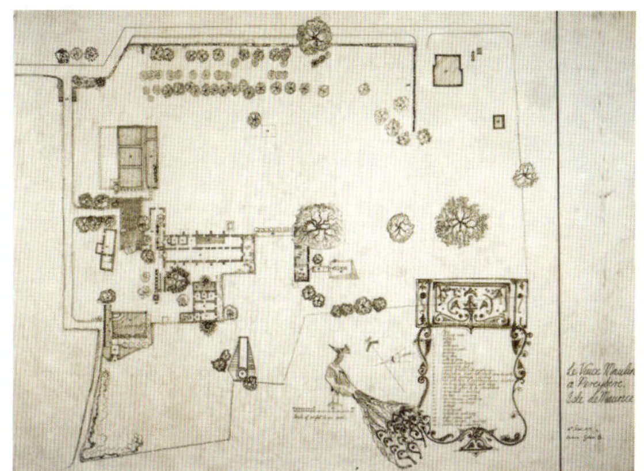

**Above** Site Plan, 1973, (Prematilleke). Bawa Archive.

### Currimjee House (1986-94)
### Florial

The Currimjee House was the first of a long line of foreign commissions that came to Bawa during the period when he was withdrawing from Edwards, Reid & Begg and starting his own design studio, though it was the only one that was eventually built. When Bashir Currimjee, a Gujarati businessman based in Mauritius, bought land for a house at Floreal on the Mauritius Plateau, his friend Peter White recommended that he invite Bawa to be his architect. After visiting the site Bawa proposed building a cluster of linked pavilions that stepped down the sloping site enclosing a series of courts and pools. He adopted a simple modern idiom that made subtle references to the Currimjees' Indian origins and incorporated artefacts gathered from around the Indian Ocean.

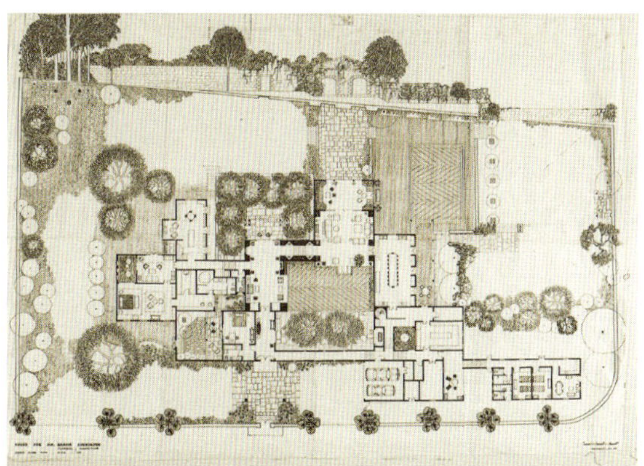

**Above** Site Plan, 1989 (Sumangala). Bawa Archive.

# Map I – Bawa's Projects in Central Colombo

# Map II – Bawa's Projects in the Colombo Region

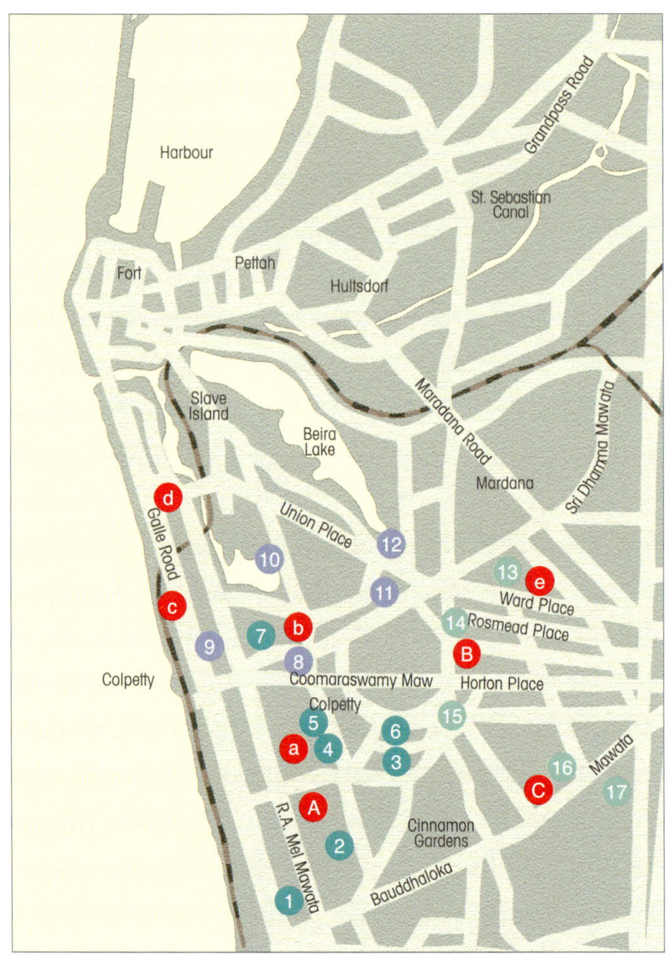


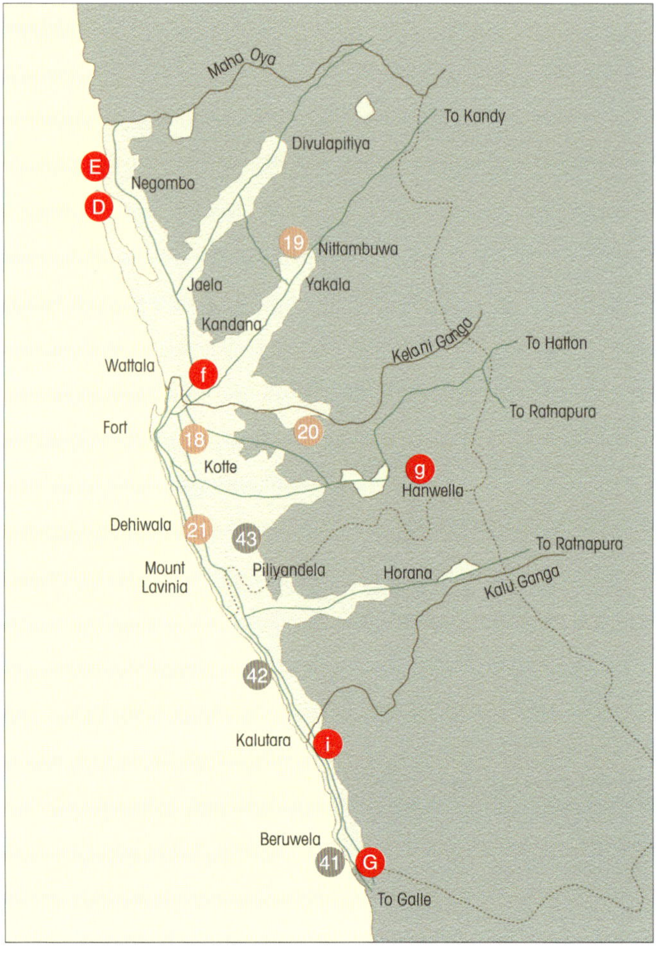


| | | | |
|---|---|---|---|
| 1 | The Gallery Café | 15 | St Bridget's Montessori |
| 2 | Geoffrey Bawa's Town House | 16 | The Agrarian Research and Training Institute |
| 3 | The Deraniyagala House | 17 | The Ratnasivaratnam House |
| 4 | Ladies' College Classroom Block | a | The Keuneman House |
| 5 | Ladies' College Vocational Training Centre | b | Classroom Block for Bishop's College |
| 6 | Stanley de Saram House | c | Two Classroom Blocks for St Thomas' Prep School |
| 7 | Chloé de Soysa House | d | Automobile Association Offices |
| 8 | Wijemanne Flats | e | Druvi de Saram Houses |
| 9 | The YWCA | A | The de Saram Row Houses |
| 10 | The Seema Malaka | B | The Fernando and Martenstyn Houses |
| 11 | The Jayakody House | C | The National Institute of Management Studies |
| 12 | The State Mortage Bank | | |
| 13 | The Raffel House | | |
| 14 | The David Spenser House | | |

| | | | |
|---|---|---|---|
| 18 | The New Sri Lanka Parliament | f | Wattala Convent |
| 19 | The Sunethra Bandaranaike House | g | Yahapath Endera Farm Convent |
| 20 | Steel Corporation Offices and Housing | i | Kalutara Public Library |
| 21 | The Leela Dias Bandaranayake House | D | The Blue Lagoon Hotel (aka Jetwing Blue) |
| 41 | The Neptune Hotel | E | The Royal Oceanic Hotel (aka Jetwing Beach) |
| 42 | The Blue Water Hotel | G | Tourist Police Station |
| 43 | The Institute for Integral Education | | |

# Map III – Bawa's Projects in Sri Lanka

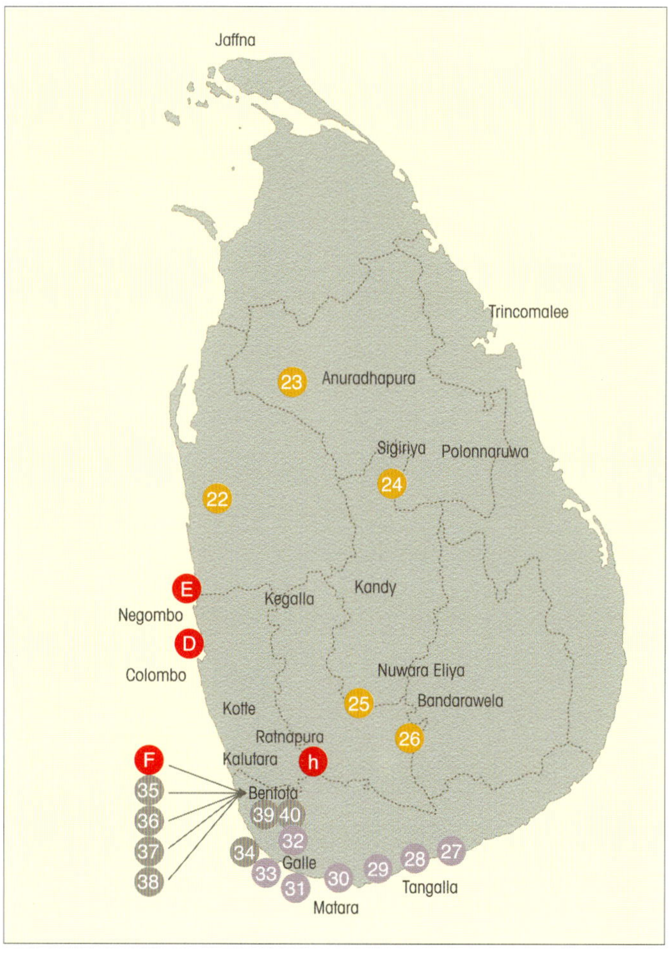


| | | | |
|---|---|---|---|
| 22 | The Polontalawa Estate Bungalow | 34 | The Triton Hotel |
| 23 | The Anuradhapura Pilgrims' Rest House | 35 | Club Villa and Mohoti Walauwe |
| 24 | The Kandalama Hotel | 36 | Villa No 87 |
| 25 | The Strathspey Estate Bungalow | 37 | The Bentota Tourist Village |
| 26 | The Nazareth Chapel of the Good Shepherd Convent | 38 | Serendib Hotel |
| | | 39 | Lunuganga |
| 27 | The Jacobson House | 40 | The Ena de Silva House |
| 28 | Claughton Bungalow | h | The Ratnapura Tennis Club |
| 29 | The Ruhuna University Campus | D | The Blue Lagoon Hotel (aka Jetwing Blue) |
| 30 | Office Building | | |
| 31 | The Jayawardene House | E | The Royal Oceanic Hotel (aka Jetwing Beach) |
| 32 | The ASH de Silva House | | |
| 33 | The Lighthouse Hotel | F | Bentota Beach Hotel |

# Image Credits

## Further Reading

Anjalendran, C, David Robson & Dominic Sansoni, *The Architectural Heritage of Sri Lanka.* Singapore: Talisman, 2015.

Bandaranayake, Senake, *Sinhalese Monastic Architecture.* Leiden: E J Brill, 1974.

Bawa, Bevis, *Bevis Bawa's Brief.* Bentota: Brief Publications. 2011.

Bawa, Geoffrey, 'Ceylon: Seven New Buildings'. London: *Architectural Review*, February 1966.

Bawa, Geoffrey, Christoph Bon & Dominic Sansoni, *Lunuganga.* Singapore: Times Editions, 1990.

Brawne, Michael, 'The Work of Geoffrey Bawa'. London: *Architectural Review*, April 1978.

Brawne, Michael, 'The University of Ruhunu'. London: *Architectural Review*, November 1986.

Brawne, Michael, *From Idea to Building.* London: Butterworth Heinemann, 1992.

Brawne, Michael, 'Paradise Found'. London: *Architectural Review*, December, 1995.

Daswatte, Channa, 'Bawa on Bawa' in *Tan Kok Meng, Asian Architects II*. Singapore: Select Publishing, 2001.

de Silva, Minnette, *The Life and Work of an Asian Woman Architect.* Kandy: The de Silva Trust, 1998.

Lewcock, Ronald, Barbara Sansoni & Laki Senanayake, *The Architecture of an Island.* Colombo: Barefoot, 1998.

Pieris, Anoma, *Imagining Modernity.* Colombo: Stamford Lake, 2007.

Powell, Robert, David Robson & Sebastian Posingis, *The New Sri Lankan House.* Singapore: Talisman, 2015.

Robson, David, *Bawa, The Complete Works.* London: Thames & Hudson, 2002.

Robson, David, *Beyond Bawa.* London: Thames & Hudson, 2007.

Robson, David, *Anjalendran, Architect of Sri Lanka.* Singapore: Periplus Tuttle, 2009.

Robson, David & Dominic Sansoni, *Bawa, The Sri Lanka Gardens.* London: Thames and Hudson, 2008.

Taylor, Brian Brace et al, *Geoffrey Bawa.* Singapore: Concept Media, 1986.

## Acknowledgments

This book draws on research that has been ongoing for the past 20 years. The author and photographer would like to acknowledge the help and support that they have received, down the years, from the Geoffrey Bawa Trust. Had it not been for the efforts of the Trust, Geoffrey Bawa's town house in Colombo and his garden at Lunuganga would not have survived and the Ena de Silva House would have been lost forever.

We would also like to thank architect C Anjalendran and photographer Dominic Sansoni for their encouragement and counsel and Jeff Bourke for his work on cataloguing and recording the Bawa drawings collection.

All new photographs are by Sebastian Posingis unless otherwise stated.

Older photographs have been taken from David Robson's archive. Drawings are reproduced from photographic images made by David Robson and Waruna Gomis in 2000 and by Jeff Bourke in 2014.

The poem 'Mirissa' is reproduced with the kind permission of Michael Ondaatje.

David Robson
Sebastian Posingis